P9-DGY-831

A Sense of Dance

Exploring Your Movement Potential

Second Edition

Constance A. Schrader, MA

University of North Carolina at Asheville

Human Kinetics

Library of Congress Cataloging-in-Publication Data

Schrader, Constance A., 1953-
    A sense of dance: exploring your movement potential / Constance A.
Schrader.-- 2nd ed.
        p. cm.
Includes index.
    ISBN 0-7360-5189-9 (Soft Cover)
    1. Dance. 2. Human beings--Attitude and movement. 3. Human
locomotion. 4. Dance--Political aspects. I. Title.
    GV1595.S33 2004
    792.8--dc22   2003019522

ISBN: 0-7360-5189-9

Copyright © 2005, 1996 by Constance A. Schrader

All rights reserved. Except for use in a review, the reproduction or utilization of this work in any form or by any electronic, mechanical, or other means, now known or hereafter invented, including xerography, photocopying, and recording, and in any information storage and retrieval system, is forbidden without the written permission of the publisher.

The Web addresses cited in this text were current as of January 20, 2004, unless otherwise noted.

Acquisitions Editor: Judy Patterson Wright, PhD; **Developmental Editor:** Melissa Feld; **Assistant Editor:** Susan C. Hagan and Maggie Schwarzentraub; **Copyeditor:** Cheryl Ossola; **Indexer:** Marie Rizzo; **Permission Manager:** Dalene Reeder; **Graphic Designer:** Andrew Tietz; **Graphic Artist:** Angela K. Snyder; **Photo Manager:** Kareema McLendon; **Photographer (interior):** See Credits on page 199. **Cover Designer:** Andrea Souflée; **Photographer (cover):** Creatas; **Art Manager:** Kelly Hendren; **Illustrator:** Brian McElwain and Mic Greenberg (anatomical art); **Printer:** Versa Press

Printed in the United States of America   10 9 8 7 6 5 4 3

Human Kinetics
Web site: www.HumanKinetics.com

United States: Human Kinetics
P.O. Box 5076
Champaign, IL 61825-5076
800-747-4457
e-mail: humank@hkusa.com

Canada: Human Kinetics
475 Devonshire Road, Unit 100
Windsor, ON N8Y 2L5
800-465-7301 (in Canada only)
e-mail: orders@hkcanada.com

Europe: Human Kinetics
107 Bradford Road
Stanningley
Leeds LS28 6AT, United Kingdom
+44 (0)113 255 5665
e-mail: hk@hkeurope.com

Australia: Human Kinetics
57A Price Avenue
Lower Mitcham, South Australia 5062
08 8277 1555
e-mail: liaw@hkaustralia.com

New Zealand: Human Kinetics
Division of Sports Distributors NZ Ltd.
P.O. Box 300 226 Albany
North Shore City, Auckland
0064 9 448 1207
e-mail: blairc@hknewz.com

Contents

X 471997

Part II   The Laws of (Loco) Motion

Part III   *The Sense of Movement*

Part IV The Politics of Dancing

Preface

This book is devoted to those entering the world of dance. It is a world you know more about than you may imagine. It is a world that will be changed by your bravery, your honesty, and your ingenuity.

In the first edition I promised that every human being has the capacity to create dances that are meaningful and personal. In the years since the first edition has been published, many readers have found this promise to be true. So I continue encouraging new dancers to explore, new choreographers to discover, and new audiences to enjoy this amazing intersection of heart, mind, and body—dance.

This edition is written for true beginners—students who are exploring the art form for the first time and are not likely to have described themselves as dancers. Through this text you will discover that dance is an accessible art form that can bring you greater self-awareness and self-confidence. Students who have experience with one form of dance will discover ways to relate that experience to new forms as they expand their dance horizons. Through almost 30 years of teaching I have learned that students are most engaged by classroom work that is interesting, enjoyable, and applicable to real life. My goal is to blend dance research and practice and turn students on to the field.

The second edition of *A Sense of Dance* is refreshed in several ways. Part I, An Invitation to the Dance, starts with the first steps of considering this art form by asking the most fundamental question, "What is dance?" If you are using this book as part of a course, you and your class will want to discuss what is and is not dance and how a person learns to dance. As you read and discuss, you will learn about others' backgrounds and expectations and finally come to a shared understanding of what dance means to you and others. New to this edition is the second chapter, The Power of Dance. Why *do* people dance? You are probably aware of several reasons

people dance: to celebrate, to commemorate, to express, to recreate, to connect with other people. This chapter takes a broad look at different aspects of dance (genres) and gives you some history, theory, and basic terminology. It is by no means an exhaustive look, but it will pique your interest about the power of dance through time and place, through culture and community. In part II, The Laws of (Loco) Motion, you'll find everything you need to be able to take a movement and play with it so that it interests and informs you. In any craft or art, an artist uses tools in creating the work. In calling this part The Laws of (Loco) Motion, I hope you'll let yourself go a little crazy with your exploration of your potential. Challenge yourself! Break new ground! What if anything really *were* possible?

The tools of the choreographer are called the elements of dance: time, space, and effort. But are these tools used only in the dance studio? Certainly not! These are the elements of any movement, whether that movement is or is not called dance. What you will find particularly useful is guidance in mining your everyday movement so that you realize its potential in your own choreography. Rather than just recycling the movements your teachers show you, why not learn to use your own experience as a springboard for your choreography?

Part III, The Sense of Movement, takes you where few other dance texts go: into the examination of what makes one person create or appreciate dance in a personal way. How do we perceive? Why are we inclined to make some perceptual choices and not others? Here's where you'll find two new chapters: chapter 10, Your Sense of Style, and chapter 11, Patterns of Coordination and Style. "Style," as you will read, is roughly defined as the impression made. The concept of style is familiar to most of us when we think of painting. An abstract style distinguishes one painting from another done in a figurative or realistic style. The impression you have from looking at a block of red color in an abstract painting is different from the impression you get from a realistic painting of an apple. But at what point does a block of red definitely resemble an apple? That is, at what point does the style change from abstract to realistic?

In dance, the style—the label of impression—of movements used to be more clearly defined than it is today. Ballet was the style of dance done en pointe in certain types of costumes to certain music. The use of generic ballet vocabulary also established that style. But in contemporary choreography not only is movement vocabulary shared among styles, but also shared are costuming, music, and technique. With such amalgamation, the notion of styles of dance needs to be reconsidered. As our sense of ourselves in a global culture evolves, so does our sense of movement.

In part IV, The Politics of Dancing, we turn our attention more fully to the challenges of crafting dances for the purpose of effective, intentional communication. Our facility with movement exploration now enables us to make more sophisticated choices in crafting work for a particular audience or effect. We now have the skills to attend to form and function of a completed choreographic project or dance.

Dance? Political? Our English word "politics" comes from the Greek word *"polis,"* a city-state of ancient Greece. Politics are matters that concern a particular community. When dance succeeds in engaging an audience, it has touched on some matter of concern, which might be as concrete as the physics of balance or as abstract as the power of love. You will once again be encouraged to use your own experience to begin your creative process. The nuts and bolts of creating a work that has unity of form are there for you in chapter 13, Composition. Evaluating not only your work but also the work of your peers and the work outside your daily sphere are explored in chapter 14, Is This Dance Good?

Features

Each chapter has elements that help you understand dance on different levels. Have you ever been on a hike and discovered a side path that took you to a wonderful view? In this text those side paths are called **Inside Insights.** They give you a glimpse into an aspect of the main chapter that is just fun to know or think about. Some of those may even provoke you to do your own research. You'll also find boxes titled **Try This Experiment.** You need to really do these. Dance has to be experienced. These are the interactive explorations that help you comprehend the main points of the text. At the end of each chapter you'll find a section called **Think About It.** These questions challenge you to go beyond nodding in agreement and put your own ideas together. These considerations give you good material for journal entries and help you begin to clarify what you think about this art form. Finally, each chapter concludes with a new section called **Your Turn to Dance.** These are two springboards for choreography that reinforce the concepts in the chapter and *boing!* you into another adventure of exploring your movement potential.

Do You Have the Power?

Dance is a creative act of expression, imitation, communication, and reflection. It is a language that has existed and operated throughout the human experience. The power of dance awaits you. Dance, then, wherever you may be!

Acknowledgments

I would like to acknowledge my husband, Clay, and my children, Gus and Mali. With their patience and support, I was able to make the time to focus on this writing.

I also thank Melissa Feld and Judy Patterson-Wright of Human Kinetics for their faith in this project and in me.

Part I

An Invitation to the Dance

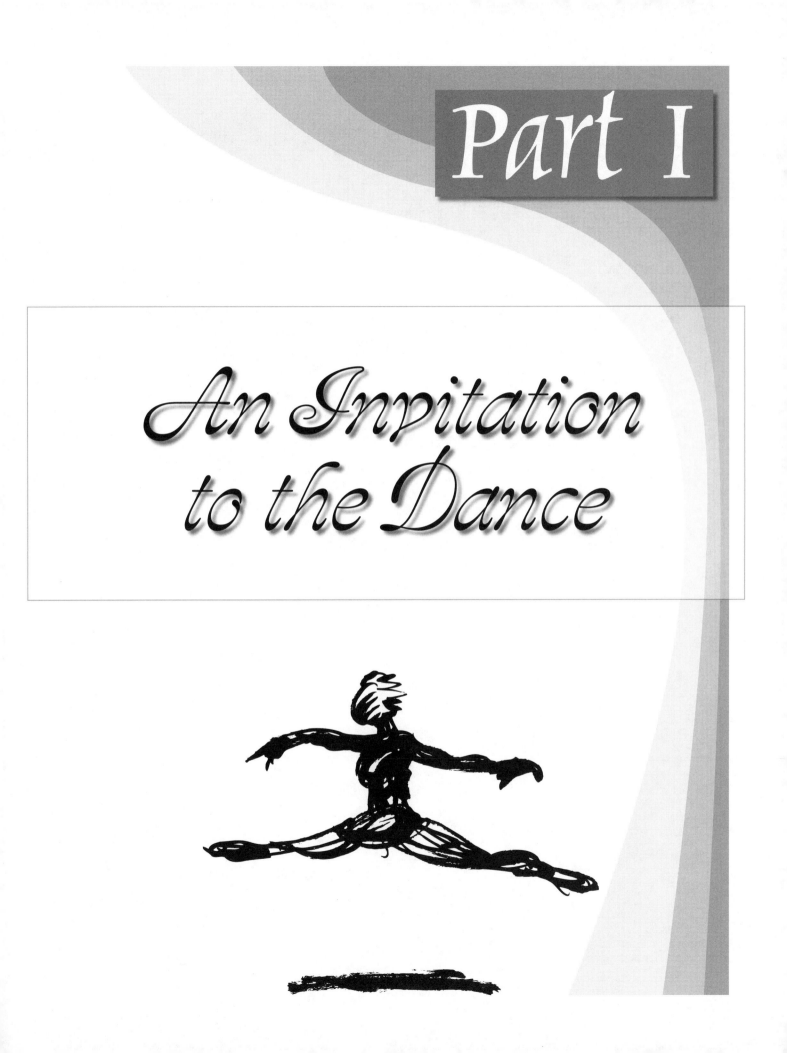

What Is Dance?

True or false: Dancing is always done to music.

True or false: You need a partner to dance.

True or false: The first ballet dancers were men.

True or false: In order to dance, you need special dance clothes and special training, and it helps if you are thin.

Only one of these statements is true. The first ballet dancers were men. When ballet developed in Europe during the early 1500s, women stood on the sidelines to admire the male dancers' grace and agility. Ballet is just one of numerous dance styles, but because of its long association with the preferences of those in the highest social status, in European-based societies it has almost become synonymous with "dance." As we come into more frequent contact with other traditions, cultures, and forms of dance, we realize that the word "dance" might as readily conjure an image of a guy balancing on his elbow as a girl balancing on her toes (figure 1.1).

FIGURE 1.1 Both of these people are dancing. What do they have in common?

FIGURE 1.2 Many social dances are done with a partner.

Every culture has its own dances—rhythmic, stylized ways of using the body to communicate and to celebrate. Although music often accompanies dance, it is not always necessary. As for working with a partner, most—but not all—social dances are done with a partner (figure 1.2).

The last dance myth—that in order to dance you need special clothes, training, and a thin physique—results from just a few of the misperceptions about dance that Western culture has developed from hundreds of years of seeing concert dance performed in special costumes, with very specialized training, and by especially thin dancers. These are not conditions for dance participation in the rest of the world. Every culture makes its own rules about what will be considered dance and who may be a dancer (figure 1.3, a and b). The function of dance differs from culture to culture. Think about how dance functions in your community. What role does dance play in religious practice? Is dance a point of cultural pride or identity? Is there an age when children no longer feel comfortable dancing spontaneously? Is that age different for boys than for girls? How specialized are the dance forms? How important is it to your grandparents that you know their dances?

FIGURE 1.3 Every culture makes its own rules about what is considered dance and who may be a dancer. (a) Polish folk dancers and (b) Hawaiian hula dancers each dance in their own way.

You probably have a few ideas about what dance is. But if you had to explain dance to someone who had not heard of it, what would you say? How would you describe why people dance? What would you say dance is for? How would you describe what a dancer looks like? Where would you say that dance takes place? And where are *you* in that description? Do you see yourself as a dancer? Why do you dance, or why do you not dance? How is dance a part of your culture? How is dance a part of your life? As you dig a little deeper into the world of dance you are likely to confront many of these questions. You may also find yourself thinking in new ways—about what it is to be a moving, responding, communicating creature in your community, in your culture, in your era.

Of course, as you explore dance you won't only be *thinking* in new ways, you will also be *moving* in new ways. Some of these new movements may feel difficult and awkward, while others may feel easy and natural. Some may appear pointless and others functional, even essential. Other movements may be appropriate to share with your friends, but some need a special circumstance for performance (on a stage or in a studio). Still other movements will either relax or exhilarate you.

Your study of dance will challenge your ideas about dance. Because you will learn about dance primarily by moving, your study will also challenge some of the ideas you have about yourself—your body image, your creative potential, your coordination. Reading and talking about dance should help you put some of these physical ideas into perspective.

INSIDE INSIGHT

Part of learning dance is being open to learning new movement patterns—new ways of doing things. Often you will find that your habitual way of moving is only that—a habit—and, if you are willing to explore new ways, you will expand your physical options. For example, cross your arms in front of your chest. Look down, and note which arm is on top. Now uncross your arms and recross them with the other arm on top. Awkward? Probably, but if you think about it, neither way is right or wrong. You have just tried a new movement.

You Are Always Moving

Freeze. Try not to move anything but your eyes as you read this paragraph. What shape is your body making right now? Are you curled up? Stretched out? Are you sitting at a desk or lying on a sofa? Do not move! Which body parts are touching? How is your head supported? Does it rest on one hand or on a pillow, or is it balanced on top of your spine? Were you aware of your breathing while you were reading? Now move. Change your posture. Change your position. Change the way you hold yourself. Change your breath.

We are, in fact, always moving. We constantly change our posture to rest different muscles. It is possible to appear to be still, but even when we are not moving our bodies through space, we still move.

You are always moving, always shifting, always balancing the opposing forces, demands, and desires in your life. Your continuous struggle against the pull of gravity keeps you moving. Sometimes the choices in this struggle are conscious; other times they are unconscious.

Even while you were absolutely still, your chest probably moved as you breathed. Was your belly moving too? What tensions did you discover in your body as you were holding the position? How did you relieve those tensions at the end of the experiment? Chances are you moved!

Movement as simple as walking involves mastering your relationship with gravity. What does that relationship have to do with dancing? Everything! When you reveal the forces acting on the body, you communicate something about the nature of the moving creature—in this case, you.

In the next Try This Experiment, you could easily use the simple sequence of falling and catching movements for a dance. By allowing yourself to begin falling, you show yourself succumbing to outside forces; when you catch your weight, the audience sees that you have willfully regained control of your body by opposing the earlier forces. Can you think of other subjects related to losing and regaining control that could be developed simply by working with gravity?

Try This Experiment

Arrange yourself in a comfortable position where you can see a clock or a watch without changing your position. Your eyes may be open or closed. Now hold this exact position for two minutes. Try to be completely still.

Try This Experiment

Let's explore the simple ways in which we respond to gravity: Stand with both feet together, arms by your sides. Without bending at the knees, hips, or waist, see how far forward you can lean before you have to move your feet to catch yourself from falling. Do this a few times to feel the pull of gravity and to find the muscles that have to work harder the farther forward you lean.

What happens when you move your feet apart?

What happens when you bend at the waist?

What would be a good title for this dance?

Tension and Release

When we move, we change the tension patterns in our bodies. Tension is not necessarily a bad thing. If we had no tension in our bodies, we would not be able to stand up, walk, or run. Without muscle tension, we would not be able to move.

Tension has acquired many negative connotations, especially when used in such contexts as "tension in the region" (preparing to fight), "lower-back tension" (pain), and "tension in a relationship" (trouble). But if we look up the etymology of "tension," we find that our English word comes from the Old Latin *tanz*, meaning "to stretch." *Tanz.* Dance. Sound similar? Although there is debate about the origin of the English word "dance," many scholars believe that in the history of our language development, to stretch meant to tense, and the word "tense" evolved into "dance."

Try This Experiment

Kneel on the floor. Now support your weight on your hands and knees. Exhale, and let your head hang. Very slowly shift the weight to your hands and one knee so that you can bring the other foot up to your hands in preparation for standing. Do you feel the pull of gravity? Did you sense how you had to rebalance or recenter your weight to accomplish this? Freeze in this position long enough to be aware of the balance of tensions required to hold this position.

When you dance you tense and stretch to show forces acting on your body. Think about social dancing. Which kinds of forces that are acting on your body do you wish to show? Do you want to look as if you are out of control? Do you want to look strong and tough? Do you want to look fluid and sensual? Remember, the forces we are referring to can be physical, emotional, social, or spiritual. As you explore creative movement or formal dance classes, remember that the way you use tension and stretch will reveal the forces acting on your body.

Imagine how it would feel if you allowed your head to fall forward and then brought it back up to a vertical position. If you were to practice this movement a few more times—letting your head fall farther and farther and letting yourself bend more and more each time—you might, finally, let your head fall so far forward that the weight would take you all the way to the floor.

If you were to experiment with that progressive shift in weight, you would probably not end up in a heap on the floor, right? Why not? Because you would have progressively balanced the tension in your body to avoid injury. Even in the final drop to the floor, you would most likely balance your weight and your speed to control the descent. We control our movements through a balance of tension and relaxation, a combination of resistance and reception.

We are continually balancing the physical, emotional, social, and spiritual forces in our lives. We breathe in, we breathe out. We are happy, we are sad. We work, we rest. We hope and are sometimes hopeless. We become tense, and we let go. In dance, some of these opposites are described as the following contrasts:

Contract—Release _____ *Bound—Loose*

Fall—Rebound _____ *Tense—Relax*

INSIDE INSIGHT

Martha Graham (1894-1991) established the Martha Graham School of Contemporary Dance in New York City in 1927. In her technique, movement originates in the center of the body with a contraction or release of the abdominal area. It is the center that motivates the movement of the spine and extremities. Try taking a deep breath, holding it for a few counts and then forcefully expelling as much air as you can. You will feel the low abdominal muscles push that air out. When you then inhale, the muscles need to release in order to let the belly expand. That exhaling sensation gives you a sense of what's referred to as a contraction, and the softening sensation of the inhalation is that of release.

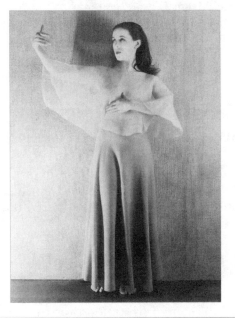

INSIDE INSIGHT

Doris Humphrey (1895-1958) and Charles Weidman (1901-1975) formed both a company and a school and gave their first concert in Brooklyn, New York, in 1928. When their company disbanded in 1945, Humphrey went on to become the artistic director of the José Limón Dance Company, which is still in existence. Both the Limón Technique and the technique that Humphrey and Weidman explored have to do with the potential of falling and the solution to rebound. Humphrey used the act of walking as an example. Each step is a potential fall from which we rebound rather than crash to the ground.

You know the muscular opposites of contract and release, fall and rebound, bound and loose, and tense and relax from your own experience. How about the way your chest and neck muscles feel just before you look at a grade on a test? You might have done well (but then again. . . .) It is a good grade! Contract—release. Think again of Doris Humphrey's example of walking down the street. If you did not rebound after each step, you would have to pick yourself up off the sidewalk between steps. Your weight falls and rebounds; you walk. Fall—rebound.

How about your body's physical change when an authority figure leaves a room? Bound—loose.

Neither state is better than the other; the balance makes for grace. If we went through life with all muscles contracted, we would move like the Tin Man in *The Wizard of Oz*. Then again, if all our muscles were released all the time, we would not even walk as well as the Tin Man's friend, the Scarecrow. At any time, some of our muscles tense or work while others release or relax. In fact, as our coordination improves with age, muscle groups are trained to contract and release so that we accomplish tasks without thinking.

Most of the time, your muscles work in harmony by making adjustments to maintain balance and comfort. Sometimes these adjustments are automatic; other times they are intentional. Surely you remember a time when you had to keep from yawning or slouching because it was not a good time to show how bored you were? And surely you have also caught yourself in the middle of a yawn or a slouch and realized, "Oops! Better straighten up!" Yawns, slouches, sighs, crossed legs, toe tapping, and pacing are all examples of personal mannerisms we use to help balance the many forces we face every day. Every day you balance your muscles' tension and release to control and to initiate movement. When you order these natural, physical, human responses, or when you use them for expression and communication, you are, in essence, dancing.

Try This Experiment

Stand on two feet and place your right hand gently on your right thigh. Slowly raise your right knee to about 45 degrees. As you do this, can you feel the muscle—the quadriceps—tighten? Check the muscles in the back of your leg—the hamstrings. Because they are not used to lift the leg, they should be loose. Now see what kind of muscle action occurs if you extend your lower leg. Finally, release all the muscles in the extended leg, let it drop, and notice how the muscles in the other leg have been working.

You Call This Dance?

The key word in creating art is "order." Any art, good or bad, is the conscious product of a person's effort to create order using a suitable medium. To repeat: When you order natural, physical, human responses, or when you use them for expression, you are dancing. Simply slumping in your chair is not, in and of itself, a dance or an artistic endeavor; however, if you deliberately use that movement pattern for effect, then you are dancing. Reflexively

tapping your toes and drumming your fingers on a desk are not artistic endeavors; these are the body's simple tension-release mechanisms. However, when you order these simple movements to create rhythmic patterns or to call attention to your personal tension by consciously repeating a tapping motion, you are dancing.

You have the skills and the facilities *right now* to consider yourself a dancer. Stretching, tensing, releasing, and all the subtle and not-so-subtle methods we use to balance the forces acting on our bodies are the source materials you need in order to begin using your body as an instrument of expression. With study comes refinement. But that is no reason to deny the value of your personal movement vocabulary as a starting point.

Let us assume you play soccer. Think about all the soccer movements that involve stretching, tensing, and releasing—all the ways that you balance the forces acting on your body. You have gravity to deal with when you time your jump for a header; you have momentum to account for when your opponent intercepts a pass and you need to change direction; you have to stretch your leg as you go for that corner kick; you experience a complete release and recharge when a goal is made—not to mention all the tension patterns that come with running, kicking, throwing, and resting. Do we call this dancing? No. We call it soccer, but the movements could be ordered in such a way that they communicate something of your perspective about the world. Take three of the movements just described: the header, the direction change, and the resting pose. Imagine what you could communicate by ordering these activities as follows:

Header to right, then left; three runs forward; quick stop; three runs backward; hands on knees to resting pose; repeat sequence.

Can you picture this sequence performed on a stage? Imagine that the dancer goes on using just those three movement patterns in a variety of sequences. Would you imagine a person dealing with physical, emotional, social, or spiritual forces? What might such a dance communicate to you (figure 1.4)?

FIGURE 1.4 Athletic leaps are not confined to sporting events. How does a leap by (a) a ballerina communicate a different perspective than a similar movement by (b) a soccer player or (c) basketball player?

To Dance Is Phenomenal

The art of dance continuously evolves. What was considered dance 100 years ago is different from today's conception. It would be lovely and tidy if we could merely define dance and move on, but the art form fairly defies definition. It is better, instead, to accept that because dance evolves to reflect the culture it serves, it is an ever-changing phenomenon. Today dance serves a wide population base—from the very young to the very old, from the highly trained to the technically untrained dancer—and there is as much controversy as there has ever been about what is, and what is not, dance.

According to Judith Lynne Hanna, author of *To Dance Is Human* (University of Chicago Press: Chicago, 1979, page 19), four components distinguish dance from nondance activities:

1. Dances have a purpose.
2. Dances have intentional rhythm.
3. Dances contain culturally patterned sequences.
4. Dances have extraordinary nonverbal movement, which has value in and of itself.

It is true that the purpose of chasing a soccer ball down a field is to put the ball into the opposing team's net. However, this activity, beautiful as it can be, is not played with an intentional rhythm, nor are the physical acts anything other than functional. We would not refer to playing soccer as dancing. While it is also true that digging a ditch has a purpose—to create a place for a new waterway—this activity does not have extraordinary nonverbal movement that has value and beauty in and of itself. We would not refer to digging a ditch as dancing, either.

Yet if you take a soccer player off the field and have her perform the dribbling and shooting movements on a stage, she would be dancing, because the act of framing her movements out of context calls attention to their being extraordinary. Likewise, put the ditch digger onstage and you have asked the audience to see something new in his activity. You could also abstract the ditch digger's movements to create extraordinary nonverbal patterns.

What's a "culturally patterned sequence"? Irish step dancing and hip-hop are distinct in many ways, but one big difference is that they come from and serve different cultures. The patterns in each are recognizably associated with a particular culture. Each combines culturally patterned sequences. Would you say the activity in a mosh pit would be suitably labeled "dance"?

Talking About Dancing

Why *talk* about dance? Have you ever heard the expression "Shut up and dance"? It is gentle chiding to get out of your head, trust your body, and go with what feels right. There are times when shutting up and dancing is going to be your best bet. But it would be foolish to categorically divorce dance from language. There are times when it will be valuable to find words that describe *how* we move and how we are moved.

Try This Experiment

Finding language to describe any movement can supply you with the start of a dance. Pick an animal and observe its movements. List the verbs, the adjectives, and the adverbs that accurately describe what you see. Then, without imitating that creature, use those words in different combinations as directions for your own movement. For instance, a squirrel might spring, freeze, or run (verbs). He might be described as being tense, agile, and light (adjectives). His movement manner might be described by the adverbs "quickly," "powerfully," "gracefully." By pairing the verbs with different adjectives and adverbs, you can discover combinations that bring you to some fresh ways of moving.

This is not an exercise to get you to imitate or mime an animal but rather a resource you can use to refresh your personal movement repertoire. And it depends on language!

Talking about dance, like talking about an encounter with any art, is a way of creating community. Differences in the way people are affected by their encounters are shared, broadening the way the people in that group know each other. Talking about dance sharpens our capacity to perceive. We use analogies and similes, we compare and contrast, and we discover connections within our experiences that come to light only as we try to articulate our perspective. All of the arts are tools we use to describe our world and our place in it. We use the "language of dance" to interpret some experiences directly as well as to invite discussion and process together our experience of the world.

Why Study Dance?

One of the biggest problems beginning dance students have is believing that they have the capacity to be phenomenal. People who are new to dance often feel that their size, shape, age, gender, and even race make them unsuitable to be real dancers. By this point, it should be clear that dance is an art form that anyone can participate in, contribute to, and enjoy. Dance is a phenomenon, and anyone can be phenomenal!

INSIDE INSIGHT

There is a great temptation, especially among beginning dancers, to plan everything rather than to explore or to experiment. All too often, students avoid movement by having discussions and asking questions. How should we begin? Who stands where? What costumes could we wear? How will it end? But what does it mean? They substitute *talk* for *action* because they are not sure what is expected and are afraid of doing the assignment incorrectly. And on a more basic level, beginning dancers, like most people, are afraid of looking like fools in front of an audience; they would rather do nothing than do something that risks making them appear inept or inadequate. Understandable. But how do we get around this? Better yet, how might you avoid this pitfall yourself?

What makes dance an art rather than a sport or a coincidence is the fact that dance is a deliberate activity that involves purpose, intentional rhythm, culturally patterned sequences, and extraordinary nonverbal movement of aesthetic and inherent value. When studying dance you will explore each of those components, and, in doing so, you will learn something about your phenomenal self.

Through your study of dance you will discover three aspects of your phenomenal self: the dancer, the choreographer, and the viewer. You will find out more about your body's limits and capabilities. You will explore not only physical but also social, emotional, and spiritual aspects of yourself. In your efforts to apply all that you know to the work you do as a choreographer, you will discover a curiosity for sights, sounds, patterns, and textures. You will learn about yourself as you try new things and experience what you consider to be failures, successes, and the risks of venturing into unfamiliar territory. You will become more aware of your creative voice as you learn about the craft of making dances. You will explore a complex idea and discover its innate simplicity. You will explore a simple idea and discover its innate complexity. As a choreographer you will experience the joy of bringing an original idea into the world.

As a member of a class you will be asked to observe other students on a regular basis. In fact, you will come to rely on the collective wisdom that develops when groups of individual dancers move together. You will learn to observe rather than judge. You will get in touch with a generosity of spirit that comes from working with classmates and supporting their efforts to discover what works for them. Learning how to be a good collaborator, how to give positive feedback, how to provide constructive criticism, and other skills has value far beyond the classroom and the theater. Learning to appreciate dance will bring you to a new awareness of yourself.

The motivation to move is a natural, instinctive response to all the forces that act on our bodies. We are always moving. To resist the pull of gravity and move about on the earth, your muscles must work to keep you in an upright position. Even when holding a still shape, you are moving—the muscles that keep your heart pumping and keep you breathing do not stop their pattern of tension and release. Movement is a measure of life, but movement is not necessarily dance. Dance is an art that uses nonverbal movement in an extraordinary way to create a form, order, or statement. Dance reveals the physical, emotional, and social forces that act on a body to reveal a sense of those forces, either for personal benefit or the benefit of an audience. To study dance is to study our phenomenal nature and to explore the personal dimensions of physical, social, and emotional strength, generosity, and wisdom.

Think About It

1. What is your definition of dance? Write it down. Underneath yours, write down the definition you find in a dictionary. Then ask three other people for their definitions. What is common to all five answers? How are they different? Create a revised definition now that you have thought more about this concept.

2. Why might your dance teacher require special clothing for dance class? Does that contradict the myth that special clothes are needed for dance?

3. If someone had been watching you as you read through this chapter, what could that person have learned about you?

4. The next time you are required to wait—for a bus, a table, a cashier—observe the way you shift your weight while waiting. How often do you stand with your whole body evenly centered on both feet? Why do so few people stand up straight?

5. Observe a moving animal, a moving, rooted object (like a tree or a flower), and a moving human. Consider how all movement reflects change, and discuss the changes evident in the movements you observe.

Your Turn to Dance

Good Intentions

Play with the following sequence: Rock forward to one foot; rock back to the other foot; then forward again to turn, step, hop, jump. Using only those movements, make a 32-count study following one of these threads:

~ Make it comical.

~ Pretend you have an important purpose.

~ Use a rhythm that is deliberate and repetitive.

~ Blend this with a dance you are familiar with in your culture.

You may repeat any element but you may use only these steps. Notice there are no limits to what you do with your arms or torso. There are also no instructions given about tempo (how fast or slow you move) or tension (how relaxed or how tense you are as you move).

Crossing Borders

Using the Internet, picture books, travel magazines, or other visual resources, choose a culture that is both intriguing and different from yours. Look for sources that have images of both men and women dancing. In the first stage of your research, work only from the images.

Using your own system of recording movement (such as stick figures or line drawings) find 10 shapes that you can roughly perform. Find two pieces of music—one upbeat and punchy and one smoother and more blended—neither of which is related to the culture you have chosen. Use all 10 shapes as the basis for movement in your study. They may be performed as still shapes or as one "frame" of a moving shape.

~ Explore the dance you can make by connecting your 10 shapes.

~ See whether you prefer the dance accompanied by fast music or slow music.

Be prepared to share your notation so that others can see differences and similarities in notation systems. After you've finished, you might keep this physical research in mind and go back to see what you can learn about the nature of the dance—its form and function, training methods, rhythmic structure, and culturally specific sequences. Observe how similar or dissimilar it is to a dance in your own culture.

The Power of Dance

*W*hat is the power of dance? Think about how you are transformed when you are having a good time dancing with your friends or when you see a beautiful dance. Can you describe that power? A close look at the way in which a dance affects an audience reveals the nature of the people for whom it has meaning. In this chapter we will briefly visit five realms of dance, each with a different kind of power.

Why Dance?

Dance is a way of knowing and communicating. All societies use dance to communicate on both personal and cultural levels and to meet physical and spiritual needs. People dance for health, pleasure, communion, expression, and profit. Dance can be both medium and message. Think of children holding hands, singing and circling, falling down, laughing, and getting up to do it all again, not for the sake of an audience, not to communicate or express, but simply to enjoy the game. In that sense, dance can be an activity that serves its own end. It can also be its own language. Human beings communicate on many different levels simultaneously, and dance can heighten consciousness to a level beyond words. Think of a pair of tango dancers, moving as one fluid organism. Sexy, sure; but watching two people move in such a deeply connected way can also be inspirational. Their connection to each other, their unity of movement, is a testament to our ability to escape our isolation. The power of dance lies in its ability to transform and transcend—to alter the heart and mind by engaging, delighting, confounding, relieving, inspiring.

What occurs to you when you dance? Stop reading and close your eyes. What answers come to you? How did you interpret the word "occurs"? Did you think of physical changes, or feelings, or how your mind works differently while dancing? Can you describe the power of experiencing dance? Your description will probably include physical, emotional, and mental changes. You may also have found yourself stuck, thinking, "Well, what occurs to me depends on what kind of dancing I'm doing"; if so, you are acknowledging that dance has different kinds of power. Depending on what you want dance to do for you, you'll seek out the appropriate form.

Different Reasons Make Different Dances

Dance can function as entertainment, therapy, a political or social tool, or a record of an experience. These functions often overlap. When people get together to square dance, it's a social event: The socializing is pleasurable, the exercise makes them feel good, and they feel fulfilled by participating in something that links them to their past. When people watch a performance of *Sleeping Beauty,* no one wonders if the princess will wake up at the end; the audiences know the story and want to experience it again. They want to compare this version to others, to see how the prima ballerina interprets her role, to share the experience with other people. They enjoy being stimulated by communion and conversation and being inspired by the performers' facility and technique. As different as square dancing and ballet are, they share some of the functions that make them valuable to society.

Try This Experiment

Before going on, write down five reasons why you dance. Don't make a list, just plop your five reasons on the paper. Now think about dances you don't do but which you know others do. On another paper write five reasons why those people dance. Some of the reasons may be similar or they may all be different. Now draw a line from one of the reasons you dance to another one. On that line, name a dance that accomplishes both of these reasons. How many different kinds of dance did you name? How is it that different dances serve similar purposes?

In this chapter we will briefly visit five different kinds of dances: social dance, ballet, modern dance, jazz and musical theater, and world dance. The word we'll use to roughly group these is *genres* (zhän-ruz) meaning "kind, sort, or style." We can make generalizations about the characteristics of each of these genres; however, the lines separating them are becoming blurred. We will touch on this again when we discuss style. This chapter summarizes the high points of the evolution of these genres and presents some of the basic positions and fundamental terms used in each genre. You are encouraged to deepen your investigation of each of these genres. The last ten years have seen a huge increase in dance scholarship, and terrific new publications offer explorations of specific areas of research. Think of these introductions as hors d'oeuvres—the full banquet awaits you!

Social Dances: Definitions and History

Social dances are recreational, traditional, and functional; often, they spring from pleasure. All contribute to a sense of belonging to a society. The dances have historical roots but largely reflect the values and beliefs of those doing the dance. Clogging, for instance, is related to its English clog dance ancestor, but the form of clogging you will find on a Southern U.S. festival stage today is the product of a contemporary culture. There are national and international organizations dedicated to the preservation of a dance at a particular stage of its development, and in those cases time stands still. But otherwise, you can expect to find social dances evolving over time.

Social dances allow people to explore and express their relationship to a group. Each dance is a bold affirmation: "I choose you," and therein lies its power. The social occasions when people dance are frequently times of transition. For example, in *Dancing*, Gerald Jonas writes that in the Middle East people dance at circumcisions; in Africa they dance at funerals; in Puerto Rico, they dance at baptisms; and virtually everyone dances at weddings. (New York: Abrams Publishing, 1992, page 108) Social dance is an enduringly popular, perhaps even necessary arena to explore the risky territory of mating through ritual. Once mated, many people continue to enjoy moving in sweet synchrony with a loved one.

Social dances in Western civilizations grew from the village dances practiced by Europeans during the 15th and 16th centuries. In the villages, circle dances and line dances were enjoyed by the masses, but court dances were more formal. There, dance was serious business. Political power rested on one's ability to dance correctly. Dance instruction gained importance and dance instructors became respected and valuable members of the court.

During the Renaissance the popular dances were rounds, ring dances, galliards, allemandes, pavanes, and branles. Western square dance and contra dance retain some of the floor patterns of these dances, which migrated with the early settlers. Colonial Americans continued to import European dances while also developing their own forms of social dances, informed by the blending of cultures in the New World. The complicated steps of the minuet tested the talents of the nobles of the courts of Louis XIV in the 17th century. The closed position that we associate with many social dances and especially with ballroom dances was, in its day, a scandalous position for a man and woman to adopt in public. In its close embrace, the waltz defied the studied politeness of the meticulous and highly mannered minuet. By the late 19th century transcontinental exchange meant even more rapid change in social dances; as social structures became more complicated, dancing as a means of connection to society also had to become more complex.

What are the social dances of today? People still enjoy some of the dances that are part of their heritage. But what about you? How are social dances a part of your life? How many of the dances you do have names? How did you learn the social dances you do? How do they function? How are they part of the history of dance?

Phases of Social Dance

In their book *Social Dance,* authors Harris, Pittman, Waller, and Dark (San Francisco: Cummings, 2003) identify seven periods of social dance in the United States, all tied to phases of popular music.

INSIDE INSIGHT

Basse danses (bah-seh doncse) were group dances that originated in Italy about 1400. They were grave and solemn, characterized by small gliding steps and bows (reverences) that were danced up on the toes, very slowly and gently, in a regal processional (in contrast to the livelier *balli,* or standard Italian court dances of the 15th and 16th centuries). In basse danses the couples stood one behind another, in columns, with partners holding inside hands. (Adapted from StreetSwing.com Dance History Archives.)

1. Between 1900 and the 1920s, during the heyday of ragtime music, dances such as the bunny hug and grizzly bear were popular.

2. During the Dixieland period, from the 1920s to '30s, the Charleston and black bottom were some of the favorites.

3. From the '30s to the '50s, social dance moved into the swing era (figure 2.1). Big band music changed the early 1900s fox-trot into a smooth dance. The lindy hop and jitterbug were not the only dances drawing huge crowds to the ballrooms of the '50s. The Big Apple, shag, and Lambeth Walk were popular among a group with growing leisure time: the college crowd.

4. The tango was a fad during the 1920s and has endured as a ballroom favorite. Other Latin dances that made it to mainstream popularity are the rhumba, samba, cha cha, merengue, and bossa nova.

5. From the '50s to the '70s, rock 'n' roll moved in, along with a host of novelty dances such as the twist, hitchhiker, swim, monkey, pony, and the jerk. A particularly interesting innovation was the new relationship between dancers: It was no longer necessary to have a partner or even relate to another person while dancing.

6. Country western, a blending of Appalachian and Southwestern arts including song and dance, was a post-World War II phenomenon.

7. Late 20th-century social dances include disco, break dance, and hip-hop.

Social Dance Positions

In social dances done with a partner you have three choices: You face each other, you stand side by side, or you don't touch at all. Within those choices, there are innumerable variations.

1. *Closed position:* Partners stand facing each other, slightly offset to their own left. Feet are slightly closer than shoulder width, with toes pointing to the partner and weight on the balls of the feet. The leader has his right arm around the follower; his hand is on

FIGURE 2.1   What is the power of social dance? For the dancers? For those watching?

the follower's left shoulder blade, offering firm support. This right-hand pressure on the back, as well as rotation of the leader's shoulders and arms (the frame), communicate direction changes. The follower's left hand is on the leader's right shoulder and the left arm rests on the leader's right arm.

  a. Latin social: Clasped hands are held at shoulder level at a 90-degree angle.

2. *Side-by-side:* In almost all Western social dance the woman or follower is on the leader's right. There are a few variations in grip.

  a. Escort style: The follower gently rests her left hand inside the hooked right arm of the leader.

  b. Conversation style: The leader's right arm reaches around the back of the follower to hold the waist. The follower's arm goes over the leader's and the hand rests on the shoulder.

  c. Cuddle: The leader's right arm reaches around the back of the follower, holding her left hand, which reaches across her body at waist level. The follower's right hand reaches over the left arm to rest in the left hand of the leader.

  d. Country western: An "opened-up" version of the cuddle with the same right-hand-to-right-hand cross. In this position, the leader's right arm is over the follower's and the leader's left hand rests near his waist.

The Language of Social Dance

Every dance has its own code words, and in social dance some of these words refer to recurring patterns. Figure 2.2 provides a few examples.

Try This Experiment

Make up a sequence using the five steps described in figure 2.2 in your own combination. First make up your sequence and then see how it would fit with music from one of the periods listed in the chronology. Does your sequence seem to fit better with big band or with ragtime music? Finally, see how well it works as a partner dance.

Selected Social Dance Vocabulary

shuffle—A light, even step. Unlike a walk, in which the weight falls heel-ball-toe, in a shuffle you stay on the balls of your feet.

two-step—Step forward on the left, close right to left. Take your weight on the right, step left again. Repeat starting right. There are three weight changes on each side.

ball-change—Standing on your left foot, allow your weight to fall backward. Catch your weight on the ball of the right foot and rebound back to the left.

pivot turn—Stepping forward on the ball of your left foot, turn your body 180 degrees and take the weight on your right foot (which is now in front of you). Again step forward on your left foot. You are pivoting around your stationary right foot. A pivot turn can go in either direction, depending on which foot is placed forward.

box step—You make a box pattern, stepping on every count. Begin by stepping forward on your left, then step right to the side. Bring the left foot beside the right, and shift your weight back onto the left foot. Step backward with the right foot, step left with the left foot, bring the right to meet the left, and you're ready to begin the pattern again.

FIGURE 2.2   Some common terms you will encounter in social dance.

Ballet: Definitions and History

The art of ballet had its beginnings in the social dances of medieval Europe. As those dances were brought into the courts, they became more and more complicated as their purpose evolved from mere pleasure to include the political and social gain of nobles and royalty. Until the advent of the proscenium stage in the early 1600s, the dances took place in the ballrooms of the courts of Europe and were viewed from platforms and galleries on three sides of the action. When dancers took to the stage, the art form began to more closely resemble the concert dance we associate with the term "ballet" today.

The terminology of ballet is in French. Although dance masters from many countries have written treatises on the correct form of the positions and movement combinations in ballet, the "language" was first systematized in the Academie Royal de la Danse, founded by Louis XIV in 1661. In his day, dance had the power to make or break careers! Through dance you demonstrated your right to be a member of the elite.

During the 18th century ballet vocabulary continued to be refined. The innovation of the pointe shoe in the 1820s brought the next big shift in ballet technique. Women eclipsed men in importance on the stage. The power of dance was in its ability to transport an audience through time and reality. With the waning of the romantic period, the power of dance as a dramatic, emotive tool changed. The skirts got shorter, fabrics got thinner, and by the 20th century, the line, or shape of the body in space, became as important an element as emoting and story had been in the romantic period of the 1800s or even the era of classical ballet in the 1900s.

The basic premises of ballet training have not changed significantly since the 1900s. The dancer's goal is to develop sufficient core strength to lift the weight of the torso out of the legs to allow maximum ease and range of motion in the legs and fluid carriage of the upper body, while at the same time achieving an ongoing balance throughout the body. Exercises designed to simultaneously strengthen and lengthen muscles are arranged in a progression set down hundreds of years ago. Class begins at the barre, then moves to the center to practice positions and transitions such as the adagio, a slow and sustained series of positions. Here one also encounters turns and jump preparations leading to petit allegro (small, fast weight changes and footwork) and grand allegro (large, soaring sequences). The class ends with the reverence, a mutual honoring of teacher and student.

Ballet has long been the domain of the aristocracy. The nobles danced for each other, and even when appreciation of the art became more mainstream in the 19th century, the world of ballet was one of privilege and class. The carriage of the ballet dancer reflects this regality. The ideal body deemed suitable for this enterprise has been discussed and defined for centuries. At one time, a dancer's size and shape determined which roles he or she was suited to present. Now, those determinations are left to the individual choreographer's tastes and interests.

As audiences hungry to be dazzled by the incredible expect more and more virtuosity, today's professional ballet dancer needs a broad range of technical, dramatic, and stylistic skills to satisfy the variety of choreographic demands. Daily studio training is essential to maintain one's instrument and prepare for the hours of rehearsal that it takes to prepare a ballet. The language of ballet is used in most contemporary Western dance forms, and it is not uncommon for dancers who are more interested in modern or jazz dance to take a ballet class every day, enjoying the thorough and consistent training ballet technique affords.

Phases of Ballet

Breaking the phases of ballet into centuries is, of course, a gross simplification. Changes occurred in different parts of Europe in different times. But the intention is to roughly place the gradual shifts from amateur to professional in historical context.

Court Ballet

➤ *1300-1400s: Social Phase. Bals,* or balls, were a part of dignified castle social life. But the dances used as entertainment in court bear little resemblance to the ballet of today. By the mid-1400s, these balls had become more and more elaborate as dukes and duchesses recovered from their difficulties in the medieval period and started amassing wealth and power. Huge spectacles were staged for the benefit and entertainment of the townspeople and impressed everyone with the importance and generosity of the host. The banquets, spectacles, and *magnifiques* that occurred in those days were lavish affairs with themed decorations, costuming, poetry, song, pantomime, and dance. These programs, often hours long, would have variety within loose thematic unity, but little thought was given to the form of the whole event.

➤ *1500s: Early Technique.* The long plays offered in court were broken up by *intermezzi*—musical-dramatic interludes that were stuck between acts. By the late 1500s these were actually related to the play and not just a diversion. Dance masters Cesare Negri, Fabritio Caroso, and Thoinot Arbeau published manuals and treatises on correct dance technique, much of which is still part of technique today. Therefore 1581 stands as an important date in the history of dance. On this date, what's referred to as the first ballet, *Ballet comique de la reine Louise* was produced. Choreographed by Balthasar de Beaujoyeulx for the French queen Catherine de Medici, it was the first production to combine elements of dance, music, set design, and poetry in a unified theme. The audience, all nobility, numbered between 9,000 and 10,000.

➤ *1600-1700s: High Court Dance.* One of the most famous dancers to influence the development of concert dance was Louis XIV, king of France from 1643 to 1715. He was an excellent dancer who insisted on working with the best musicians, poets, and choreographers. The King named Pierre Beauchamp as the first ballet master of L'Academie de la Danse. We have M. Beauchamp to thank for the five positions used in ballet today.

Try This Experiment

Find a place where you can move six to eight feet in any direction. Keeping your shoulders and hips facing front and your feet in a parallel position, move forward and back with grace and elegance at a moderate speed. Now, keeping your feet in parallel and your body facing front, add sideward motion, still moving with grace, elegance and speed. Now try it again, but work in rotation (that is, position your feet with heels together and toes angled out 45 degrees). If your status at court depended on your grace and fluidity of motion, which position of the feet would you use?

Birth of Classical Ballet

A classical ballet is a dramatic production that tells a story using the movement vocabulary of ballet. Some of the most familiar classics are *Swan Lake, Giselle, Sleeping Beauty,* and *La Bayadère*—all of which came out of the Imperial School of Ballet in Russia during the 1800s. The ballets of the romantic period concerned supernatural worlds and ethereal creatures who could float and fly and cross between the real and "other" worlds. The ballon (the lift and lightness) of the ballerina was an enviable quality enhanced by the innovation of the pointe shoe. With the invention of the pointe shoe, interest in the ballerina rose and stage dance became increasingly associated with women.

Ballet in the 20th Century

Toward the end of the 1800s audiences were exposed to a new kind of ballet, one that was less dependant on formalized mime and more concerned with exploring the art as a complete entity. These ballets had unity of costume, subject, and scenery, an integrated corps de ballet, and choreography that expressed the state of mind of the characters. One name is associated with the shift from classical to contemporary ballet: Serge Diaghilev (1872-1929). Diaghilev (deeAHgilev) was neither a dancer nor a choreographer; he was an impresario, a producer who brought together some of the greatest choreographers, dancers, scene and costume designers, and composers to create ballets for his company, the Ballets Russes. The choreographer Michel Fokine (1880-1942), often created *ballets d'èpoque,* or period ballets, set in exotic places and periods. The costumes were stunning, the sets were magic, the music was cutting edge, and the movements were new and daring. Fokine believed that the whole body should be expressive, that the power of the dance came from its ability to reveal the inner life of the individual.

A list of the collaborators during the 20 years of Diaghilev's Ballets Russes (1909-1929) includes the names of most of the major figures of the modern period. You have probably heard of some of the famous ballerinas: Anna Pavlova, Tamara Karsavina, Bronislava Nijinska, and Lydia Sokolova, to name only a few. Although there were several strong male dancers, Vaslav Nijinsky's name is one of the most well known. As choreographer and main character in the 1912 debut of *L'Après-midi d'un Faune* (*Afternoon of a Faun*), Nijinsky presented shockingly sexual and unconventional movement. Ballet? Many said no.

When Diaghilev died in 1929 the Ballets Russes collapsed, but his innovative spirit lived on. Léonid Massine had worked with the Ballets Russes on several ballets and he continued to choreograph. In England, Ballet Rambert, founded in the 1920s by Marie Rambert, who had worked with Diaghilev, gave choreographic opportunities to Frederick Ashton and Antony Tudor. In Russia, ballet continued to push the limits of technical rigor. One particularly bright young pupil in St. Petersburg, George Balanchine (1904-1983), was to take ballet around yet another bend. Balanchine came to the U.S. in 1934 to establish the School of American Ballet and the American Ballet Company. His interest was in reviving classical lines, not what we've referred to as classical ballet, but the idealized lines revered by the ancient Greeks. With cool, logical, mathematical attention to space and proportion, he created a new aesthetic and called for a new title for his works: neoclassical.

Ballet in the 21st Century

The 20th century may have been the high tide of classical ballet, but where does ballet go from here? Audiences ask for the classic story ballets but also demand novelty and innovation. "The biggest crisis facing ballet at the end of the 20th century was the question of identity," writes Nancy Reynolds in *No Fixed Points.* "The classics had their place as did the Balanchine corpus [all of the ballets he created], but neither had provided a spark for further development" (New Haven, CT: Yale University Press, 2003, page 603). As we will see in the next section, social, psychological, and financial influences contribute to a blending of a once distinct aesthetic.

Ballet Positions

1. *Positions of the feet.* There are five fundamental positions of the feet (see figure 2.3). The positions described represent perfect turnout. It is important to remember that the feet achieve these positions due to outward rotation of the whole leg in the hip socket. Your turnout may not be 180 degrees. You should turn out only to the extent that you can keep your knees straight without strain. A more natural turnout is pointing the toes 45 degrees out from parallel and keeping the heels together.

First position: The heels touch and the toes point away from the center to the left and right of the body. In perfect turnout the heels and toes form a single straight line.

Second position: The balls of the feet and the heels form a single line and the heels are approximately one foot apart.

Third position: One foot is in front of the other, with heels touching the middle or arch of the other foot.

Fourth Position: From third position, slide the front foot forward about 12 inches, still in rotation, so that it is directly in front of and parallel to the back foot.

Fifth position: There are two variations of fifth position depending on whether you are in the Russian method or the Cecchetti (cheKEtee) method. In Cecchetti, the heel of the front foot is directly in front of the big toe of the back foot. In the Russian method the legs are crossed even further and the front foot crosses to the tip of the back foot's toe. The feet touch at all points and the knees are fully extended.

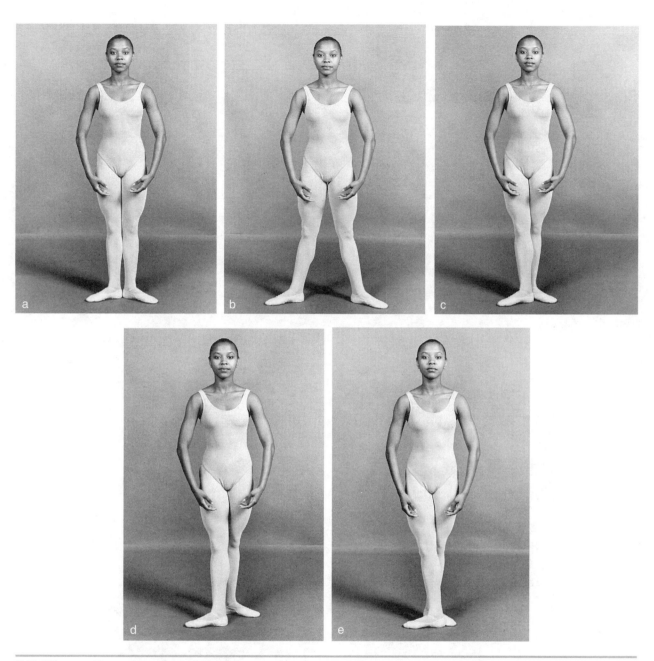

FIGURE 2.3   Foot positions in ballet: (a) first position, (b) second position, (c) third position, (d) fourth position, (e) fifth position (Cecchetti method).

2. *Positions of the arms.* Remember that as early as the 1500s there were "definitive" treatises on correct positions in dance. There remain several variations even in the oldest academic traditions. Learning the following names is a good start, but be prepared to discover variations in expectations among different ballet schools.

The preparatory position is illustrated in figure 2.3: Arms are rounded low in front of the body, with the fingertips in front of but not touching the thighs. The other arm positions are illustrated in figure 2.4.

First position: Arms round in front of the mid-torso.

Second position: Arms stretch from shoulder level sloping downward, and are slightly rounded, immediately in front of the side of the body.

FIGURE 2.4   Arm positions in ballet: (a) first position, (b) second position, (c) demi-seconde position, (d) fourth position en haut, (e) fifth position en haut. Note that figure 2.3 shows arm positions in the preparatory position.

Demi-seconde (half-second): Arms stretch at the side of the body, half the distance between first and second.

Third position: One arm rounds high over the head while the other stretches to second position.

Fourth en haut (fourth on high): One arm rounds high over the head while the other curves in front at the waistline.

Fourth en avant (fourth in front): One arm curves in front at the waistline; the other arm stretches in second position.

Fifth en haut (fifth on high): Both arms are high and rounded, framing the head, extending diagonally upward from the hairline.

The Language of Ballet

Ballet classes throughout the world are taught in the same vocabulary. You could go into a class in Tokyo and, although you might not understand the corrections, you could understand the sequences. When a teacher asks the students to "Glissade, pas de bourrée, jeté, assemblé," whether they are in Paris, Tokyo, Istanbul, or New York City, the dancers will do the same movements. The names of steps and combinations of steps take years to learn. Figure 2.5 provides some examples.

Try This Experiment

Select two or three steps from The Language of Ballet section and put them into a sequence using both sides of the body. Knowing what you now know about ballet's characteristic carriage of the torso, take yourself back in time to the 1700s, the period of the minuet. Imagine yourself wearing the costume of that period and see how you might transform your sequence so it would blend with the folks wearing the big wigs, the cinched waists, and the ruffled blouses.

Selected Ballet Vocabulary

plié (plee-AY)—French for "bend." You are already familiar with this word. If you want to bend a piece of metal, what's the name of the tool you use? Pliers! The plié is the key to elevation, landing, and many of the connecting steps of ballet. It is the lowering of the pelvis by bending the knees. The whole foot maintains contact with the floor on both flexion (descent) and extension (ascent).

battement (baht-MAHn)—Beating, clapping (swift leg lift).

tendu (tahnDOO)—Stretch. (As the foot stretches to point along the floor, the gesture leg also stretches away from the supporting leg. The foot stretches fully but does not leave the floor.)

battement tendu—Stretched beating of the leg and foot. Standing on one leg, stretch your other leg in front as far as it will reach without moving your hips. Keep your toe on the floor. That's a tendu en avant. If you stretch the leg to the side, you are moving à la seconde.

dégagé (day-gah-ZHAY)—Release. (In a dégagé, the foot of the gesture leg slides on the floor as the leg moves away from the supporting leg, and, at the last reach, the foot releases from the floor to point just off the floor.)

battement dégagé—Like the tendu, but now the fully stretched moving leg disengages from the floor two or three inches.

rond de jambe à terre (rohn duh zhahnb ah TAIR)—French for "round leg on the ground." Standing with your weight on one leg, extend the other in front of you. Now, as if drawing a circle in the sand, make a half circle from front to back, then close the leg under. Take care to extend your whole leg throughout, as if trying to draw the biggest circle possible. This can be performed circling front to back (en dehors) or back to front (en dedans).

cambré (kahm-BRAY)—Bent, arched, bowed (back bend above the waist).

demi (duh-MEE)—Half.

grand or grande (gran)—Great, big, large, noble, majestic, wide. A grand battement goes above 90 degrees, and a battement is below that level. (In a grand plié, the legs bend fully.)

FIGURE 2.5   Some of the vocabulary you will use in ballet.

Modern Dance: Definitions and History

At the turn of the 21st century experimental dance had no single name but was referred to as pure dance, expressional dance, fancy dance, barefoot dance, art dance, and other descriptive terms. To this day the term "modern dance" encompasses a variety of techniques and styles. Some modern dance companies perform works that were choreographed before the dancers in the company were born; others experiment with new forms or new combinations of movements and styles from all over the globe.

Modern dance rejected the rigidity of the body, the unnatural lines and training, the hierarchy of the ballet schools, the star system, and the politics of ballet. But modern was not just a reaction to ballet; it was also a rejection of another popular dance arena, the vaudeville circuit. The exhibitionism was offensive to these early artists who felt that dance could serve more noble means. Dance could be social comment; it could lead to political reform. And it could make people think, not about fairies and fantasies and frills, but about this life, this time, this society.

In spite of modern dance's original rejection of the training and terminology of ballet, most dancers in any genre are familiar with and employ the language of ballet and its principles of training. In modern dance, unlike ballet, there is no set curriculum, no regular order of exercises, no "modern music" (as there is "ballet music"), no particular costume, and no body type that is considered optimal. You may not even know whether you'll start class standing on your feet or lying on your back.

In the 100-plus years of modern dance, thousands of forms and styles and techniques have evolved in response to a person's interest in creating a personal statement. In many cases, what begins as a revolution turns into an institution. Not all modern companies are experimental, but it is probably safe to say that modern dance dedicates itself to experimenting. Nor is experimentation the exclusive domain of modern dance—all creative acts are experimental in some form. The dedication to exploring the manipulation of time, space, and effort without the constraints of codified positions defines modern dance.

Phases of Modern Dance

You will notice that the phases of modern dance are not chronological; they overlap. There was great exchange and influence between innovators in Europe and the United States, with one experiment sparking a series of others. Some sparks would turn into bonfires, the embers of which would still be glowing years later. Other sparks would ignite a slow-burning root fire with flares simultaneously appearing in multiple places.

New Dance (1900-1940)

The pioneers of modern dance were both critical and idealistic. Social, economic, and political changes raised new questions about morality, rights, freedom, and the nature of the human condition. New times called for new dances. But for patrons accustomed to tutus and pointe shoes, this new dance was difficult to understand. It wasn't beautiful in the same sense that beauty had been defined. The music that accompanied it wasn't "dance music." There was no fancy scenery. There was no story. Some said this new form wasn't dance at all.

The forerunners of this new dance were Loie Fuller (1862-1928), Isadora Duncan (1877-1927), and Ruth St. Denis (1878-1968). The title "mother of modern dance" is most often bestowed on Duncan because of her avowed dedication to reclaiming dance from the grips of escapism and exhibitionism, reestablishing it as a serious art.

The artists working with Diaghilev were busy pushing the limits of dance as an art: Nijinsky's *Le Sacre du Printemps* (*The Rite of Spring*) was so shocking and new that fights broke out in the concert hall as people argued and heckled and cheered and booed at the premiere in 1913. In 1917, Massine's *Parade* was received with outrage. Artists in Germany were going deeper and deeper into the human psyche, searching for a dance capable of revealing the inner self, the true self. Early modern choreographers experimented with the potential of dance outside of the conventions of ballet: Mary Wigman's (1886-1973) harsh, dramatic, almost violent solos; Oskar Schlemmer's (1888-1943) mechanical, dehumanized ballets; Valeska Gert's (1892-1978) uninhibited and often outrageous solos; Rudolf Laban's (1879-1958) exploration of systematizing movement; and Harald Kreutzberg's (1902-1968) virile, theatrical dances.

The Big Four (1910-1945)

The Big Four, the most influential pioneers of modern dance in America, were Martha Graham, Doris Humphrey, Charles Weidman, and Hanya Holm. (See figure 2.6.) These artists worked only slightly after the artists of the New Dance and have been much influenced by them. They are pioneers because they helped define American sensibility through their dance. As much as any homesteader in early America, these four made dances that were about the American spirit. Graham presented her first concert in 1926. Humphrey and Wiedman joined forces to create both a company and a school, making their debut in 1928. When Holm, a pupil of Wigman's, came to this country in 1931 to start a school to teach the Wigman technique, her emphasis was on the power of "absolute dance"—dance that relies on the lines of the body and the lines it makes in space rather than on pantomime or facial expression. Throughout the 1940s, these four dominated the concert dance scene in the U.S.

The Second Generation (1935-1980s)

Revolution results in new institutions. The students of the Big Four struck out on their own. Pearl Lang, Anna Sokolow, and Jane Dudley were first to leave the Martha Graham Dance Company and explore their own movement styles. Eleanor King and Sybil Shearer set out from the Humphrey-Weidman group. José Limón, a former Humphrey-Weidman principal, started his own company in 1942. A list of names and dates is almost meaningless without discussing the changes in the contributions to dance that occurred through these people specifically but also within this rich time of empowerment. These second-generation dancers were the ones who had been trained by—or, you might say, had been the guinea pigs of—the Big Four as they built and defined their techniques. The exponential explosion that occurred when these folks went off to figure out their own techniques resulted in a fertile climate of exploration—of aesthetics, training, presentation, subject matter, and audience interest.

Look into the techniques of Paul Taylor, Merce Cunningham, Alvin Ailey, Lester Horton, and Erick Hawkins—all techniques still referenced and performed today!

Postmodernism (1960-1980)

In the 1960s and '70s, in the midst of another period of social and political upheaval, dance got turned on its ear again. The postmodernists ("after-moderns"), as they are called, rejected the techniques and theories of modern dance and experimented with a whole new host of movement structures. They challenged the

FIGURE 2.6   Doris Humphrey and Charles Weidman delight in the dance.

conventional performer–audience relationship, the notion of training, and the politics of choreography, and once again caused audiences to wonder if what they were calling dance was really dance at all.

Chance dance, happenings, contact improvisation, dance theater, performance art—all manners of performance that had been experimented with in the early 1900s were shaken in their sleep and tried out afresh. The casting about for a good name to describe these forms of dance art reminds us of the dilemma dancegoers were in at the turn of the century. What they saw wasn't ballet, but what *was* it?

The new dance's use of pedestrian movements, movements that any ordinary person could and would do, was particularly unnerving to audiences accustomed to seeing, well, *dance.* The postmodern choreographers were considering movement in its most elemental form. How much can be stripped away from movement design before it's not dance anymore? At this time the idea of performing tasks rather than steps was novel. The idea of creating and solving a physical problem spontaneously during a performance was shocking. The idea of doing nothing and calling it dance was infuriating to some and refreshing to others.

Internationalism: The Merging of the Disciplines (1950-2000)

As opportunities for encounter with traditions, languages, images, and concepts outside our own cultures have grown, so has our embrace of new ways of dancing. The lines between genres have blurred into a new kind of internationalism. Contemporary concert dance has no particular national face, no particular cultural face, no particular aesthetic that defines it. The dance boom of the 21st century that started with a few big names has exploded into a thousand sparks.

Modern Dance Positions

1. *Foot positions.* Modern dance uses the same turned-out positions as ballet plus a full repetition of those positions in parallel. In the parallel positions the heels are where they would be in the rotated positions, but the toes point directly front.

2. *Arm positions.* Depending on the technique, arms may or may not have a set position or follow a set pattern. The arms tend to follow ballet positions, but they may be fully extended or rotated out (palm up) or in. The "true side" position was introduced as a term by Merce Cunningham. In true side, the wrists and elbows are fully extended directly to the sides of the body, rather than using the curved arms of other techniques.

3. *Floor positions.* Some classes begin on the floor rather than standing. There are four basic sitting positions in the Graham technique, around which many variations exist:

   a. Beginning position: Toes touching, feet arched, heels lifted, knees and thighs lifted, back fully extended;

   b. Second position: Legs extended to sides in a *V*, knees facing ceiling, feet either flexed or pointed, back extended, arms in second;

   c. Fourth position on the walk (legs are bent one in front and one in back): Front leg knee is up and the foot is on the floor, back leg inner thigh is on the floor;

   d. First position: Legs fully extended front, back fully extended. In the Humphrey technique the soles of the feet touch and the knees fall open to the floor. Here too the back is extended and balanced over the "sitz" bones.

In release technique, of which there are many variants today, the class might begin by lying on the back, then folding into a ball on one side and opening again onto the back to fold into a ball on the other side. A contact improvisation class might begin by having partners sitting back to back, one partner leaning forward to support the other, and then changing to allow the other person to be supported. So, as you might gather, there is huge variety in the structure of a warm-up depending on how the body needs to be prepared for its tasks.

The Language of Modern Dance

Many of the terms you will encounter in modern dance are techniques developed by the Big Four. Figure 2.7 describes some of these techniques.

Jazz and Its Cousins, Tap and Musical Theater: Definitions and History

In jazz dance, the entire body is engaged in simultaneous movement, in contrast to classical ballet in which shapes are made by moving the

Selected Modern Dance Vocabulary

contraction—A curving of the torso into a concave (C) shape by engaging the muscles in the front of the body. To get this sense, make a fist and do a slow-motion "punch" to your own gut. Feel how your abdominals suck up and cause a change in your low back and pelvis? That's a contraction. The contraction is fundamental to the Graham technique.

release—Used to mean "the return of the body to its neutral position" from a contraction. You will find instructors encouraging you to release muscles that may be unnecessarily holding a joint or joints; by releasing those muscles a more fluid and relaxed movement becomes possible.

fall/rebound—Fundamental to the Humphrey-Weidman technique. "When the act of falling reaches its choreographed conclusion, the immediate reaction is the rebound. In contrast to a 'bounce,' in which the downward movement is a deliberate repetitive attack, the rebound becomes a natural release of energy reversing the timing of the speed of the fall from fast to slow." (From *The Dance Technique of Doris Humphrey* by Ernestine Stodelle, Pennington, NJ: Dance Horizons, 1978, page 33.)

successional motion—Flow of energy within the body in a given direction. Suppose your head and throat are an empty container now filled with seed beads. Starting with the top of your head, bend forward and feel them all pile into the top of the skull. Then slowly restack the vertebrae, carefully pouring the beads back down the throat and into the ribcage. In order to keep them from getting jammed up in the throat area you had to move each vertebra slowly and successionally.

music visualization—When a dance matches the dynamic, rhythmic, and phrasing aspects of the music, one might say it is a study in making the music visual. Merce Cunningham, who contended that the music and the dance need not be related, challenged this intimate pairing of dance and music.

FIGURE 2.7   Some of the vocabulary you will encounter in modern dance.

limbs around a still or designed torso. It is an American form, born in the early 1900s when African and European peoples first began to mix their dance traditions. Throughout its long history, jazz and its cousin arts, tap and musical theater, have struggled for legitimacy as "real art," fighting a bias against dance that "merely" entertains. The power of jazz and its relatives is direct, often sensuous, and lively. Its roots are in the vernacular dances of the people. Most of all, these forms are essentially tied to their music. The play between the dance and the music is often all the dance is "about."

Jazz is rooted in the rhythms and movement styles brought to this continent by African slaves. Slaves were also shipped to islands in the Caribbean before being transported to the United States so dance traditions from Caribbean islands have made a distinctive contribution to jazz dance as well. Denied their ceremonies and traditions, the slaves were initially still allowed to dance and play music, but eventually even those practices were prohibited (when the slave owners figured out that they were using the drums to communicate). The slave owners could take away the drums and the music, but they couldn't take away hands and feet, and all manner of stamping, clapping, and body percussion continued. When that rhythmic play met the footwork of the Irish immigrants, the clog dances of the English, and the American soft shoe, there was a lot of sampling, swapping and borrowing among the forms. Tap dance is informed by all these traditional dances.

Oh, and don't forget about song. Many of the dances had songs that went with them. Variety shows that included songs, skits, dances, and burlesques were a popular diversion, especially for the middle classes. Starting in 1866, a show called *The Black Crook* ran for over 400 performances in New York. Although the musical and dramatic standards were low, the scenery and dancing seem to have been its main allure. "Auxiliary ladies" (the forerunners of the Radio City Music Hall Rockettes) established the kick line as standard musical theater fare. Held together by a very thin thematic line, the shows incorporated some chorus work with featured stars who held their fame only as long as they could distinguish themselves from other aspiring entertainers. Jazz "technique" included a repertoire of tap steps and elements of social dances and ballet.

Phases of Jazz, Tap, and Musical Theater

Jazz, tap, and musical theatre forms have gone through and continue to go through phases of development influenced by cross-cultural encounters, popular tastes, and commercial viability. "Jazz" is a word that came into the English language to describe the music of the early 1900s, a time when the European and African music traditions met and mingled in rich cross-cultural fertilization. New music invited new forms of dance.

New World: New Forms
First let's look at the dance traditions that were imported with the African slave trade. According to well-known choreographer and technician Gus Giordano, writing in his *Anthology of American Jazz*, "In Africa every tribe and sub-tribe has its own set of dances, each with its own dance rhythm—one for every occasion. No two are quite alike, even in part, though many take over four hours to perform in full. Consider, therefore, the countless rhythms and tempos that are to be found in Africa" (Evanston, IL: Orion Press, 1978, page 9). Consider what then happened when these tribes were shattered and scattered and intermixed in the New World. Consider finally, that there were no common languages among the slaves and that dance was the one thing they did have in common.

Now think about the plantation and the kinds of music and dance that were enjoyed by the upper class—reels, minuets, and other refined, ordered ways of socializing. European-based classical music uses a sophisticated interplay of melody and harmony. African music focuses on the interplay of rhythms. It is characteristically polyrhythmic, meaning there are many rhythms going on at the same time. The dance that goes with this can be described as polycentric, meaning it moves in many different body centers simultaneously. These different centers of movement (head doing one thing, pelvis another, arms another) are dancing the various rhythms of the music. This was a lewd, vigorous athleticism that was shocking and possibly frightening to the Puritan mind and body accustomed to moving in harmony with a flowing tune.

The cakewalk developed around harvest time on plantations when the slaves, dressed in their own finery danced as couples along a straight path balancing buckets or glasses of water on their heads. The winner was awarded a cake, often as simple as a corn cake. Later, this dance changed, first to become an entertainment for the slave holders and then, during the vaudeville days, as a staple element in the vaudeville shows with antics and apeing and showing off being essential to the success of the number. This kind of challenge dance included high kicks, fancy struts, and antics (many of which were mocking the unwitting slave owners). The competition inspired by these performances gave rise to steps that remain in the tap curriculum, such as the buck-and-wing. The cakewalk was included in minstrel shows, with white performers donning blackface to imitate the black dancers. When the Fugitive Slave Act passed in 1850, many of the slaves migrated north and many talented performers moved to Europe, where color was less of an issue. One famous dancer, William Henry Lane, found fame in both Europe and the United States for his use of body percussion (slapping his chest and legs and feet) while chanting verse, the most popular of which was "Juba," a name that became associated with him.

Vaudeville

Vaudeville came from what had been called "variety"; it had its roots in Europe, where itinerant performers trouped from town to town and village to village, says Charles Stein's *American Vaudeville* (New York: Knopf, 1984). In the early 1900s new dances emerged and disappeared from American ballrooms as they went in and out of vogue. Vernon and Irene Castle helped popularize the fox-trot, a social dance that has stood the test of time. A significant invention played a central role in the development of the music of the period and

the dances that went with it: the record player! People were able to dance whether or not there was a band to play for them. When the troops came home, worn out from World War I, they wanted to enjoy the freedom they felt they'd earned. The vaudeville shows took musical theater a little farther down the road with more elaborate sets, more integrated stories, and more sophisticated audiences. Entertainers such as Bill "Bojangles" Robinson, a black tap dancer, took tap to a new level of sophistication and style. Ballroom/show dancers Fred Astaire and Ginger Rodgers danced right along with the new technology, and dance crossed over to film. Astaire had been a popular performer throughout the '20s, and when musicals expanded into the movie industry, he became one of the most popular figures in the business. In *Jump Into Jazz: The Basics and Beyond for Jazz Dance Students,* authors Kraines and Pryor write: "He blended the flowing steps of ballet with the abruptness of jazz movements and was the first dancer to dance every musical note so that the rhythmic pattern of the music was mirrored in the dance steps" (Mayfield Press, 2001, page 180).

Broadway

During the 1940s Broadway saw such premieres as *Oklahoma!* (1943), *Carousel* (1945), *Brigadoon* (1947), and *Paint your Wagon* (1951). What's significant about these is that they were each choreographed by ballet dancers. In the 1940s, jazz music got so complicated that it was no longer possible to dance to it. Social jazz dance waned and professional jazz dance began to emerge as a form of its own. Modern jazz dance was the amalgam of ballet and modern with the strong rhythms and percussive and sensual music of jazz. When Agnes de Mille choreographed *Oklahoma!* she was determined not to have dance be a trivial part of the production. Her success in elevating dance in the musical theater to an art of its own was a turning point in dance history. Jerome Robbins, equally at home in the ballet studio, brought elements of ballet and modern jazz into his Broadway hits. His *West Side Story* (1957) is an excellent example of the range of styles he brought together in a single production. In 1960, Alvin Ailey premiered *Revelations,* a modern dance that made significant use of jazz dance styles.

Jazz Becomes a Technique

To feed the film industry with the dancers it needed, Los Angeles became a center for jazz dance training. Two men in particular made huge contributions to the solidification of a formal jazz technique. In 1951, Luigi (Eugene Louis Facciuto) created a system of jazz training that was both rigorous and lyrical. Gus Giordano developed a similar system of training and positions, but his technique reflected a stronger modern dance influence. It still used isolations and percussive qualities, but in a more natural style than Luigi's. Then in the '70s, Bob Fosse's distinctive jazz style developed in several Broadway shows. The "Fosse hand," flexed at the wrist, is one signature, but his work is also known for being slick, erotic, and intense.

Jazz, Tap, and Musical Theater in the 21st Century

The popularity of such Broadway hits as *STOMP, Bring in 'da Noise, Bring in 'da Funk, Tap Dogs,* and *Riverdance* (and its variants) have established "rhythm shows" as a new genre of dance-based theater. Tap dance is serious fun. And music videos have brought jazz dance to new definitions. From the early days of *Soul Train,* dance has become an essential element in the sale of popular music. The current trend is moving away from the "long shot" dance videos of the era of Michael Jackson's "Thriller" and "Smooth Criminal"; instead, short, quick cuts of dance sequences are sprinkled in. In the '90s hip-hop emerged out of the break dancing of the '70s. "New school"—a style of hip-hop that evolved when the music began to combine rap and singing—is popular all over the world. It is a style that goes beyond dance to form a complete aesthetic, including associated music, clothing, language, and visual art. And jazz dance technique continues to be developed as private dance studios across the country participate in dance competitions. Because of the high level of athleticism and competition, some people have speculated that jazz dance might one day become an Olympic event (Kraines & Pryor, 2001)!

World Dance

During the 20th century, major changes in our access to networks of communication, transportation, and media have fundamentally changed our cultures. We are no longer isolated from each other in the ways that we were at the start of that century. The arts that we once used to define ourselves and preserve our histories are now accessible to anyone. Rituals, once privileged, private, and sacred, can now be viewed, in some form or fashion, by anyone who wants to buy a ticket. Ceremonies in which dance played an important part are now offered outside the community, off the hallowed ground, and sometimes are even open to audience participation. What remains of the original power of these dances?

We need to understand the kinds of power those dances had in order to think about how or if their power has changed. Although space once again precludes an in-depth analysis, we can profitably address some broad categories.

Dance-Dramas

Whether presented in a Balinese temple or a Ugandan dance ground, the purpose and power of the dance-drama is to reenact the stories and legends of a group's history. Dance-dramas are performed for the benefit of the tribe or community. The performers are often members of a particular family whose social role is to maintain the dances and share them at the proper times.

These dances date back to the beginning of civilization, when prehunt dances ensured the safety of the hunters and the survival of the group. There are figures pictured on pillars in a Cambodian temple dating as far back as 1180 BCE doing movements that are still in the traditional dances of the *Ramayana*—the ancient Vedic stories of the Hindu tradition. The classical dances of India are not only for entertainment. They serve to attain the yogi's state of supreme bliss. Bharata natyam, the oldest of the Indian classical dances, perfected and stylized over 2,000 years, still remains fresh and fascinating in its richness, traditional movements, and aesthetic appeal. And in the mountains

INSIDE INSIGHT

The Kung Bushmen have a medicine dance ceremony that begins in the evening and sometimes lasts until dawn. Women sit on the ground, clapping and singing and occasionally dancing a round or two, while men circle around them, singing and stamping rhythms with their feet. The songs are wordless but named: "Rain," "Sun," "Honey," "Giraffe," and other "strong things." The strength of the songs is their *ntum*, or medicine, thought to be a gift from the great god. Ntum is also in the fire, and even more so in the "owners of medicine," or curers. Most Kung men practice as curers at some point in their lives.

of Tibet, on the eve of the new year, dance dramas that go on for hours are performed in the lamaseries.

Ceremonial and Ritual Dances

Ceremonial and ritual dances may or may not tell a story. The rituals bring favor to the event. They have a focus but not necessarily a narrative. They may be specific (circumcision, wedding, rite of passage, illness, funeral), or they may be cyclical (seasonal, lunar). Curt Sachs, author of *World History of the Dance*, tells us that ritual dances may be harmonious or ecstatic. In harmonious dances the motions and rhythms are repetitive, possibly hypnotic, and the patterns are simple. Typical movements include shuffling, hopping, lunging, stamping, sliding, or stepping with a bent knee. The spine is relaxed and the arms, hands, head, pelvis, and trunk may swing or sway from side to side. In ecstatic forms the intensity of the dance builds as it goes on. Movements include whirling and spinning; every body part may shake or tremble. Heads roll, legs and arms thrust into the air, vibrating with energy, sometimes leading to convulsion. Ecstatic dances demand great strength and facility. The climax is the trance state for one or more of the participants. Sachs writes: "Ritual dances are mimetic but imageless. The power comes not from the gesture but from their rhythmic repetition in the midst of other ritual aspects. The dancer jumps to inspire the gods to make the crops grow high." (New York: Norton, 1963, page 21).

Folk Dance

"Folk dance" is a label often used to include characteristic national dances, country dances, and figure dances performed in costume to folk tunes. Many of these dances may have begun as ritual or ceremonial dances—dances believed to hold magical power—but have survived as a sources of national pride and social pleasure. You'll find song dances, village dances, and figure dances in most parts of the world. These dances strengthen social bonds.

The forms and figures of folk dance vary; within a particular nationality you will likely find line dances, round dances, snaking dances, or square dances. Each one serves a different purpose in creating or celebrating community, so looking at how the people of a culture dance often provides insight into the values they hold important. Who dances? Does everyone do this dance or just the adults or the children or the women or the men? How do they dance together? Do dancers take turns or does everyone dance together? Can a couple go anywhere in the room or does the dance work better if people follow a particular path? Does everyone have to dance at the same pace? Is this dance closed (a circle or square) or open (a line or a dance with no fixed paths)?

For instance, Finnish dances are never competitive or showy. The Finns have no war dance. In their folk dance traditions, men and women are on equal terms—there are no "women's dances" or "men's dances." What might you guess about their values?

Dances are important in Turkish life. They are a part of weddings, festivals, and religious and national holidays. The dances have varying characteristics based on region and location, and they demonstrate the different social roles of men and women. Some are reenactments of daily activities while others tell stories.

The Mexican Danza de los Viejitos is danced by young men who move like very old men and entertain with antics and caricatural hobbling and wobbling. In contra dance, partners face each other in two lines and meet in the center when it is their turn to dance. In square dances, four couples face each other to form a square and then move as couples or according to gender. In the Israeli misirlou, dancers arranged in a male/female chain, connected by pinkie fingers, perform the snaking floor pattern moving next to each other. In the United States's Cotton-Eyed Joe, short lines of dancers move around the room like spokes of a wheel, connected by arms crossed either over the shoulders or behind the back.

Because they serve many functions, folk dances also fit into the categories of social, recreational, and concert dance. For instance, the samba has been called the national dance of Brazil, so it would logically be labeled a folk dance. But it is also a social dance and the foundation of the spectacles performed for millions of celebrants at Carnaval. The polka was originally a Czech peasant dance, developed in Eastern Bohemia (now part of Czechoslovakia). After World War II, Polish immigrants in the United States adopted the polka as their "national" dance. Does that make the polka a Polish folk dance, an American folk dance, or a Polish-American folk dance?

As traditional dances have moved out of their traditional settings, their power has changed very little in some cases; in others it has changed dramatically. Tourists arriving for a Hawaiian holiday may be entertained by the hula dance being performed at the airport, but that dance has a different power for the tourist than it does for someone who understands its traditions.

In some folk dances the original, historically accurate choreography is still danced; in other cases the duration, performance, performers, context, and even the floor patterns have changed or been dropped as traditionally performed elements. For instance, the polka is a social dance with Bohemian roots, but anyone can polka as long as they imitate the step-together-step-hop pattern. Major hit shows such as *Riverdance* and its imitators brought Irish step dance into the international spotlight, but would you say that what is performed in such shows is folk dance?

To conclude, the term "folk dance" is one that can be applied to a dance that is rooted in a specific cultural heritage. It is performed to music also rooted in that heritage and is often costumed in a historically specific way. As the dances naturally evolve, the movement, costumes, and accompanying music may represent a particular point in their evolution. The power of the dance may therefore have changed with time.

INSIDE INSIGHT

The song "Misirlou" was published as sheet music in the 1930s by Nicholas Roubanis. In the 1940s, the Mitchell Ayers band recorded the tune. Dick Dale and His Del-Tones, as well as The Beach Boys, recorded it in 1963, and other surfer bands subsequently put it in their repertoires. "Misirlou" was featured in the opening scene of the movie *Pulp Fiction*.

In 1945, a Pittsburgh, Pennsylvania, women's musical organization asked Professor Brunhilde Corsch to organize an international dance group at Duquesne University to honor America's World War II allies. She contacted Mercine Nesotas, who taught several Greek dances, including the Cretan syrtos haniotikos, which she called "kritikos", but for which they had no music. Because Pittsburgh's Greek-American community did not know Cretan music, Pat Mandros Kazalas, a music student, suggested that "Misirlou," although slower, might fit the dance. The rest, as they say, is history. The misirlou is danced all over the world, even by the local Pittsburgh Greeks. (Adapted from http://www.phantomranch.net/folkdanc/dances/misirlou.htm)

The steps of folk dances are basic locomotor movements: step, hop, run, jump, slide, leap, and combinations such as skip and gallop, which are covered in more detail in chapter 4. A few of the named combinations are shown in figure 2.8.

Dance has the power to transform, inspire, depress, or entertain. The same dance may invoke reactions ranging from delight to disgust in different people. It may confirm or confuse. Dance can create community or reinforce "otherness." We have merely glanced at five genres that are incorporated in Western concert dance. As you review the material in this chapter, think about how history repeats itself. Keep this in mind as you attempt to make something completely new. Chances are, somewhere in the history of dance, something similar has already been done.

Knowing about trends in dance history may help you research examples of other people's solutions to danceable subjects. How have other people danced about death, or friendship, or humility? How has the element of time informed dances in other eras? Who else has been interested in dances that tell stories? Who has been interested in dances that do not tell stories?

What is our power as dancers? As choreographers? As dance appreciators? Your task is not to be novel but to be *you*. Your task as a dancer is to explore the power of dance so that you can inform and transform. Your task as a choreographer is to develop skills so that the power you wish to communicate through your dance is intentional. Your task as an appreciator is to make room for new images and sensations, allowing their power to work their magic on and in you.

Selected Folk Dance Vocabulary

chug—A sudden drop of the weight forward by bending the knees, done on one foot or two. In some dances the hips also move forward to tuck; in others, the leg moves independently.

grapevine (aka "karaoke step")—This sequence travels sideways by crossing the feet alternately in front and behind. The hips rotate to accommodate the placement of the feet. Side step to the left by crossing the right foot behind the left one; step side with the left and continue moving sideways to the left by crossing the right foot in front of the left.

paddle turn (aka "buzz step")—If turning to the right, keep the weight on the ball of your leading foot (or right foot), alternately push against the floor using the ball of your left foot and rotate your right heel approximately 90 degrees to the right (clockwise), making a weight change each time until you complete a full turn. To turn to the left, reverse the movement: Your left heel moves counterclockwise as you alternately push using the ball of your right foot to complete the turn.

polka—There are four weight transfers in the polka: a hop and three steps. The step alternates from side to side and is done within two beats of music. Hop (left), step (right), close (left), step (right).

schottische—Three steps and a hop. The three steps can be left, right, left, hop, or right, left, right, hop while moving in different directions—forward or backward is most typical. The schottische usually gets one beat of music for each action.

stomp/stamp—A stomp is a step that strikes the floor heavily without a transfer of weight. A stamp strikes the floor heavily with a transfer of weight.

slide—Combines a step and a leap, typically done to either side.

FIGURE 2.8   Many of the common steps in folk dance are combinations of movements.

Think About It

1. Which trends do you find repeating in the development of ballet and jazz dance?

2. What influences people's preferences for watching dance?

3. How does the role of the audience differ among these genres?

4. Have any of these genres been central to society as a whole in their time? What is the power of dance in defining a culture?

5. In your opinion, are some dance forms "higher" or "lower" than others? On what do you base your opinion? Give specific examples that support your claim.

6. Research one particular thread of one genre by investigating one famous person. What political, social, personal, and historical events were important in the person's development? What were their contributions? What is their legacy? (Who followed in their footsteps?) How did their students go in different directions?

Your Turn to Dance

Many Centers/One Center

Following up on the idea of polycentrism introduced in the jazz history, you will make a solo dance that explores moving from many centers at once. Start by playing around with the possibilities of multiple centers. First, work without music to discover what your natural inclination is in tempo and rhythm. Can you move your head in a 4-count pattern and add your shoulders in a 2-count pattern? Can you keep that going and use your hips to make a rhythm that's different from the ones made by your head and shoulders? How complicated a combination can you sustain?

Take this polycentric movement to its fullest expression, then switch to moving from a single center. Initially, locate this single center in your abdomen. Experiment with going back and forth between many centers and one abdominal center. Then see if you can locate a center in another part of the body—your shoulder, your wrist, your chest—and see what it feels like to try to move from that place before returning to your polycentric motion.

Play with timing so that these poly/single switches are neither balanced nor predictable. Add in stillness.

Now explore this improvisation with different kinds of music. What is this dance's power?

What Kind of Folk Dance?

How might you use these typical folk steps in your own choreography? Try playing a chance game to create some movement themes. Tear a piece of paper into 12 pieces. Write a different locomotor movement on each piece, then write a different folk step on each remaining piece. Turn them over. Make up a pattern of repetition or use this one: 2-2-2-1-1. Turn over one piece of paper. That's your first move. Let's say it says "schottische." If you're using the pattern given, you'll begin your sequence by doing the schottische two times. Let's say your next choice reads "step." You take two steps. You might end up with something like this:

schottische (2)-step (4)-slide (4)-paddle turn (8 pushes or 2 full turns)-hop (2)-jump (1)

Now decide how many people are going to join you. Is this a couples dance, a line dance, or a circle dance? Finally, make up a reason for doing it. What could be its power?

How Do You Learn to Dance?

A woman was preparing a report on folk dancing. While doing her research she met an 88-year-old man who had been clogging (an American folk dance) all his life. Thrilled to have found such an authority, she asked him to show her some of his steps. He danced for her, and she was very impressed. "That one with the swipe," she asked, "would you please show me that one again?" She tried to duplicate the man's pattern. "Excuse me," she interrupted, "is that shuffle-step or shuffle-hop?" He started over, a little slower, and again she interrupted, "Is it a flap or another shuffle before the scuff?" Sighing, the polite man started over, and again the eager scholar stopped his dance. "Oh, I see!" she said. "But do you change your weight on the 2 or the 3?" The man stopped again and simply asked, "Darlin', do you want to dance or do you want to talk about it?"

Learning to Dance and Learning About Dance

You signed up for a dance course because you wanted to move, but now you may be frustrated because the course requires you to read. Then again, you may be a research-oriented person who prefers to gather information before beginning, or you might just be confused about what reading has to do with dancing.

Both learning to dance and learning about dance can be approached from several different angles. Learning about the dances of other times and places will take you into history, anthropology, sociology, politics, and psychology. Learning about dance is a fascinating way to explore human nature. For instance, in the previous example, what sociological observations might you make? How would you have gone about learning some of the clogger's steps? Would you say that learning movement is a kind of research?

Learning about dance and learning to dance involve asking questions. What is the purpose of this dance? Can anyone do it? How does a person train to do this dance well? Is there an audience for it? How is an audience meant to respond? Where did this dance come from?

Chances are, the veteran clog dancer learned to dance not by reading about it or asking a bunch of technical questions but by imitating and experimenting with what he saw. This is the *dive-right-in* approach to learning about dance and learning to dance. Others include the *creative movement* and the *technical* approaches.

Using an analogy to clarify these three methods, let us say that you are interested in working with wood. You would use the dive-right-in approach if you decided that the best way to learn about woodworking was to hang around the shops of some woodworkers and see what tips and skills you could pick up. By watching them, talking with them, and helping them with their projects, you would eventually get the hang of woodworking and feel confident about starting your own projects. The creative movement approach would include collecting pictures of woodworking designs that interested you and, possibly, checking out an instructional book from the library. You would read about different kinds of wood, joints, and tools, collect some materials, and play with what you have in order to see what you can make. The technical approach would land you in a class taught by a master woodworker who would lead you through a series of skills and give you constant feedback to correct your developing skills. If you wanted to build a house, you would probably draw from all three of these approaches. Each has its merits and appropriate applications, but each also has its pitfalls.

Dive-Right-In Approach

The dive-right-in approach is usually the one used to pass down folk dances, including the dances you and your friends do. There are studios that teach social dances, such as the jitterbug, the mambo, or the fox-trot, but contemporary dances are learned by doing. No reading, no writing, and no special classes. You go to a dance, and you dive right in. You normally find this approach used in dances that have limited movement vocabularies or a minimal selection of basic steps. Clog dancing, for instance, is based on eight basic steps that the dancers modify according to their individual styles. Clogging is done more for recreational and social purposes than for concert performance. Although there are teams and competitions, clogging is, in general, a social dance that encourages and celebrates individual stylistic differences. In fact, these innovations keep the dance alive. As with other popular social dances, one movement pattern (usually very repetitive) will be slightly varied (either by intention or by accident), giving birth to a new pattern. The dance evolves as others try out this new movement and, invariably, add their own flair to the pattern.

On the other hand, many folk and other ritualized dances are valued for their celebration of tradition. It's the performer's responsibility to honor that tradition by repeating the dance in a form that resembles the original as much as possible; therefore, many dances of this type are not a good outlet for choreographic creativity. However, traditional dances have long been a source of material and inspiration for choreographers who have adapted traditional patterns to fit their own work.

Try This Experiment

If you have friends or classmates who are familiar with a line dance, have them teach you that dance, not by explaining it or "breaking it down" but just by moving with them as they do the dance.

Creative Movement Approach

The creative movement approach celebrates spontaneity, originality, and individuality through structured movement opportunities in which the dancer continuously invents movement according to personal preferences. Most of the time this opportunity is not a free-for-all; it is structured to encourage personal investigation into some particular aspect of movement. The creative movement approach is an incredibly useful way to learn about your personal movement preferences, analyze your strengths and weaknesses, and explore new territory. That new territory may be physical, social, emotional, or a combination of all three.

The next Try This Experiment is an example of a creative movement exercise. Which of the steps do you think would be the most challenging? Or, to put the question another way, with which of the steps could you most challenge yourself? Would those explorations present you with a physical challenge? Would you feel awkward or uncomfortable making those explorations in the presence of others? Would you be afraid to put yourself in that exploring frame of mind no matter who was watching? Would you be afraid that you were doing the exploration in the wrong way? These physical, social, and emotional challenges are the very reasons that some dancers are attracted to the resources of the creative movement approach to dance. It assumes no previous dance training, encourages innovation, and honors the experience and resources of individuals at whatever stage they arrive. However, dancers must be careful not to get too comfortable with one mode of creating and moving—if this familiarity continues, everything they create will be very similar. Instead, dancers interested in this approach should continue to find challenging structures and push themselves to generate new solutions and refine their movements.

Try This Experiment

Being able to perform a series of quickly changing isolations is a skill that will help you in dance techniques related to concert jazz dance and many popular forms of dance. To improve your "quick-fire" ability, try this creative movement approach. Turn your head on one count. Keep it there and raise and lower your shoulders as you count "and 2." Shake your right hand, then your left on "and 3"; clap and look front on "and 4." Create four more counts of isolations so you have a sequence of eight counts. How quickly can you complete your sequence?

Technical Approach

Traditionally, learning about dance and learning to dance has required you to be a copycat. We call this the technical approach because you copy a dance technique that has been identified and valued as worthwhile for training. This technical approach to learning dance celebrates the history and traditions of time-honored training methods; it is devoted not to inventing new movements but to accurately repeating a movement syllabus that has been recognized as a distinct style (figure 3.1). It is the student's

FIGURE 3.1 By imitating the forms demonstrated by the tai chi master, the student discovers a rhythm of breath and weight and a grace that comes from their integration.

duty to master the nuances of movement necessary to continue the historical tradition. You achieve this goal by rigorously repeating specific movement patterns for hours and by practicing those patterns as strictly physical skills. Although a teacher might offer an image that helps clarify a movement pattern, it is still up to the students to repeat the patterns as closely as possible to the way they have been demonstrated. For instance, a teacher might suggest that the students imagine a soft breeze lifting the arms, but it would not be appropriate in a ballet class for students to let their arms float up wherever their imaginations dictated. No student could sustain interest in such repetition without being curious about the possible nuances of the exercises. Students need to commit to increasing their skills and range of motion as well as recognizing and executing the given patterns.

In many situations some aspects of the dive-right-in, creative movement, and technical approaches will add variety to the learning process. As you work, bear in mind that whichever style you are interested in pursuing, the dance has a tradition and a history. Even the newest dance craze has its roots in some moment in the history of dance. Reading and talking about that history are valuable to a complete understanding of the art form, but the most critical source of knowledge will come from moving, doing, and dancing. Regardless of which approach you choose, as a beginning dancer you will work with five fundamental movement experiences.

Fundamental Movement Experiences

Whether you want to learn a grand jeté or a time step, whether you want to break old habits, learn old patterns, or create new ones, your job is to integrate these five fundamental movement experiences as you work: analyzing the actions of the spine, determining locomotor versus axial motion, working with rhythmic coordination, moving with functional alignment, and moving from your center.

Try This Experiment

Explore your spine's potential to bend by lying on your back and slowly bringing yourself up to a curled, sitting position. Then roll down onto your back by trying to let each vertebra touch the ground, one at a time. Imagine what your spine would look like if the room were dark and only your spine glowed in the dark. What other ways can you bend your spine? You have done forward flexion and back flexion. How about side flexion?

In a sitting position, twist your head as far as you can without moving your shoulders. You are twisting your cervical spine. Now, without moving your pelvis, continue to twist, allowing the action to travel down through your thoracic spine. Let your hips move, allowing the twist to also occur in your lumbar spine. Rewind, keeping your head as twisted as possible.

Have you ever played with one of those toys that collapse when you push the bottom and then stand up again when you let go? If you have seen one, you remember that the little creature is held together with rubber bands that relax when you press and go taut again when you release the button. Using that same image, slump over so that your spine is bent and twisted. Now bring yourself back to vertical. You just extended your spine.

Actions of the Spine

The spine can perform three actions: It can bend, twist, or extend. You just did all three in the previous Try This Experiment. Your spine is composed of 26 vertebrae, and any of the three actions is possible at each of the joints. Pretty amazing potential! Remember that the three actions can be useful in two ways. First, as a strategy for copying other people's movements, begin by recognizing the actions of the spine. Is the spine vertical? Is only the lumbar spine (the lowest third) vertical and the rest bent? Is the spine bent and twisted? When trying to read movement, look for what the action of the spine might be.

Second, apply the bend, twist, and extend motions to your creative efforts. If you want to make your movement patterns more visually interesting, try changing the shape of your spine as you move. Use these actions as a condition of movement; that is, work with a continuously bent or twisted shape. In a technique class you will find that your spine determines the basic shape of your movement and establishes the particular relationship to gravity that the technique honors. The audience will perceive the line of force acting on a body as perpendicular to the line of the spine. Therefore, a spine that is vertical will create an image of balance or freedom from strain against gravity. A bent spine will create an image of a weakened or submissive form. A twisted spine will create an image of mutually opposing forces (see figure 3.2).

Ballet, for instance, displays a freedom from the force of gravity, so the spine is generally vertical. Jazz dance, which often deals with the contrasts of power and submission, uses the spine to indicate those two conditions. Modern dance makes shapes that may or may not pertain to the force of gravity. This may be one of the reasons people find some modern dances inherently confusing—their intuition tells them one thing, and the dance says something else! As a dancer and a dance appreciator, you can use this information to clarify your intentions and those of a choreographer.

Locomotor Versus Axial Movement

Another fundamental movement experience distinguishes between moving through space and moving in place. In dance, when we say "moving through space," we are not talking about rockets; we are referring to the volume of the dance area in which the dancer works. This space could be a classroom, the stage area, or even a parking lot or field. Dancers have two options when it comes to moving: They can move through space by walking, running, leaping, or skipping, or they can move in place. Actions that take the body through space are called *locomotor* movements. Actions that do not take the body through space are *axial* movements. This distinction serves two purposes: You can use it to read dance more effectively, and you can use it as a tool for improvisation.

Try This Experiment

To explore the distinction between locomotor and axial movement, try this experiment (you will need a fairly open space in which to work): Imagine there is an *X* on the floor, and you have your hands and

FIGURE 3.2   How many different ways do you see the spine being used?

feet on each of the four points of that X. With your pelvis off the center of the X, and your hands and feet glued to their spots, move as much as possible as you count to four. Then, cover as much space as possible as you count to four, moving anywhere except on the X. When you get to four counts, freeze with two feet and one hand glued to the floor. Again, move as much as possible as you count to four, then move anywhere else (running, leaping, rolling) as you count to four, this time ending on one foot. By bending, twisting, and extending, move on this new spot for a count of four, then move anywhere else as you count to four, ending on your bottom for a final count of four during which you move however you can. Conclude by making a still shape. Anything you did while you were not on an X was a locomotor movement. Everything you did with one or more points fixed to the ground was axial movement.

Rhythmic Coordination

Athletes are aware of the importance of rhythmic coordination, and they use rhythm in their training. Rhythmic coordination helps a basketball player achieve elevation and timing for a lay-up. The rhythm of the step-step-jump pattern has been practiced repeatedly and helps the player to time when to shoot the basket. Competitive swimmers use the rhythmic coordination of their stroke patterns to pace themselves and sense their speed. The use of rhythmic patterns in motor activities—from competitive sports to vacuuming a rug—enables the participant to settle into a groove, put the body on automatic pilot, and free the mind for decisions, such as when to shoot or pass. In dance, as in the martial arts, we seek this freedom for its own sake, as an end in itself. There is a difference between the application of rhythmic coordination in dance and its use in sports; the rhythm is intentional in dance while it is functional in sports (figure 3.3).

Rhythmic coordination is a fundamental movement experience that will be explored in any of the three approaches to learning dance. Intentional rhythm distinguishes dance from other movement activities. As you learn to dance or as you learn about dance, you will

FIGURE 3.3   Similar movements can have very different functions.

become aware of the importance of rhythmic coordination. It can mean moving to the music, but let us not limit ourselves to working with music. Sometimes dance is performed in silence, to a text, or to music that has no recurring pattern of beats. Likewise, in many dance activities rhythmic coordination, through its predictability and familiarity, invites an ease of movement and a freedom of mind.

Functional Alignment

If you needed to dig a ditch, you would not hold your shovel with both hands on the end. Depending on what you needed to dig up, you would move your hands closer to or farther from the head for maximum leverage. Becoming aware of functional alignment in dance is a bit like learning to choke up on a shovel. The more you work and the more you come to understand your personal strengths and weaknesses, the more you will discover how important it is to work in the most balanced, relaxed manner. You are constantly balancing the forces of nature, resisting the pull of gravity, and responding to millions of muscular changes in the course of the day. When you begin forming your dance movement, you need to be conscious of working so that your joints are protected and your strength and flexibility are most easily accessed.

Moving From Your Center

Moving from your center is probably the most elusive of the five fundamental movement experiences. The concept of center is an intriguing one. Anyone who has cornered on a motorcycle or ridden a surfboard will tell you that your center is not a specific X-marks-the-spot place on the body. In the same way, a dancer's center is not a spot you can put an X on, nor is it a place you can feel with your hands. When you dance, your center is your physical, emotional, and spiritual source of strength and balance. Martial arts rely on this sense of center for power, speed, and effective movement. It is not a power that comes with bulky muscles but one that comes with grace, agility, and a cultivated ability to choose the right movement option at the right moment.

Moving from your center means having the ability to be completely invested in your movement.

So when we talk about centering, we are not talking only about the physical spot slightly below the navel. That region is more than just a center of gravity; it's also your center of power, the root of your deep breathing apparatus, and your psychic "throne." A dancer or any efficiently moving person can move with both power and grace by mobilizing that throne; they can then move with an ease of physical options—direction changes, weight shifts, fluidity in the spine, ease of breath. A person moving from the center is both balanced and present.

Here is a concrete example: The teacher asks the class to imagine and explore the experience of being surrounded by flies. The dancer who is not working from her center will be the one standing in a corner half-heartedly waving her arms while looking around to see if anyone is watching her. The dancer who is working from his center will be the one turning, ducking, swiping, going to the floor, and running from the spot he started on. One person attempts the motion of swatting but is too nervous about what other people think to become emotionally motivated by the image of flies. The other person is completely invested in manifesting the movement physically, emotionally, and spiritually.

In another example, the teacher asks the class to make an interesting dance presentation using the following sequence: Take two steps forward, one step back to turn, and spiral to the floor. The dancer moving from her center will create a reason for being drawn forward, then back, then to the floor. She will explore different feelings of force that could be responsible for such a sequence. Pushing, pulling, balancing, and tensing will be part of her explorations. She will allow herself to have an experience and will therein discover a compelling, personal investment in the sequence.

The person who is not moving from his center will be more mental, checking the mirror (if there is one in the room) to see how he looks, probably trying to move according to some idea about how a dancer should look.

He will be looking around, not trying to pick up ideas but self-consciously checking to see if anyone is watching him. This caution is entirely normal, especially among beginning students. Unfortunately, it is not a productive work habit, and it generally results in inhibiting access to the magic that waits to be discovered in each individual.

Learning to move from your center means learning to trust your own resources. As these centered moments come to you, you will realize that moving from your center is not only a fundamental movement experience, it is a fundamental life experience.

The five fundamental movement experiences are important for a beginning dancer but are equally important to a more advanced dancer who is learning to take new risks and pushing to new levels of dance mastery.

What Does It Mean?

Perhaps you sympathize with the girl standing in the corner half-heartedly swatting but not willing to get any more involved. It might be that you have been asked to practice an exercise that does not seem to have any purpose other than pain and frustration. You may find yourself thinking, "Sure, I could do that, but what does it mean?"

Purpose of Dance

In a Nigerian village the women perform a special dance as they lay a floor in a new hut, but it would not be accurate to say that the purpose of the dance is to lay a floor. The purpose of the dance is to make the floor-laying a magical experience. When the young girls of a European village are collected to skip around a maypole holding ribbons, they do eventually cover the pole in bright colors, but that is not the purpose of the dance. The maypole dance celebrates spring. In our increasingly utilitarian culture, many of those who are new to dance wonder what purpose dance serves.

The purpose of dance will vary for different people. Those who enjoy social dance probably find that they like being with other people; they enjoy moving with other people, and they like the way they feel after dancing. Those who enjoy taking creative movement classes want to use their imaginations and learn about themselves by solving problems using their bodies. Those who are attracted to formal dance classes appreciate the rewards of rigorous training as they discover more physical potential.

Among those who create (choreograph) dances, there are different ideas about the purpose of presenting their efforts to others. Some wish to share the thrill and joy of moving. Some hope that the movement patterns they have put together will be so impressive to a viewer that simply to watch will be an exhilarating experience. Other choreographers deliberately avoid the use of highly trained movement, hoping instead to establish fellowship with their audience by using a vocabulary that is within the average person's capability. There are choreographers who are interested in exploring an aspect of the human physical potential and presenting the fruits of these explorations. There are also those whose work draws on each of these agendas.

Finding Meaning in Your Own Dancing

Your purpose for dancing will be personal. The meaning you get from watching a dance or from dancing will be a personal response. As you study, you will find memories, emotions, and ideas being triggered. You will find that your capacity to sense the world becomes more acute; you will see, hear, and feel more, and generally be more alive to your world.

Learning to observe the movement (and stillness!) in the world is a lifelong practice—the more you know, the more you see. Reading movement is an important skill, not only in your dance class but in other aspects of your life. It is your job, as a student of movement, to collect interesting patterns, postures, gestures, and movements from nature, friends, strangers, animals, and every aspect of your experience. It is your job to discover what fascinates *you* about the moving world.

As you begin to apply that fascination to create dances, even short dance studies will require that you develop your capacity to hone your ideas and to make a gift of those ideas to others. You will find both the frustration and the satisfaction of trying to create order out of what could be a chaos of ideas. Developing your creative capacities will be beneficial in many areas of your life beyond the dance studio or auditorium.

Training, Exploring, and Forming Your Own Style

Regardless of your approach to dance—dive-right-in, creative movement, technical, or some combination of these approaches—your efforts to become proficient will involve three processes: training, exploring, and forming. And as you integrate these processes, you will be developing a *style.*

Style

In *Webster's New World College Dictionary*, there are 25 different ways one might use the word "style." Within these 25 different usages are even more distinctions, such as in the one most pertinent to our application, which reads, "specific manner or mode of expression, execution, construction, or design in any art, period, work, employment, etc." As you are finding and forming your own style, you will be incorporating patterns of coordination that you have been taught or have discovered on your own. In some cases, you'll hear the dance form you're studying referred to as a style. Later in this book we will devote more specific attention to the notion of style so that, as an informed student of this art, you can use the word accurately and intentionally. We'll look at style and body intelligence, style and patterns of coordination, and style in identifying dance in history. But here, in the early part of our introduction, let's think about what it might mean to have your own style.

"Dance" is a word that describes an enormous range of movement activities, which are grouped and categorized by many different titles. Some of these titles (or categories or genres or styles—these words are often used interchangeably) were useful at some point in history but are no longer accurate, so when you hear the word "style" you would do well to pause and ask whether it fits. You are likely to find that the word is used to describe what something is *not* as often as it is to describe what something *is.* There is a broad category called folk dance, in which you find thousands, possibly millions of dances "of the people." When you hear someone say that they "do folk dance" you may not know what steps they actually do, but you know they do not dance about dying swans and princes, nor do they create original choreography for self-expression. You will also hear folk dances referred to as "ethnic dances." The electric slide, hula, schottische, morris, Jarabe Tapatío (Mexican hat dance), and the sword dance are

INSIDE INSIGHT

What's modern dance? It is true that all art is modern at the time it is made. But the title "modern dance" more accurately refers to dances that were made during the period between the 1860s and the 1970s, a period art historians refer to as the modern period. If you watch video or film versions of some of the choreography from the original modern dancers, you will see that the style of movement is no longer of our time. How would you describe the difference?

all dances that grew out of a cultural group. Would you say that the tango or the salsa or hip-hop are "folk dances"? Why or why not?

Every moving person has a style of dance. Trained or untrained, we all have a personal signature to the way we move and dance. Granted, many people claim that they do not dance, but if these people relinquished their inhibitions long enough to share a tiny bit of their dancing spirits, you would see that they too have a dance style.

Style comes from your soul as well as your body. You can train your body to execute movements and patterns, but the way those are actually performed reflects the physical, emotional, social, and spiritual aspects of your unique nature.

Ultimately, or let's say, ideally, your study of dance will open up new possibilities of expression for you, and through that process, help you realize more of your potential as a human being. As you are exposed to ways of moving that are new to you, you will absorb what you are ready for and your options will be expanded. Know that, unlike a sponge, which eventually reaches saturation, there is no limit to what you can absorb. So as you encounter new patterns and new coordinations other than your familiar "manner or mode of expression, execution, construction" (aka style) of movement, at least explore what you might be able to integrate into the style you already have.

Try This Experiment

Close your eyes and picture a dancer. What image came to mind? What was this dancer wearing? Was this dancer still or moving?

Now close your eyes and picture yourself dancing. In what ways are these two images similar? In what ways are they different? How much of your dance style is an imitation of dancers you have seen and how much is your own?

Finally, close your eyes and picture one of your parents dancing.

Three different people. Did you imagine three different dance styles? Three different ways of moving and expressing? If you drew a blank on any of these images, why do you think that might be?

Training

Training is important if you want to achieve mastery in a particular skill, but bear in mind all of the skills that are available to pursue through work in dance. Physical, emotional, social, and spiritual growth are all a part of learning to dance as well as learning about dance. Physical training will help you develop your instrument—your body—so that you have the possibility to physically realize a great diversity of movement. Rigorous physical training is not a prerequisite for being able to enjoy dance or to choreograph a dance, but both an awareness and acceptance of your physical limits and strengths are needed.

Training is nothing more than dedicating thought and attention to some aspect of personal development in order to direct the growth of your skills. You are training if you repeat technical skills, if you try to develop more strength and flexibility, or if you attempt to access a new level of creative potential (figure 3.4).

Training might mean paying attention to the way you sit, stand, or run. You are directing the growth of your powers of observation in everyday activities. Training might mean that you deliberately choose to work with a new partner in class. You might wish to use your dance class as a place to direct your social and emotional growth. Training might mean keeping a journal of sights, sounds, smells, thoughts, reactions, feelings, and other food for choreographic thought. Training might also mean something as simple and spiritual as learning how to fall, how to move backward without looking, or how to share your work with your classmates.

Your dance training involves observation not only of your teachers but also of your classmates. We learn so much from watching other people. But try as we might, we can never be just like Paula Abdul, Fred Astaire, Mikhail Baryshnikov, or even the best dancer in the class. You can certainly benefit from their imagination and inspiration, but if you ignore or fail to develop your own creative voice, your dances will lack the very spark you so admire in others. Ultimately, you must be able to use ideas you have gained from others and enjoy the uniqueness of your own ideas.

Exploring

A sense of adventure is disappearing from daily experience. It is impossible to avoid advertising, so much of which is geared to sell solutions to problems rather than encourage investigation of how those problems may have occurred in the first place. Much of education is geared either to reiterating the correct answer or to deducing what it is that a teacher wants to hear. Given the present information overload from all the media, it is easy to be seduced into believing that there is nothing new to explore. In fact, nothing could be farther from the truth. You are in charge of cultivating your creative curiosity. You are responsible for finding magic in who you are and what you do, and dance class is a great place to develop those skills—skills that will also impact other aspects of your life.

Exploration in dance might mean that as you repeat a movement pattern, you explore reaching a little farther or rotating a little more. It might mean that you play (yes, play!) with the tension you are working with or the forces that motivate your movement. Exploration might mean that, when given creative flexibility, you see what it is like to move more quickly than you normally would, or more slowly. Exploration might mean that you allow yourself to begin whether or not you are sure you will succeed. Allow yourself to process without worrying about product. It is a bit like playing with a piñata: To get to the goodies inside, you have to be willing to use a creative approach: swinging at the target without being able to see it.

FIGURE 3.4   External guidance and correction are often essential parts of the training process.

Forming

When you rolled clay between your hands to make snakes, you were forming. When you scoop and drizzle sand to make a castle, you are forming. Forming is part of any artistic pursuit. In any of the three approaches to learning dance, you will find yourself forming patterns and sequences that have physical, social, emotional, and sometimes spiritual significance for you. Training, exploring, and forming are interconnected aspects of the creative process. While you train, you explore new ways to form your body into desirable shapes and to accomplish new goals. When you explore, you train yourself to operate with curiosity and suspend judgment, and you form unique patterns motivated by your personal interests and skills.

When you bring form to your work, whether that work is a 4-count study or a 40-minute piece, you bring your training, and the fruits of your exploration, into focus. For the sake of an audience, your classmates, and your own satisfaction, forming is the springboard of the art of dance.

In subsequent chapters we will look at how daily life applies to dance, and how the art of dance applies to daily life. We will examine the elements of dance and the differences between dance statements and dance reactions. Finally, we will look at the process of using dance for thoughtful, deliberate self-expression. We will explore perception and creativity in an effort to awaken you to the possibilities of using dance as a valuable, functional way of expressing your humanity.

INSIDE INSIGHT

Dance etiquette in the class. In a dance class, as in any other group activity, every participant should be considerate of the needs of others. This includes being considerate of other people's need to see the demonstration, hear the instructions, and explore the tasks required. Each teacher will have his or her own particular ways of conducting a class, and it is the job of the student to honor that teacher's style. Some teachers will solicit questions before beginning the exercise; others will allow questions only at certain points. Some will expect you to mark (indicate but not fully do) the combination during their demonstration; others will require you to be still. Respect for the instructor is critical to the success of the class. Because it is assumed that each person's focus will be devoted to the tasks of the class, chatting or being off task during the class is a distraction not only to others but also to the teacher. Arriving late, leaving early, being inappropriately dressed, and sitting down between repetitions are also no-nos. It is appropriate (and often expected) to show gratitude and respect for the instructor by applauding him or her at the conclusion of each class.

INSIDE INSIGHT

Dance etiquette in the theater. You may assume that if you are seeing a dance in a theater, the performer has willingly offered the dance as a gift to the audience. Whether or not the piece matches your expectations, it is polite to accept it as a gift and then look for how you might benefit from that gift. To get full benefit you will need to attend with an open mind and a generous heart. Side comments during the performance distract your attention and that of the others you draw into your commentary. Just as talking disturbs the magic in a movie, so too does talking during a live performance. Your interpretation of a dance's form, its meaning, and the role you see it playing in society will be determined by your depth of familiarity with compositional techniques, dance history, and personal preference. Guidelines for responding to and evaluating dance appear in chapter 14 of this book. Figure 14.4, titled "Some Considerations for Critical Feedback," will help you to identify aspects of a dance you found particularly successful.

Think About It

1. If you enjoy social dancing, think about the kind of dancing you do and focus on one movement pattern that you feel you do well. How did you learn that pattern? How is the way you perform it different from the way other people do it? (You may have to look very closely, but you will find a difference.) Which of the approaches did you use to learn that pattern? Are you still improving on it? What made you want to learn to dance to begin with?

2. Think about some of the ways in which you use rhythmic coordination in your daily life. Name at least three activities. How is it that these activities lend themselves to rhythmic movement? If you were to impose a rhythm on an activity, such as brushing your hair, how would that activity change? Would you now call this activity a dance?

3. How can a dance have meaning?

4. If you had to choose, would you rather watch a dancer who could

   a. perform amazing acrobatic feats,

   b. reveal to you a sad or beautiful aspect of being human, or

   c. present intriguing patterns and shapes with no literal or narrative reference?

5. Is dance timeless or does our ability to appreciate a dance depend on circumstances of culture? In other words, when we watch a modern dance choreographed in 1953, is there a difference between the way we see it today and the way audiences saw it then? What is different? What is the same?

Your Turn to Dance

Limits and Parameters

Sometimes the best way to start a piece is to set some parameters limiting what you can and cannot do and then see what's possible within those limitations. In this dance you'll be investigating the movement of the spine as the basis of a dance. You'll be working with axial rather than locomotor motion.

If your instructor has not already specified a piece of music with which to work, choose a piece that is sparse rather than orchestral, perhaps a solo instrumental piece.

~ Set limits on how big or how small you will allow yourself to move. For instance, your bottom never leaves the chair or your right foot never leaves the spot, or you never move either of your feet.

~ Initially explore the actions of the spine as the music plays. Consciously *name* the action as you employ it ("now I'm bending, now I'm twisting, now I'm bending to the side"), working mechanically rather than emotively.

~ If you can get a friend to work with you, ask that person to randomly call out actions *without looking at you* so that the sequence is not predictable. If no such partner is available, write out a sequence of tasks (twist, twist, bend, twist extend, bend), then try to complete that sequence by articulating your movement in a specific vertebra, changing the point of articulation each time.

~ Continue rehearsing so that you can repeat the piece accurately. Give it a title.

~ How is what you've made dance?

Sports Break

Observe a sport being played. Write down the action words as they occur. For instance, if you were observing golf, you might write, "walk, stand, bend, stand up, straddle, swing, twist, lean." Using those tasks, construct a rhythmic sequence. In cases where you might be inclined to mime, such as swinging a golf club or a tennis racket, transfer the action to another body part, perhaps swinging a whole arm or upper body. Try to disguise the sport you observed so that it is difficult to guess where the movement came from. Set it to music.

Your Moving Body

*I*f it seems to you that we keep flipping back and forth between discussing dance as separate from daily life and as part of it, you are exactly right. We have established that there are aspects of dance that separate dance activity from similar physical activities. We have discussed the differences we might expect to find among various kinds of dance, such as social, concert, and creative movement dance. In chapter 5 we will look at the elements of dance and discover how they are part of daily activities. When creating or appreciating dance as a performance art, we intuitively apply our experiences with these elements by relating the use of time, space, and effort with our personal experiences.

In this chapter we continue to draw from information that you are familiar with—your own body. You will be asked to consider the mechanics of movement, basic movement patterns, and some simple anatomy so that you will have a better understanding of your movement potential.

Each body is unique. Your ability to imitate another person's movement will be determined not only by your skill in reading movement but also by the physical potential that you have developed. Likewise, your ability to create movement patterns will be determined by what you have seen or tried in your lifetime. This chapter will help you both to realize how much you already know and to build on that knowledge in a healthy, personal way.

The Body Is an Instrument

You need a musical instrument in order to make music. Whichever instrument a musician chooses—flute, guitar, synthesizer, violin, harmonica, even the human voice—he must become familiar with it if it is to be played with control. You can pick up any instrument and elicit sound, but in order to make music with skill you need to learn the instrument and practice playing it. For dance, your body is your instrument. We are all able to use our bodies as instruments to express feelings. Studying dance is like practicing an instrument; by sharpening your natural skills and increasing your range and potential through practice, you improve your playing.

Let us begin by investigating the art of moving, starting with movements as simple as walking or bending. These are movement patterns you mastered as a child, patterns that are so familiar you may not even know them by name. We will look at movement for the sake of accomplishing a goal or a task, and movement done for the sheer pleasure and satisfaction it can bring. We will consider the ways a body might move from one place to another and the ways a body might move on one spot. Finally, we will consider the moving body as a unique instrument to be explored, played, and celebrated for its potential.

The use of the body as an instrument of expression is less respected and encouraged in Western culture than in other cultures, so it is often the case that, beginning in adolescence, people start to feel uncomfortable exploring their physical potential. This is unfortunate

FIGURE 4.1   We learn the fundamentals of movement, such as leaping and running, as children.

because, as we discussed in the first two chapters, the expressive use of the body is a natural part of living. Most children enjoy running, leaping, sliding, spinning, and imitating the ways things move in the real world and in their imaginations (figure 4.1). Animals, clouds, kings, queens, bugs, fish, ghosts, armies, and fairies are all found in children's play. They enjoy moving for the sake of moving and creating for the personal mastery it brings. They enjoy sharing their efforts with admiring audiences. To them, moving is magic. It is possible to recapture that magic as we explore in a more mature way all the potential we have for using our bodies.

INSIDE INSIGHT

What's primitive about "primitive dance"? There can be a temptation to look at dances from other traditions, observe their use of repetition and basic locomotor patterns, and lump them under the label "primitive." But before resting with a culture-bound notion that these dances are somehow less sophisticated, take time to explore the function of the dance, the role of the dancer, and the underlying assumptions of what is and is not sophisticated. In the same way, do not underestimate the power of the so-called simple movements of your childhood. Do not underestimate your own power to use your body to make magic.

When considering your own movement potential, be aware that there is a temptation, especially among beginners, to be negative—to focus on all the things that feel wrong, awkward, or make you feel incompetent. Use the body as an instrument to focus on the kinds of sounds that you make easily and well, then gradually build your repertoire by practicing, experimenting, and refining your physical voice. You can bet that John Coltrane and Miles Davis made one or two squeaks before they mastered their horns. Be willing to observe without judging. Be willing to explore. Leave your mind and body open to discovery through trial and error. The way you work with your instrument will be your unique gift to the world. That is worth working on.

When you learn an instrument you start out with the fundamentals and build from there, so let us take the same approach. Let us break moving into two categories: *moving in one place* (axial movement) and moving from one place to another (locomotor movement). We will call the second category *moving through space* and start our exploration there.

Moving Through Space

"Space" usually means off the planet or outer space, so the idea of moving through space brings images of weightlessness, white oxygen suits, and walks on the moon. Let us look at moving through space in a more earth-centered way. Let us think of space as synonymous with area, volume, or room.

Try This Experiment

Try these experiments and begin to explore the potential of just one body part in space.

~ Move your hand up, down, toward, and away from the book.

~ Make your hand float, now dart, now squirm.

~ Lead with your little finger up to the top left corner, and then use your thumb to lead the hand to the bottom left corner.

~ Using your left hand, imagine that there is a strong force that you need to overcome as you press your hand to the right.

~ Now try holding your arm still so that your hand stays in one place in the space between you and the book. What movements can your hand make with your wrist fixed in space? You can open and close your fingers, move only one digit at a time, fan the fingers and stretch them up.

When we think of moving through space, it is easy to imagine moving in a wide, open space such as a field or a huge room; but you just proved that there are a lot of ways to move through even a very small space!

INSIDE INSIGHT

Some complex patterns are common in childhood but disappear as people become more cautious about expressing themselves in public. For instance, when was the last time you skipped or galloped? You just do not see many people over 15 years of age skipping, sliding, and galloping. Because complex locomotor patterns are less functional ways of moving through space, people who skip, slide, and gallop through life are generally viewed as silly or, at the very least, not functionally oriented. What do you think?

What is the space between you and this book, between you and the nearest window, and between your feet? What is the space from the floor to the ceiling and from the ground to the lowest limb of a tree you can see? When you consider space you are evaluating not just distance but volume, all the air and the straight or jagged perimeters that define the space in question.

Look at the space between you and the nearest door. Can you name three ways of moving that would take you from your chair to that door? Write down a series of steps, including how many of each one, and in which order these steps should occur. Try your series and find out what it takes to accomplish the whole series in the space available, or use your imagination to predict how the sequence could be performed. Remember, space equals volume, not distance. Moving through space can involve moving close to the ground, through the air, moving side to side, doubling back on your path, pushing, pulling, and so on. Moving through space can be as challenging and interesting as you care to make it. Reconsider the space between you and the door, and imagine all the possible ways that you could work with the three words you chose.

If you included the words "run," "walk," "jump," "hop," "leap," "crawl," or "roll" to describe your movement through the space to the door, you named one of the seven basic locomotor patterns—movement patterns that are used to transport the body from one place in space to another. Each of these patterns is a different way of moving your body through space. To accomplish any of these locomotor actions, and thus move through space, you need to transfer your weight from one place to another.

Each of these locomotor patterns is a specific way of transferring weight so that the body moves through space. As a child you probably used all of these patterns in your play without even thinking about the distinctions among them. As a dancer you will also use these patterns, but you will probably be more conscious of which pattern is which. When learning patterns in class it is useful to recognize such distinctions. When making creative choices as a choreographer it is useful to recognize one pattern from another so that you can repeat or refine your choices and work more clearly with other dancers.

Basic Locomotor Patterns

The first locomotor movement an infant makes is a roll, a transfer of weight from one side to the opposite side that causes the body to flip. Another infant-related movement pattern is crawling, where the weight of the body is transferred from one leg and its opposite arm to the other leg and arm. Next comes walking, which, like crawling, involves transferring the weight from one foot to the other while counterbalancing with the opposite arm. A run is related to a walk in that the weight of the body is transferred from one leg to the other; although the body never completely leaves the ground in a walk, in a run there is a moment of air time. Check this out for yourself. If your weight transfer keeps you in the air even longer, you are leaping. What happens in a hop? Do you transfer your weight to the other leg? What is the difference between a hop and a jump?

Because these locomotor motions are the basic vocabulary of natural, human movements, they are the building blocks of dance. Any dance step that involves moving through space can be described in terms of the basic locomotor patterns. Test this by taking one of your popular social dances and writing down the names of the movements that make up the pattern you recognize. If you keep this simplicity in mind as you try to imitate dance moves, you will discover that you are really trying to learn new ways of combining steps you already know!

Complex Locomotor Patterns

Within locomotor movement, we find basic patterns combined to form more complex ones. Some of these patterns are personal or cultural; some are found all over the globe. As a student of dance you will find it useful to learn movement sequences by recognizing the locomotor patterns within complex movements. Eventually, you will find that some of the basic patterns are frequently combined in the same order; by recognizing these complex patterns, you can simplify your learning.

Take, for instance, a complex pattern called skipping. A skip, which is a combination of a walk and a hop, is a good example of a complex movement made up of basic locomotor patterns. Because you learned to skip as a child, you no longer see that sequence as a step-hop combination but rather recognize the whole pattern as a skip. When learning a sequence of steps that includes this complex pattern, you simply plug in the skip as one pattern instead of two.

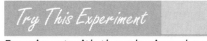

Try This Experiment

Experiment with these basic and complex locomotor units, then fill in the blanks describing the nature of the weight transfer in each one. The first one is done for you.

Basic movements

Walk: transfer of weight from <u>one foot</u> to <u>other foot</u> on the ground

Run: transfer of weight from ____ to ____ in the air

Leap: transfer of weight from _____ to _____ ____ with maximum height

Slide: transfer of weight from _____ to _____ without leaving the ground, yet moving through space

Hop: transfer of weight from _____ to ____ ____ in the air

Jump: transfer of weight from _____ to ____ ____ in the air

Roll: transfer of weight from _____ to _____ _____ on the ground

Complex movements

Skip: combination of _____ and _____

Gallop: combination of _____ and _____

In each style of dance you study you will find complex locomotor patterns that move the dancer through space using the same, repeating series of basic locomotor patterns. Some of these patterns have names, and some simply come and go with fashion.

Many of the named patterns describe some special activity or effect that the pattern creates. For instance, a pas de chat, a common, complex pattern in ballet, translates to "step of cat." The quick action of the feet folding under the body as the weight is transferred from one leg to the other in the air gives the step a catlike feel. Balancé (bah-lahn-SAY) means "to swing" and is a step that swings front to back or side to side. A jazz square is a pattern the feet make when one foot crosses over and in front of the other, followed by a step back and an open, or side, step.

Remember your chair-to-door sequence? Repeat the sequence you just made with one addition: Instead of moving from one place to the next, find three places in your sequence where you will move not *through* space but *in one place*. Movements that occur on a fixed

INSIDE INSIGHT

Contact improvisation is a dance form that grew out of the dancers of the Judson Dance Theater in the early 1970s. It is a form that relies on sharing and transferring the weight of the body in what were then very unconventional and improvisatory ways. Thanks to the groundwork laid by contact improvisation, concert dance now regularly employs a rich repertoire of movement in which weight is transferred not through the floor but through other bodies!

base are called *axial* movements. By developing your eye for basic locomotor patterns and combinations, you will find that it becomes easier to read movements that travel through space. Likewise, your understanding of some of the principles of axial movement will help you read and reproduce movements in which the body does not move through space but rather moves on or around an unchanging point in space.

Basic Axial Movement

When we talk about axial movement we refer to movements that occur on or around an axis. You already know a few things about the concept of an axis. An axis has a fixed point; using the Earth as an example, the fixed point is the planet's center, around which it rotates. To begin this chapter we looked at movements that occur through space, which, to continue the analogy, would be like the Earth moving around the sun. Now we are going to look at movements that occur *in* space, like the rotation of the Earth on its axis.

Take a pencil and stand it on its point. What movements are possible without moving the point from its place? The pencil experiment can give you a good idea of the human body as an axis that can lean in a 360-degree arc around the fixed point—the standing base. Because it is rigid, the pencil can lean or rotate only on its fixed base. Let us create an axis that is more flexible. Find three paper clips and hook them together to make a chain. Hold the chain over the center of the following grid. The grid is labeled to make you consider the chain as a body that is standing on one spot.

Experiment with actions of the chain that can be accomplished without moving the axis off

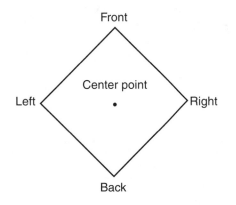

the center point. Be aware of how you have to support the parts of the chain in order to make the whole shape bend, twist, shrink, or stretch. What other movements are possible with this chain? What movement is possible if you pull it very tight and tall and do not allow the top to move (not even a millimeter)? What happens if you allow some flexibility among the clips but still maintain the vertical shape? Although the proportions are not quite exact, imagine that your body is like those paper clips; your legs are the lowest clip, your hips are the middle clip, and your waist, middle spine, and upper spine are the top clip. Play with the clips to create a series of four actions that go off and return to vertical. Get up and feel these axial movements in your own body. Find the fixed point in each one.

Finding the Fixed Point

"Fixed" means set or stationary. When you were experimenting with the movement possibilities of the pencil, the fixed point was the end of the pencil touching the paper. Once you started working with the string of paper clips, you could decide if the fixed point was at the bottom, middle, or the top of the chain.

Finding the fixed point within an axial movement will allow you to be specific about how you are making or supporting a shape. As you probably discovered in this last experiment, some joints allow more options for movement than others. The joints of the spine allow you a great deal of axial movement options.

Take a few minutes and explore the options available in specific parts of your spine. Begin by establishing the base of your neck as the fixed point. How can you twist, bend, and stretch your neck without moving from the shoulders down? Now move that fixed point lower, to just below your ribs. Giving yourself total freedom above this point, what movement is possible? What movement is possible if you keep this bottom point fixed and also fix the base of the neck? This allows you to move only your ribs. Can you make this isolation interesting?

Space, Place, and Body Holds

These concepts—space hold, place hold, and body hold—are useful to a beginning dancer because they can help the dancer to read and reproduce movement patterns and shapes. During the pencil experiment the fixed point was the tip of the pencil. That was the part that was immobile, and the rest of the pencil moved around that place. If you were to fix one foot on a point on the floor and then lunge in every possible direction without moving that foot, you would be moving with your foot fixed in one spot or place. This is fairly easy to feel when the fixed point is on the ground, but what about when it is fixed in the air?

Try the next experiment to get a sense of space hold.

Try This Experiment

Hold your arm in front of you, and, leaving your arm just where it is, see what kinds of movement are possible with the rest of your body.

Now explore the movements that are possible if you fix only your hand in space.

Now explore your range of movements if you put a space hold on a foot in the air.

What kind of dance can you make by putting a space hold on your head and moving the rest of your body? Remember, space hold means fixed in space—no level or direction change for that fixed part.

If a space hold means that some part of your body is fixed in space and does not change, what do you think a body hold is? A body hold is an act of maintaining the position of one body part relative to another body part while the rest of the body moves through space. It is better to learn this by doing rather than by sitting and reading.

Try This Experiment

Stand up and point your nose in the same direction as your toes. Now turn your head so that your nose is over your right shoulder. No matter what, do not change that relationship of your nose to your shoulder. Walk in a circle to the left. Lower to the floor, then lie down on your back. Roll over to your stomach and come to your knees. Move your right shoulder to twist, to bend. As long as you keep that nose-to-shoulder relationship, you have a body hold.

Knowing what a body hold is can be very useful in recognizing patterns and shapes in dance and recreating these patterns and shapes yourself. For some people it is very easy to learn movement by using guides outside the body. Others find it easier to use their own bodies as a reference. Do you know which comes more easily to you?

Whether you are moving in space using locomotor patterns or using all your joints to make interesting shapes on one spot, you are applying your natural, human abilities to combine what you know about gravity, tension, and relaxation to make a pattern of movement that is challenging to you or inspiring to others. Whether you are moving through space or in place, you are using the elements of dance that we talked about in the previous chapter. The pleasure or satisfaction that this activity brings you will have a lot to do with your appreciation of your physical capabilities. That pleasure or satisfaction will also depend on what you find challenging or inspiring in the movement of others.

Earlier in this chapter we likened the dance instrument—the body—to other instruments, and we stressed that the more familiar the musician is with the instrument, the more likely it is that the sounds produced are pleasing. Your job is to become familiar with your capabilities as a moving body and as an interpreter of movement so that the dance you bring to life is as pleasing as possible to you.

Understanding the difference between moving through space and moving in place is important for developing self-control and movement clarity. We have seen that there is an infinite variety of ways one can move through space and in place.

Realizing the Potential of Your Instrument

It is important to understand both the potential and the limits of your instrument so that you can learn to challenge yourself appropriately and make the most of the instrument you are.

No matter how talented and dedicated a pianist might be, he will never get a piano to sound like a tuba. Likewise, not even the most talented tuba player will be able to make her tuba sound like a piano. How wonderful that both of these sounds exist in the world! How wonderful that each musician strives to bring out the unique character of the instrument!

Anatomical Considerations

Different people are built in different ways. Bones have different lengths, ligaments that connect the bones have different lengths, and muscles that make movement have different lengths and varying strengths. Some people can easily hold a leg in front of their chest but have little side extension. They can touch their toes with straight legs, touch their chin to their chest, or curl their tongues; others cannot perform these movements.

It is possible to make some changes in our physical capabilities through training. However, some differences between instruments need to be celebrated rather than fought. A piano will never sound like a tuba.

Functional Considerations

Bear in mind this question as you pursue your relationship to dance and movement training: What do I want from this? If you have hopes of becoming a professional ballet dancer, your training goals and regimen need to be very dif-

ferent than if your hope were only to become more coordinated. If you expect to be able to read music and play "Heart and Soul" from memory, your training will not need to include hours of scale practice and years of diligent repetition. However, if you want to be able to interpret the masters, your training must approach not only the level but also the nature of their training. If it is your goal to play a piece by Liszt as well as Liszt himself played the piece more than 100 years before, then you must train in a comparable manner. If it is your goal to dance the role of Odette/Odile in *Swan Lake* as well as Margot Fonteyn did in her prime, then, to prepare for such comparison, you must train in a comparable manner.

Competition and comparison can be motivating factors in a person's training. In sports, if you know what time you have to beat, you have some idea whether that time is within your reach and how you might wisely reach the goal. It is unfortunately frequent in dance education that competition and comparison become ruinous tendencies that keep students from realizing their unique potential. Dance training is not a race. As you pursue your movement training, continuously clarify how that training both suits and serves you. Keep yourself open to new physical challenges and use the achievements of others as resources and inspiration. Learn to be a resource and an inspiration to others, not by mirroring or besting their efforts but by identifying and developing your own potential. To that end, let us turn now to some basic anatomy that will help you.

Basic Anatomy

You do not need to have a degree in anatomy in order to be able to apply some common sense to your movement training. The human body is an absolutely incredible entity worthy of a lifetime of study, but we are going to limit ourselves to basic talk about bones, muscles, and joints. We will look at 15 different muscles and muscle groups and talk about functional alignment and injury prevention.

If you're learning to play the piano, it can be useful to know how the sound is produced so that you can maintain your instrument properly and play it with sensitivity. If you want to do extraordinary movements like flips, splits, back bends, and high kicks, you need first to understand your human limits, so that you can train your instrument specifically and safely and recognize what makes those movements attractive or valuable to you. Then training becomes both feasible and worthwhile.

Bones, muscles, and joints support your body against the pull of gravity. In addition to providing structure, bones form boxes that protect the vital organs of your body. Muscles and ligaments hold all the bones together; ligaments do the primary stabilizing, and muscles actually move the bones by contracting. All movement occurs at joints. Because of the different joint structures, different joints allow different lines of movement.

Bones

The adult human skeleton has approximately 206 bones. The skeletal system is divisible into two parts. The axial skeleton consists of the bones that comprise the skull and face (22 bones), the spine (26 vertebrae), and the thorax or chest (25 bones). The axial skeleton is the axis of the body.

The appendicular skeleton is comprised of the bones of the upper and lower body that are attached either to the spine or to bones that are distal (farther away from the spine). These are the bones of our arms, legs, shoulders, and hips (figure 4.2, a and b).

The structure of each of these bones—their relative lengths and strengths—contains important variables when it comes to determining movement potential. For instance, a person

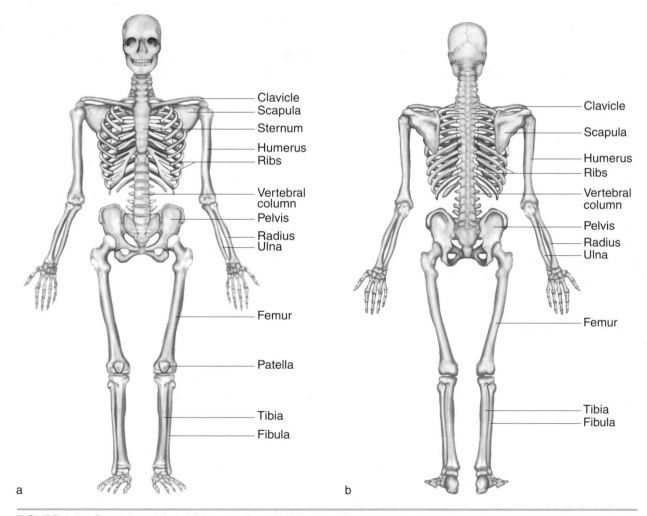

FIGURE 4.2   Front (a) and back (b) view of an adult human skeleton.

INSIDE INSIGHT

Did you know . . .

~ your wrist is a 15-bone joint?

~ children have more bones than adults?

~ your foot is a 26-bone structure?

~ approximately 35 percent of living bone tissue is soft tissue?

~ bones are not just the joists and girders of the body? They also produce blood cells, store nutrients, and provide protective housing for our organs.

with long toes (relative to the rest of the bones) is likely to be a good jumper. A person with a wide pelvis (relative to the rest of the bones) is likely to be good at quick direction changes.

Muscles

All muscles, shown in figure 4.3, a and b, move bones by producing three actions:

1. Extension
2. Flexion
3. Rotation

Assuming you are sitting down, we will use the hip joint as an example. Slump so that your pelvis tips back toward your spine. Now sit up straight. That act of sitting up straight, bringing the lower spine into line with the rest of your back, is called extension. If you were to continue taking your lower spine forward, out of line with your upper spine, you would be going into forward flexion. Slumping would return you to backward flexion. You could rotate this same part of your body by twisting your pelvis to the right or left.

Muscles contract and bones move to accomplish any of these three actions. Muscles are tissues composed of fibers that are grouped to attach one bone to another bone. The arrangement, size, and shape of these fibers vary considerably from one muscle to another based on its function. Muscle length and muscle strength vary greatly from person to person, so we are each endowed with special potentials for different tasks. Some

people have relatively short hamstrings (technically, biceps femoris, semitendinosus, and semimembranosus) and therefore are not as adept at movements, such as splits, that require length in those muscles. Some people have very tight hip flexors, which means that it is harder for them to put their ribs on their thighs. People with long muscles, however, are often prone to joint injury because the muscles are less protective. You must remember that everyone's muscle structure allows both strength and weakness, and it is up to the individual to train in order to protect weaknesses and enhance strengths. Flexibility training will improve a muscle's ability to contract and stretch, but such training needs to be done carefully, sensibly, and consistently in order to be effective.

Both muscles and ligaments connect bone to bone. Muscles, however, also contract and stretch to produce motion. Ligaments only stabilize.

Joints

All human movement occurs in the joints. When you bring your hand from this book to your face, this movement occurs in the elbow joint. True, the arm moves through space, but the action is in the joint. Watch a mime perform the standard mechanical-person routine and, if the mime is good, you will clearly see this joint articulation.

Knowing where movement occurs can be very useful when training because it can help you to focus not on the outcome of a gesture,

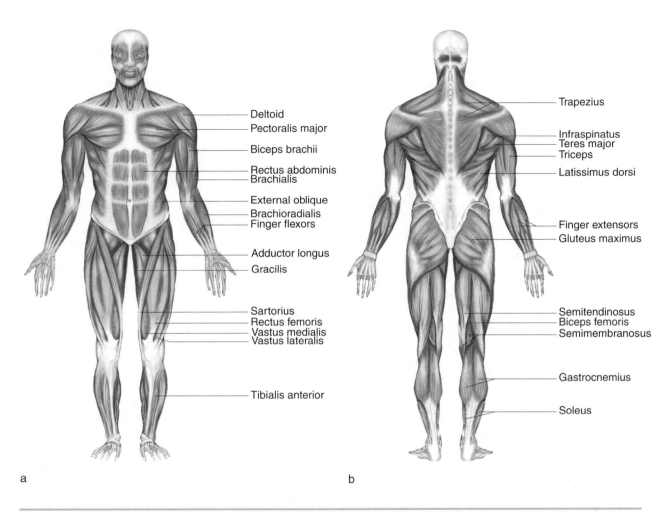

FIGURE 4.3   Front (a) and back (b) view of adult human skeletal musculature.

such as a leg lift, but on the source of that movement—the muscle action that produces movement in the hip joint. Once you start looking at movement from this perspective, you will be able to refine, simplify, and streamline your own movement.

Accepting and Training Your Body

Your abilities to flex, extend, and rotate depend on the length of your bones, the structure of your joints, and the length and strength of your muscles and ligaments. You can train yourself to be stronger and more flexible, but you cannot train your bones to grow or shrink, nor can you train your ligaments to stretch or contract.

Accepting your body does not mean giving up because some physical task is difficult on the first attempt. Rather, you will want to apply all that you know to solving a difficult movement problem. You may want to specifically design a training program so that you will have a greater range of movement available. With work you can improve both your strength and flexibility.

Understanding Flexibility and Strength

Flexibility is the range of motion in a joint or group of joints. What kind of flexibility do you have in the top joint of your little finger? That is, what range of motion is possible around that one joint? Now see what kind of flexibility you have at your wrist joint. What about at your shoulder? Go back through these three joints and determine what *limits* your flexibility in each of those joints. Flexibility can be limited by these things:

1. Length of a muscle
2. Length of a ligament
3. Contact with another bone or group of bones

Some of the constraints that feel like muscular limits to movement might, in fact, be ligamentous limits. For instance, your femur is attached to your pelvis by (among other things) the Y ligament. This ligament limits the distance you can move your femur straight back, behind your pelvis. If that ligament is long, you will have more range of motion than someone with a shorter ligament. This is a physical limit you must accept. A flexible back might be the product of long ligaments and muscles not only in the back but also in the front of the body.

Muscles stretch; ligaments rip. Through stretching and flexibility training you can increase your range of motion around your joints, but throughout such training you need to bear in mind that your unique physical structure may suit you better for some kinds of movements than others. If you have a short Y ligament, you cannot train or work out to add to its length. To imitate a position that has the leg straight behind the body, you need to find another way to achieve that height.

Strength is, technically, the power to exert or endure. Strength is measured by the amount of force you can produce with a single, maximal effort. Strength and flexibility are closely paired in dance work. Your ability to jump high depends not only on the strength in your legs and hips but also on the flexibility, which allows you to prepare for a jump by deeply bending your legs. Your ability to hold your leg close to your ear depends not only on the strength of your leg and abdominal muscles but also on the degree of flexibility in your leg and hip joints.

Through repetition, gradual overloading, or pushing your previous limits, you can improve both your strength and flexibility and increase your range of motion and physical capabilities.

Flexibility and strength are developed as well as inherited. Through use and practice a body can gain flexibility and strength. You do not have to choose between being strong or flexible; in fact, you would be wise to develop both aspects of fitness. A person who has inherited a very loose joint system will have more difficulty controlling placement than someone with shorter muscles and ligaments. On the other hand, a person with loose joints will easily accomplish stretches and extensions while a person with shorter muscles will have to train to accomplish the same movement. Training is key. Take a few minutes now to evaluate your basic strengths, flexibility, and aspirations as a moving body (see figure 4.4).

FID—Your Recipe for Training

Have you ever gotten a new pair of sneakers and not put the lace through that thing that positions the tongue in the middle of the shoe? What happened to the tongue? Most likely, it *never* stayed in the middle of the shoe properly from then on, right? Like the tongue in a new shoe, it's easy to get off track in your training if you don't have a guide or a plan to follow. But if you know what you're doing, you can easily accomplish the changes you want.

Face it: Training means attending and repeating. It means paying special attention to something you want to improve and then diligently and patiently repeating and repatterning the muscles and ligaments in the desired manner. There are three aspects to this repetition that you can vary depending on the results you are trying to achieve. You can change the *frequency*, the *intensity*, or the *duration* (FID). By varying the frequency of a training practice, the intensity of the work, or the duration of the exercise, you will achieve different training results.

To a large degree, physical training is what we call "task specific." In other words, if you want to become more proficient at holding your leg in a high second position, the most direct training would be to practice holding your leg in the highest second position possible and gradually increasing the height. You can approach this training challenge by varying the

Name Your Strengths and Weaknesses

Before we consider the importance of the splits, flips, or back bends in your movement vocabulary, think back to the first section of this chapter and make a list of your personal strengths as a body simply moving through space.

The three most flexible parts of my body are
  1.
  2.
  3.

The three most inflexible parts of my body are
  1.
  2.
  3.

The three strongest areas of my body are
  1.
  2.
  3.

The three weakest areas of my body are
  1.
  2.
  3.

The three moves I would most like to be able to do are
  1.
  2.
  3.

I am impressed when I see someone who can
  1.
  2.
  3.

FIGURE 4.4   Discover your own strengths, flexibilities, and aspirations as a dancer.

frequency, intensity or duration of the task. You can vary the number of times, or frequency, you attempt that form. If you work on that position only while you are in class, your frequency of repetition would probably be too low to gain much improvement. However, if you stopped once an hour throughout the day and did a few stretches and extensions, because your frequency would rise, so would your facility.

What might you do to increase the intensity of your training? *Progressive resistance* is a con-cept used in training programs to describe a regimen in which one gradually increases the difficulty or load on the muscles being trained. Suppose you wanted to build up the muscles in your arms and back and the only equip-ment you had was a wheelbarrow. By adding a little more dirt every time you hauled a load, you would be progressively adding resistance to the task. So getting back to our second-position extension, how might you progres-sively increase the load on the muscles that support the leg as it rises? You've got two choices: You can increase a weight that moves with the leg, or you can "lift" the leg against a static object like a bar or a flexible resistance band. How about some extra-heavy shoes!

To increase the duration—you guessed it: Hold your leg up for longer and longer periods. If you parked your heel on a window-sill and watched a half-hour TV show, you would be training your hip flexors to relax while the muscles along the back of the leg were allowed to stretch. But if you periodi-cally lifted your leg even an inch and held it for three seconds, you would be combining flexibility, intensity, and duration into one training session.

Now think about the ways of moving you would like to improve. What kinds of chal-lenges are you ready to set for yourself, and how willing are you to work and concentrate to meet those challenges? Think about what changes you would like to work on, then answer the questions in figure 4.5.

You have already taken the first step in developing your ideal moving body: You have begun to explore how your joints, bones, muscles, and ligaments allow you to move. You will begin to identify your personal strengths as you continue this exploration. (Look back at your answers to the questions in figures 4.4 and 4.5.) The moving body is an exciting instru-ment. *You* decide how to play it.

Set Your Challenge

The change I would like to accomplish by _____ (pick a date) is to increase my _____ in my _____. To accomplish this I am setting the following regimen for myself:

Frequency:

Intensity:

Duration:

Don't forget the reward! When I achieve my goal I will treat myself to _____.

FIGURE 4.5   Your challenges will change over time. Come back to this as you progress in your dancing.

Think About It

1. Observe a person who is either injured or less able to move because of age or illness. How is that person's movement adapted because of a special, fixed point? Is that movement done to protect a body part or to compensate for a lack of movement in that joint? Explore to discover whether the person is using a body hold or a space hold in order to make coordination.

2. Create a short dance based on the concept of a body hold. Pick a body part and explore the options you have if you maintain a particular relationship with another body part. Repeat your exploration using two other body parts. Repeat using a third relationship. Find a way to incorporate locomotor movements into your explorations, and develop your discoveries into a dance.

3. Create a short dance based on the concept of a space hold. Explore establishing the fixed point at different levels and in different body parts (not just the hands and toes). Explore creating and dissolving these fixed points. Explore moving as a *result* of fixed points (like a marionette). Find a way to incorporate locomotor movements into your explorations, and develop your discoveries into a dance.

4. If you were to string 26 paper clips together, you would have an axis with many possibilities for movement. In fact, that is how many bones you have in your spine. The joints between each vertebra, each bone in your spine, are capable of the following axial movements: bending (flexing), twisting (rotating), and stretching (extending). Create a short dance based solely on the axial movements of your spine. Deliberately confine yourself to one spot, and explore as many movement options as you can.

5. Using what you know about different ways of moving through space, basic locomotor patterns, and complex patterns, create a series of four locomotor patterns that take you through space. Make two that have even rhythms and two that are uneven. Each time you change to a new pattern, change your direction. For instance, you might take six walking steps in one direction, turn right and skip four times, combine a step and a jump five times in a row in a new direction, and end by going in a fourth direction by rolling three times. Remember, you have seven basic locomotor patterns to build with: roll, crawl, walk, run, leap, jump, and hop. The possibilities for combinations are infinite!

Your Turn to Dance

Phone-Number Dance

1. Assign a number to each of the seven basic and two complex locomotor patterns. (Walk = 1, Run = 2, Leap = 3, and so on.) Then take your phone number and correlate the digits. A zero equals stillness. The number also dictates how many times you will repeat each movement. If your phone number started with 212, your dance would begin with two runs, one walking step, and two more runs. Keep the actions very direct and undecorated at this point.

2. Further complications for this dance might include the following:

   ~ Choosing a digit to use as a floor pattern

   ~ Combining two phone numbers to make a duet

   ~ Creating two "rules" to give to another dancer such as "Never face front" or "Keep your focus on the front right corner as much as possible"

   ~ Performing the dance in waltz time (3/4)

Hold It!

1. Applying the concepts of place and space holds, set for yourself the challenge of getting from one place to another by fixing one body part in place, moving the rest toward your end point, and then fixing another part and moving the rest. For instance, anchor your right foot as you lunge from A toward B; land with your left hand on the floor and leave it there as you move everything else toward B, and so on.

2. Explore the same notion using space hold.

3. Combine the two.

4. Create a duet in which two dancers are either racing each other or converging.

Part II

The Laws of (Loco) Motion

5

The Elements of Dance

$\mathcal{A}$s we mentioned in chapter 1, there are many similarities between dance and other physical activities. We differentiated dance from these by noting that dance alone is defined by four components: aesthetic function, intentional rhythm, culturally patterned sequences, and extraordinary nonverbal movement. In chapter 2 we explored the power of different dance forms. In chapter 3 we looked at different ways a person might approach the study of dance; we noted that there are traditions as well as new options both for training and how to apply that training. We looked at the fundamental movement experiences that are part of any dance experience. In chapter 4 we considered the mechanics of movement, basic movement patterns, and anatomy to help us understand and accept our physical capabilities and limitations. We now move on to consider the elements, or simplest principles, of dance. Think of the elements of dance as analogous to the elements listed on the periodic table. Water is composed of hydrogen and oxygen. Without either, you do not have water.

Time, space, and effort are the elements of dance. The human body exists in time and space, and it exhibits some effort. At the very least, without the muscular effort of the heart and respiratory system, breathing—human life—would cease. A body has mass and occupies space. If you think about the fact that you are older now than when you began reading this chapter, you will recognize that time is also a fact of physical existence. As hydrogen and oxygen make up water, so time, space, and effort constitute dance.

An understanding of these three elements, along with the infinite variety of movement that can be created by varying each one, will help you not only in your dance-making but also in your dance training and appreciation. By looking at the ways you consciously and subconsciously manipulate these elements in your daily life, you can also begin to use your daily experiences as resources for your dance work.

Dance Elements in Daily Life

You may not have thought about movement in this way before, but the elements of dance are facts of movement that you have worked with since you were born.

Try This Experiment

Take a moment and consider the time, space, and effort of your movement—right now—as you read this book.

~ Your chest expands, though only by a few centimeters, each time you breathe. The space you occupy, therefore, changes.

~ Change your posture by sitting back, crossing your legs, or lowering this book. How much time passed during that shift? Could you perform the same shift more quickly or more slowly?

~ Are you holding the book? Is the weight of the book partly resting on something? These are different kinds of effort. Are you using your neck muscles to hold up your head, or are you supporting your head with your hands, arms, and back muscles?

Time, Space, and Effort

Think about your day in terms of the elements of dance. Do you spend a lot of time rushing around, or are you more likely to spend your days moving slowly or sitting still? What effect does the space you occupy have on you? Do you like sitting in close proximity to others or

do you prefer to "have your own space"? Do you look forward to being outside? Do you balance the time you spend being observed by others by choosing to be where no one is watching your behavior? Do you rush to the door when class ends just for a change of scenery? How do you summon the effort necessary to stay alert in a meeting or a lecture that you find boring? In a circumstance in which you have a strong difference of opinion from those around you (or those who are in authority), what kind of effort is required to keep your opinion to yourself? These are all examples of how time, space, and effort are part of your daily life (figure 5.1).

In chapter 1 we discussed the fact that movement is a response to needs, either physical, mental, or spiritual. Walking into the kitchen to get a drink during a television commercial is one example of a movement in response to a physical need, as is stretching your legs under your desk or bolting from your chair for a quick breath of fresh air between classes. In your daily life, time is usually an issue. You are told how much time you will have for a test, lunch, task, and so on. You are required to schedule your own time for homework, recreation, private time, and family duties.

Space is also an element of daily life. Can you think of an example of how your movements are affected by the space you occupy? How do the chairs that you sit in most of the day affect your movement? How about the designs of the rooms in which you spend your day? How might they affect your movement? How about the distance you live from school or work? Are you close enough to walk, or do you have to take a car or bus? Are you an indoor or outdoor person? How does the space you occupy affect how you feel?

To get a sense of who you are as a mover—what your movement needs are and where these needs come from—let us look at how you use time and space in some of your daily activities. Begin by setting up a piece of paper with three columns, marked "Activity," "Place," and "Time" (see figure 5.2 on page 72 for an example). Under "Activity," list five activities that are part of your required daily routine. Be as specific as possible; instead of writing "go to

FIGURE 5.1 Space and effort requirements vary depending on your daily activities.

store," choose the verb that describes how you go to the store, such as "walk to the store" or "drive to the store." Under those five, list five more activities that are not required in your daily routine but that you choose to do. Now go back over the whole list, and next to each of the 10 activities that you just identified, start another list under "Place" that describes where your activities occur.

Look at your list again and notice what (if any) patterns exist in your day. Are your required activities mostly active or passive? When given a choice, do you engage in active or passive activities? Do you consider yourself an active or passive person? Do you consider yourself a small-space or large-space person? Do you prefer long-term or short-term activities?

The elements of dance are part of daily life because movement is part of daily life. When you think of time, space, and effort, remember that these are not just dance elements; they are, in fact, elements we use to make our movements communicate the effect life has on us. What can you learn about yourself by considering the way that you deal with the elements of movement in daily life? You bring this awareness with you to your study of dance. Do you prefer slow, sustained movement? Do you always stand in the same place in class? Do you prefer to move by yourself or with another dancer? Do you prefer to move in straight lines or in curving pathways? Do you change levels easily (go down to the floor and up in the air), or are you most comfortable at one level? Do you move in spurts—moving very quickly and intensely, holding still, and moving very quickly and intensely again—or are you more comfortable with an even activity pace? Do you like to take risks when you move, or are you more comfortable moving with complete control at all times? Do you prefer to be watched, or would you rather dance only for yourself?

Manipulating Time, Space, and Effort in Daily Affairs

We often manipulate the elements of movement without thinking about them, yet we do

Daily Activity Chart

List 10 activities that are part of your daily routine, 5 that are required and 5 that you choose to do. Then list where each activity occurs.

Activity	Place
1. Drive to store	In car
2. Sit in class	At desk
3. Change clothes	In locker room
4. Wash dishes	In rear of restaurant
5. Walk home	Outside
1. Play soccer	Outside
2. Practice piano	In living room
3. Meet friends	In mall
4. Watch TV	On sofa
5. Eat snack	In car

The next column we will label "Time." List how long you were in that space without a break.

Activity	Place	Time
1. Drive to store	In car	10 minutes
2. Sit in class	At desk	55 minutes
3. Change clothes	In locker room	5 minutes
4. Wash dishes	In rear of restaurant	5 hours
5. Walk home	Outside	15 minutes
1. Play soccer	Outside	1 hour
2. Practice piano	In living room	30 minutes
3. Meet friends	In mall	1 hour
4. Watch TV	On sofa	1 hour
5. Eat snack	In car	10 minutes

Last, indicate whether your activity was physically active or passive using an *A* or a *P*.

	Activity	Place	Time
(P)	1. Drive to store	In car	10 minutes
(P)	2. Sit in class	At desk	55 minutes
(A)	3. Change clothes	In locker room	5 minutes
(A)	4. Wash dishes	In rear of restaurant	5 hours
(A)	5. Walk home	Outside	15 minutes
(A)	1. Play soccer	Outside	1 hour
(A)	2. Practice piano	In living room	30 minutes
(A)	3. Meet friends	In mall	1 hour
(P)	4. Watch TV	On sofa	1 hour
(P)	5. Eat snack	In car	10 minutes

FIGURE 5.2 Example of a filled-in daily activity chart. Create your own to determine who you are as a mover.

so to achieve a specific effect. Let us look at some examples of ways that you might direct your use of time to create a particular effect. You might humor a child by pretending to take a lot of time to think about the answer to a well-known joke. How about communicating frustration or drudgery by dragging out your performance of some assigned task beyond the time it should take? How about expressing impatience by speaking in a clipped, shortened manner?

The sense of time varies with each person in every situation. Parents and teenagers are known for having different senses of time when it comes to the telephone. Workers and their superiors often seem to have a different sense of how much time is required to do a job well.

We have touched on some examples of the effects of space on daily activities; now let us consider some of the ways you might deliberately manipulate the space available to you for a specific purpose. For instance, you might choose to invade someone's personal space as a subtle way of asserting yourself. In Western culture, polite social distance is about 4 to 6 feet, but if you stand closer than 4 feet from someone with whom you are not intimate, you offer a nonverbal challenge to that person's power. Have you ever had to sit next to someone, maybe on a bus or plane or a movie theater, who spilled over into your seat, hogged the arm rest, crossed his legs, and crowded you? Maybe you are the kind of person who shrinks and accommodates this sprawler, or maybe you are the kind of person who subtly expands to reclaim your rightful half of the available space (figure 5.3).

The beach can be a fun place to watch territorial claims. It is an unwritten code that each party should give other parties maximum privacy by setting up as far away as possible from each other. Perhaps you have had the experience of being one of the first to arrive on a giant expanse of sand. But as the day goes on, more and more people arrive, and the beach space changes from a broad, private expanse to a crowded scene. The space you had at 10 a.m. is entirely different from the space you are left with by 4 p.m. You can watch some people deal with this by moving their towels and chairs to expand their own turf, or maybe they turn up their stereos to aurally impinge on other

FIGURE 5.3   Have you ever used your size to intimidate a smaller person?

people's space. Like one's sense of time, the sense of space, and the need for a lot or a little of it, will vary for each person.

We can manipulate the elements of effort for a specific effect. Can you think of a time when you appeared to exert more effort than you actually were exerting? How about when the teacher is going to call on someone, and you deliberately display signs of deep concentration and effort even though you have no idea what is being discussed? Even if these examples do not describe your behavior, you may observe them in others. We intuitively use the three elements of dance in our daily lives.

Applying Elements to Dance Training and Choreography

With what you already know about movement, you can use the elements of dance to describe familiar movement, analyze new movement, and create original choreography.

Recognizing the Familiar

Reading dance is a skill that involves learning to recognize certain signs and symbols. Obviously, one difference between reading a dance and reading a book is that if you are unfamiliar with a word in a book, at least the book stays in one place while you go look up the new word; if you encounter a new sign or symbol in dance, it is gone before you can do any research. Applying what you know about the elements of dance will help you read dance more effectively. Applying your intuition about the ways the dancer uses time, space, and effort will help you recognize what is familiar about the dance (figure 5.4). Recognizing the familiar may mean that you notice a pattern of movement that is repeated; it may also mean that you notice that the dancers are continuously moving, that they appear to be drawn to one part of the stage, or that they rarely appear weak. Recognizing the familiar may mean that you see steps that you have encountered before, or that there is something predictable in the way that the dancers move.

Recognizing the familiar may mean that the choreographer has chosen images from daily life—child's play, street people, bowling pins—and has put those images on the stage for you to ponder. The time, space, and effort contained in those images will trigger your memories.

Recognizing the familiar can also mean using the elements to assist your dance class work. Whether you are using this text in conjunction with a class that emphasizes technique or creative movement, you will find yourself being called upon to read other people's movements. In a technique class you are guided through the repetition of certain movement patterns designed to improve your strength, flexibility, and sequence memory. In a creative movement class you might be asked to recall a movement pattern that you have created, or you might be asked to incorporate patterns created by other students. As you learn and repeat these patterns, try to identify what is already familiar about the movements and patterns being presented. You will find the learning process much less intimidating!

FIGURE 5.4   For hundreds of years, aspiring ballet dancers have repeated virtually identical exercises. We recognize these movement patterns and shapes as part of classical ballet.

Using the Elements to Analyze New Movement

Part of learning to recognize familiar movement is learning to recognize what is not familiar. I have seen this before; I have never seen that before. This I can predict, but how did they do that? If you spend too much effort trying to analyze a dance while you are watching it, you are liable to miss the whole effect of the dance. But afterward, as you recall the dance, it can be helpful to look at what you remember in terms of the elements of dance and consider your intuition about how those elements were used.

Analysis is more necessary in situations where you are trying to master a pattern or sequence (see figure 5.5). You can use what you know about the elements of dance to help you read dance so that you can reproduce what has been demonstrated. In your learning process it may help to ask yourself some of these questions:

➤ How is the pattern structured in time? Is it all fast, all slow? Does it ever really stop? Is the rhythmic structure even or uneven? Does it ride or oppose the music?

➤ How is the pattern structured in space? What directions are used? Does it switch from side to side? Does it move from high to low? If it travels from one spot to another, is the path straight or curved?

➤ How is the pattern structured in effort? What kind of tension is being used? Does the movement seem to be bound or free? What seems to be important about the effort of the pattern? Are there accents? How is this pattern different from other patterns? How is it the same?

You can use the elements when reading movement and also when asking your teacher questions to help clarify what is intended.

FIGURE 5.5   When learning a line dance, you pick up a little more each time the whole pattern repeats.

Using the Elements to Create Original Choreography

When we try to create something new we have to acknowledge that we are simply reworking what we have been told and taught into the context of our experiences. The deeper you can investigate your experiences, the more you will have to offer as you create your own work. In terms of the elements of dance, the more you allow yourself to explore what you know about the time, space, and effort of your experience, the more you will have to offer as a choreographer. For instance, consider the experience of sitting in a waiting room. (Which waiting room? You decide!) Think of this experience in time, space, and effort. Are you early or late, hopeful or dreadful, calm or nervous? Are others in the room calm or nervous? Are there enough chairs for everyone? Is there reason to focus on someone else in the room, and is this socially appropriate? Are you all gathered for the same reasons? Using your experience, you can define the room and the nature of its occupants by focusing on the ways that time, space,

and effort are evident. Never mind that there have already been dances created about waiting rooms; the circumstances that you create will be unique and valuable if you apply your experiences to your investigations of the situation's potential. When striving to create original work, do not worry about trying to be inventive. Focus on identifying what you intuitively know about the time, space, and effort of your subject matter, and share that with your audience.

When making a dance we use the elements to create a particular choreographic effect. Choreographers depend on an intuitive understanding of these elements when they create dances. Consider flamenco dancing. Whether or not you have ever studied this style of dance, you can appreciate that the dancer needs the skill to be able to create so many sounds so quickly. If you were to study flamenco dancing, you would learn even more about the subtleties of the arm movements and the complicated rhythmic patterns, but even without such training you could intuitively sense that while the dancer is swooping gracefully forward and back, a lightning-fast profusion of sound is coming from the dancer's feet—a powerful force underlying the dancer's grace.

INSIDE INSIGHT

Maria Taglioni and Helen Tamiris each performed dance that was novel in its time. For Maria Taglioni (a), "toe-dancing," as it was called, was a shocking and delightful novelty in 1909. Helen Tamiris (b), who gave her first concert in 1927, presented work that was very different from the ballets and the review-style dance of the day. Audiences were equally puzzled but came to accept the new form of expression in time.

INSIDE INSIGHT

We are the benefactors of the postmodernists' experimentation. Thanks to their explorations, both of what dance might be and what might be dance, we have even more options to work with today. You are being asked to consider how, in your daily life, you intuitively or subconsciously employ the elements of dance to make a statement, not necessarily an "art" statement, but a statement about your circumstances nonetheless. Yes, you use these elements intuitively, but now you can begin to use them intentionally and experimentally.

Similarly, a choreographer can expect some intuitive reaction to the choices made about the use of space. A Japanese performance company, Dairakudakan, opened its performance with a special ceremony performed outside the theater in which it would later appear. In this ceremony the six men in the company would cover their bodies with white powder, wrap themselves completely in rope, suspend themselves from the side of the building, and then slowly unravel the rope as they descended to the ground. The danger that these performers chose to assume was intuitively obvious to all those who gathered to watch the performance. The dance was slow, beautiful, and organic; it directly addressed the audience's intuitive sense of space. Or, for another example, consider Trisha Brown's dance performed by dancers on several rooftops in Manhattan. Would

you feel that the time, space, and effort were different if the same dance were performed on the ground?

All movement occurs in time, through space, and with effort. We intuitively manipulate these elements in our daily lives to serve our physical, mental, and social needs. The dancer intentionally manipulates the elements of movement to create patterns of form or feeling. By consciously manipulating the three elements, it is possible to produce an infinite variety of movement. These movements may be familiar, purely sculptural, or dramatic. Others are consciously designed, spontaneous, or natural. Some can be executed only after years of training.

The elements of movement can be useful to anyone interested in recognizing, analyzing, or creating movement.

Think About It

1. Try to design a movement sequence that moves through space, with effort, but uses no time. We have said this is impossible. Do you agree?

2. Using the elements of dance, make a snapshot description of each of the following: a stranger, a friend, a family member, and an animal. For instance, you might describe a woman walking a little dog as "moving straight ahead, stopping and starting frequently, with the dog providing slight resistance on her left side." The same woman walking a huge dog might be described as "moving in a zigzag pattern, lurching and resisting, always being pulled to one direction."

3. Choose one activity of your day, such as studying, driving, walking, or bathing, and find ways to investigate as many aspects of that activity as you can by exploring the time, space, and effort it requires. As you work, allow yourself to leave the literal or real world behind, and discover other intriguing aspects to these heretofore mundane affairs. For instance, as you explore the activity of studying, you might get in touch with movements that pertain to feelings of anxiety and your inability to retain facts, or you might find yourself stuck to the chair or the books. When you consider driving, one look at the way that cars are designed will assure you that fantasy is a big part of some people's driving experience. How could you use time, space, and effort to bring such fantasies to performance?

Your Turn to Dance

On/Off Clothes

This improvisation appears in Ruth Zaporah's book *Action Theater: The Improvisation of Presence*, (Berkeley, CA: North Atlantic Books, 1995). It is a group improvisation. What about this dance is characteristic of the postmodern style? What about this goes beyond postmodernism?

You will need to have on tight-fitting dance clothes over which you can put your street clothes. From *Action Theater*, page 2:

Everyone, put your street clothes back on. Change the speed of your movements as you handle your clothing. Sometimes move very quickly, sometimes slowly, sometimes pause altogether, stop moving, staccato movements, tremble, wave. Focus on each moment as it comes into your awareness. Even within a 5-second time frame, change your speed three or four times. Pretend that someone else is directing your movements, so that you are not thinking about it. Don't get serious. We're playing!!

Be aware of your eye focus. Choose what to look at. Do you always want to be looking down at the floor? You may want to look ahead of you, or behind you, or off to the side.

Now repeat this with half the group watching, the other half doing.

Dance of the Daily

Look at your list of activities and see which are actually active. For instance, washing clothes involves moving clothes around, but watching TV does not involve any significant activity. The previous choreographic improvisation gives you some options to explore as you change clothes. What options might you explore as you pour water into a glass or fix yourself a sandwich or fold towels?

Pick an activity and play around with doing just that activity as you vary the elements of dance. Do not pretend to do the activity; really do it, but do it in such a way that you attend to and transform the activity into a movement study rather than a dramatic, narrative, or even comic subject. Just do it. Would you call this *dance*? How can it be said to possess the four aspects of designed movement that qualify it as dance? What is the relationship between invention and intention?

Further complications: Experiment with adding text by talking as you do your activity.

~ Tell a phony, fantastic, autobiographical hero story.

~ Recite text from a scholarly journal or encyclopedia.

~ Recite the words to a popular song as if each sentence has very deep meaning.

#

6

*H*uman movement occurs in time, through space, and with some kind of force, effort, or energy. In the next three chapters we will look more closely at each of these elements, but don't be deceived by the exclusivity suggested by the chapter titles. These are not separate camps with fences around them. Think of these elements as aspects of a phenomenon that can be examined or described in different ways. How would you describe yourself? Is there only one description? Of course there isn't. In describing yourself, you would emphasize aspects that are especially relevant to whatever strengths you want to highlight. In describing the ways that you are an intellectual, you are not renouncing your physical or social strengths; you're just not focusing on a particular set of strengths. In thinking about a dance, we might emphasize the effectiveness of rhythmic manipulation or the appeal of a sustained gesture or the importance of using the upstage area—but we can't detach one element from another any more than you can take hydrogen out of water and still have water.

Each element has its own set of concepts. As we explore the aspects that make up time, space, and effort, keep some curiosity active about the kinds of combinations that intrigue you or come easily to you. Are you most likely to manipulate the way time is used in a study? Or perhaps you are more curious about the ways in which you might use the space? Or do you find yourself intrigued with varying tension patterns? After gaining more familiarity with these elements you will begin to discover what drives your own artistic vision.

The Basics of Time

All movement and stillness occur in time. It is remarkable how differently people sense time, either as a very precise monitor or a very loose construct. It should not come as a great surprise, therefore, to discover that in working with time as an element of dance, people have different preferences and strengths. Some are most comfortable working with music that has a very clear rhythm, and others prefer their movements to be independent of a specific beat. Some are stimulated by music that drives them, others by music that allows them to float free of a beat. Dancers have been exploring the use of their own voices onstage in increasing numbers, using text, poetry, or sounds to accompany their movements. In such cases the structure of time is very different than it would be if they were moving to the sounds of popular music. Some dances are meant to be performed in silence; they leave the dancer free to speed up or slow down appropriately. In order to choose the most effective use of music, or let's just say sound, you need to be familiar with the basic terminology that allows you to attend to all aspects of sound in time. By the end of this chapter you'll have a better idea of how to describe sound and music in terms of pulse, beat, tempo, rhythm, and meter.

Tempo

One consideration of movement in time is how fast or how slow the movement is. The speed of the movement is the tempo. When dancers ask for the tempo of the phrase, they are asking how fast the movement will need to be. Like many other words used to describe the element of time in dance, tempo comes from music vocabulary. There are words to describe different speeds in music but these are not speeds as much as they are moods. A piece marked "vivace," which translates loosely as "lively," is meant to be played fast. Make that *very* fast, like the speed of beads of water moving on a hot griddle. A piece marked "adagio" would be played slowly. In dance, an adagio is a slow movement phrase, which is often used to build or display strength and control. "Allegro" describes a brisk, lively musical tempo; in dance, the grand allegro is a movement phrase with great leaps and lively movement. See figure 6.1 for additional musical vocabulary in dance.

Selected Musical Vocabulary

adagio—Slowly, leisurely, softly
allegro—Fast, lively
allegretto—Playful, slightly slower than allegro
andante—Moderately slow, at walking speed
dolce—Softly, sweetly
largo—Large, broad, slow, and dignified
legato—Smooth and flowing
lento—Slow
presto—Fast, rapid
tempo—Rate of speed at which a musical composition is performed
vivace—Spirited, bright, energetic

FIGURE 6.1   Notice that the definitions indicate the quality combined with the element of time.

INSIDE INSIGHT

Are 2 1/2 minutes a long or short time? It depends on what occurs during that period. In 1976, there was an earthquake in Guatemala that lasted that long and was responsible for the nearly complete destruction of a city and the deaths of 23,000 people. Butoh (see photo) and Noh are theater traditions that use the element of time very deliberately. In those forms, 2 1/2 minutes might not be enough time to turn the head from front to side.

INSIDE INSIGHT The vocabulary of concert dance is French, but the vocabulary of music is Italian. Catherine de Medici, the daughter of the powerful Florentine banker Lorenzo the Magnificient, was married to the French king Henry II to create a political alliance between Italy and France. When she came to France she brought with her the more developed arts of music and dance and established those in the royal court. The language of music was established. The language of dance continued to be developed and eventually was codified for the court.

Some composers will put metronome markings on their sheet music to give the performer a sense of how quick they intend the pace of the piece to be (see figure 6.2). In many cases you will find a composer suggesting the tempo by describing a mood or attitude. "Brightly," "With compassion," "Broadly," "Sustained and melancholic," "With courage." In music as in other time-based arts, the interpretation of time is subjective.

FIGURE 6.2   The metronome marking indicates that the music should be played at 80 beats per minute. The time signature indicates that there are 4 beats per measure and each quarter note gets one beat.

Try This Experiment

Find a piece of music that is performed with a drum machine. A lot of popular music is produced with what's called "sampled" sound—sounds that were originally created by a human musician but were then stored in a computer to be reproduced by a computer, not a live musician. As you listen to the music, pay particular attention to the quality of the tempo. Using the terms of composers, how do you describe the tempo? Keep that experience in mind as you seek out either a live performance or the recording of a live performance. What is different about the tempo in a live performance?

Beat

When asked to provide the tempo, the choreographer will respond by producing a beat—a steady, recurring pulse. These words, "beat" and "pulse," are hardly new concepts. Your heart beats and creates a steady, recurring surge of blood through your veins—your pulse. What may be new to you is their application as dance terms. When we think of a beat, we think of something we can hear; for instance, a drumbeat or a sound of a faucet dripping. But we don't merely hear a beat, we sense it with other parts of the body as well. When we hear a series of beats, we organize the sound so it makes sense to us. We find patterns. When we hear several beats, we sense the amount of time between each of the beats, and we can then determine the tempo. Thereafter, we might or might not actually *hear* a beat to be able to keep in time.

Get a pencil and tap an even rhythm on your table or desk. Start out at a pretty quick tempo. Are the beats even? No accents? Slow down the tempo a hair and add one accent every five counts. Now slow it down just a little more and try this pattern: accent and four more beats, then five beats in your head but no sound, then back in with the pencil, alternating sound and no sound. Where do you "hear" the beat when there's no sound to hear?

Now just play around with random beats keeping no consistent interval between taps. What do you find yourself doing? Do you find yourself wanting to make a repeating pattern? Do you find yourself trying to sense a repeating pattern? Do you prefer this to the 5-count exercise listed previously?

Here are a few other experiments to be sure you understand the difference between a beat you can hear and a beat you can sense:

~ Find your pulse by lightly pressing on the artery in your wrist or neck.

~ Once you have found your pulse, tap that beat on your leg.

~ Keep tapping the same beat, but tap audibly every *other* beat. You will have to sense the beat without making an actual sound.

~ Keep tapping that same beat, but tap audibly only on every third beat. You will have to sense two even beats between your taps.

If you now got up and did 10 jumping jacks, or some kind of exercise that increased your heart rate, you would find a different, faster pulse in your body. Imagine this faster tempo, and tap a faster beat on your leg, gradually working up to sensing this new beat in groups of four. (You will have to sense three beats between your taps, or TAP, beat, beat, beat, TAP, beat, beat, beat.) Was it easier for you to sense a slow or a fast beat?

When we sense a series of beats, either in active listening or in our subliminal experience, we sense whether the interval between the sounds is regular or irregular. If it's regular we try to find a larger pattern it fits into. If it's irregular we keep casting about mentally and perceptually to try to find a pattern. Pause right now and listen carefully to all the sounds and patterns that are in your environment. Can you hear the ventilation system? Can you hear the fluorescent lights? If you are outside, is there a recurring beat to the sound or din of traffic? Unless we are put in an isolation tank, our brains are constantly processing sounds and translating them into sound patterns. Some fit, some do not.

Rhythm

Were you aware of the pattern you made when tapping only one beat and sensing the others silently? This pattern of accented and unaccented beats is called a rhythm. You first accented every other beat and created a rhythm that recurred every 2 beats. Next, you established a 3-count rhythm. Finally, you established a 4-count rhythm, meaning on every fourth beat you created an accent. Look at this written out another way:

➤ Tap, clap, or walk in the room creating 12 even and equal accents. We will represent these 12 marks in time by making evenly spaced marks on the page, indicating that the sounds occur at regular, equal intervals.

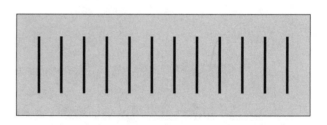

➤ Repeat your 12 beats *and* make one continuous sound for the duration of the 12 beats—sing a note, inhale, exhale, drone, or make whatever noise you want. Be sure that this sound can be sustained for the entire 12 counts. This addition we will note by drawing a long line through the 12 time marks, connecting all the lines together. When you combine the 12-beat rhythm with the drone you are creating a polyrhythmic structure. You have one rhythm that cycles in 12 counts and another rhythm, in this case a pulse that cycles

12 times. This will feel more clearly rhythmic if you add an accent every fourth beat. Your rhythm will cycle three times. Combined with your sustained drone or gesture you have an even more complex polyrhythmic structure.

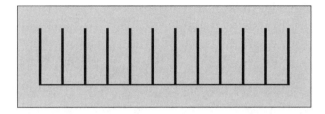

➤ Before you repeat your 12 regular beats by walking or clapping, look at the next figure, and you will see that an X has been drawn over one of the 12 marks. This indicates at what point and for how long you will make your vocal sound. The sound you add will last only as long as the time it takes for 1 beat to pass.

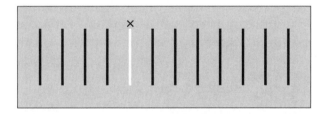

➤ Now it is your turn to decide when your sounds will occur during the 12 counts. Do this by making separate Xs over 3 of the 12 marks. Rather than making a long, continuous sound through all 12 beats, as you did previously,

make your accompanying sound when you get to those beats. Repeat your 12 regular beats by walking, clapping, or tapping, and add your sound during the beats that have Xs over them. If you had a long sound, you will have to make it shorter to fit in the time available.

Try these patterns:

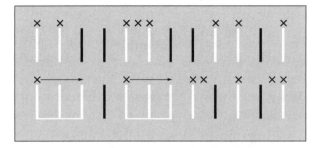

An interesting dance might be made by combining three or four sound-accent patterns and performing them simultaneously. What if one dancer made the "sound" of "yes," another "no," and a third "maybe"? Can you imagine a dance with that music? What other interesting sound or word combinations can you think of?

In the previous exercise, different sounds would be better suited to different tempos and accent strengths. The "yes-no-maybe" dance might even change rhythm (that is, change the recurring pattern of accents), as emotions evolved. The appropriate rhythm for a dance does not necessarily come from music. Rhythm—a recurring pattern of accents—can arise from a number of sources, including nature, emotions, machines, and

INSIDE INSIGHT

We are continuously integrating rhythmic patterns into our experience. We've just touched on the musical rhythms, but did you know that your own body is a polyrhythmic entity? We mentioned the heartbeat. That's one rhythm. Can you think of another rhythm? How about the breath rhythm? You have a digestive cycle, a kidney cycle; women have menstrual cycles, and we all have waking and sleeping cycles. As you probably know, your brain goes through different cycles even while you are sleeping. And, speaking of your brain, there are different cycles of brain activity that both create and induce varying levels of attention. When you are in the presence of sounds that allow all those different rhythms and cycles to be in harmony with each other, you experience a sense of well-being. When your body is unable to create that kind of harmony, because of an overload of input, or dissonance among all the cycles that are in your experience, you feel a sense of unease.

music. A choreographer works intentionally with time by manipulating the duration and the speed of movement. The intentionality of duration and speed will result in one of the following kinds of rhythm: organic, metric, or mechanical.

Organic Rhythm

Organic rhythm surrounds us—it is within us and is something we work with every day—but we seldom give it our attention. You may have noticed the way the wind starts to stir before a heavy rain. It picks up speed, the temperature drops, and the rain comes, first in big, scattered drops, then in a downpour. Soon it tapers off to a light rain or no rain at all. Only the leaves or other objects drip water. This build and decline is rhythm. It is an increasing and decreasing intensity that forms a pattern of accents over time.

Have you ever watched a trail of ants discover a piece of food? First one, then two, then hundreds of ants arrive and devour the food. Afterward, the number of ants decreases, until none remain. This is another example of organic rhythm. Your heartbeat and pulse are also organic rhythms.

Try This Experiment

While sitting comfortably, become aware of your breath's rhythm—the rhythm of your relaxed inhalations and exhalations. At first, your breath may be affected by your attention. Sit quietly until you can merely observe and not interfere.

When you feel you are ready, use the inhalation to expand your upper body, chest, and arms, and use the exhalation to relax your upper body and chest, and bring your arms back to your center.

Experiment with increasing the range of your movement, but always keep your movement motivated by your breath.

You will probably find that as the work increases, the tempo of your breath's rhythm increases; this cycle builds on itself. Organic rhythms evolve through natural causes, such as effort or intensity. They almost have a life of their own. The rhythms of a lightning storm, a person involved with heavy labor, and a basketball player are organic. Organic rhythm is not measured in units of time that are consistent from beginning to end. Instead, the rhythm evolves or emerges from the effort required.

Metric Rhythm

A parking meter measures how long your car has been in the space. A gas meter measures how much gas you have used since the last reading. A speedometer measures how fast your car is traveling. A meter measures how much and how fast.

In music, the metric system measures time. Metric rhythm is not part of the metric system used for weights and distances in most of the world. In music, meter indicates how the music is divided and how fast the notes must be played relative to each other. Go back to the experiment on page 84 to get a better sense of how this system works.

INSIDE INSIGHT

If breathing were just an inhale and exhale activity, we'd be exhausted from the effort after about 10 minutes. Are you aware of the four parts of the breath cycle? How do we really breathe? There are four parts to the breath cycle: *inspiration, utilization, return,* and *emptiness.* Breathing in, you inspire yourself. The in-breath moves to your lungs and your lungs utilize all you can absorb. What you can't use is returned to the air as you exhale. Then there is a period of quiet and respiratory inactivity, which eventually becomes your next inhalation (inspiration). Depending on the demands you are placing on yourself, physically and emotionally, you will need some parts of this cycle more than others. What do you need right now?

➤ Use both hands, one to accent the first beat and the other to keep the beat going through all 16 counts. Have both hands make the first beat, then continue to tap out the remaining 15 beats using only one hand. Play this pattern through twice. When the tapping hand finishes count 16, the accent hand comes in again, and both hands play to restart the pattern.

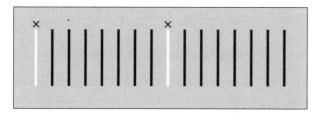

➤ Now divide the following 16 beats into 2 groups of 8. As before, use one hand to make the accents and one hand to keep a consistent beat.

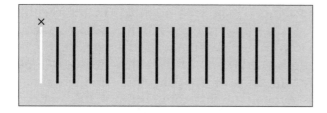

➤ Now divide the 16 beats once again, this time into 4 groups of 4 counts. Your accent hand will join your tapping hand 4 times.

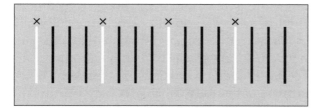

➤ Now divide the 16 beats into 8 groups of 2 counts. Your accent hand will join your tapping hand 8 times (every other beat).

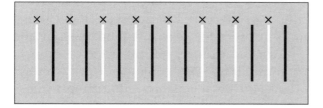

You have just played 4 meters of music! You have just divided time in four ways. Play each one through again, at least twice. Each time you come to an accent, *actually say,* "One," and then sense or say the rest of the beats.

Meter in music is based on finding that "one." It is the place in time when you can hear or sense a return, a new beginning. Go back to the 4 meters you created previously. Instead of letting your accent hand rest between accents, keep it moving like the hand of a clock, so that it hits the "one" accent at the right time and is immediately launched again into a new circle.

We have said that the meter tells you both how many beats and in how much time. Consider the second aspect of the definition (in how much time). In the first meter you had one accent, or one "One." In musical terms this would be called a *measure* of 16 beats. That is a long measure, and one not usually found in music. In the second meter, you still have 16 beats of time, but you have divided the time into 2 measures of 8 counts. In the third effort, you still have 16 beats of time, but you have divided the time into 4 measures of 4 counts. How much time? It depends on the meter.

Do all measures of 8 counts need 8 sounds? Do all measures of 4 counts require 4 sounds? This is the tricky part of understanding metric rhythm. You do not have to actually hear the beat all the time in order to sense it. If a piece of music is divided into measures of 8, each measure will last for 8 equal counts of time, but there can be *any number of sounds* during that time. Consider an example. The following pattern is 4 measures long. Each measure has 6 beats.

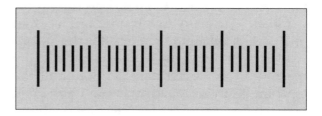

Trace over the previous pattern on a separate piece of paper. In each measure place a mark over any 4 of the beats. Make a different pattern of marks in each measure. When you have made your marks, play your pattern by tapping the marked beats and sensing the unmarked beats inside.

Add 4 more marks in each measure, placing some marks between the beats. You still have 4 measures of 6 beats, but you have a rhythm that has 8 sounds to it. How are you going to squeeze all those sounds into the same amount of time? Play between the beats!

Metric rhythm is the description of how sounds are organized in regular, specified measures of time. If you study music theory, you will learn how to read music and interpret musical symbols that are used to indicate different meters. This introduction is intended not to make you a musician but to help you understand how metric rhythm can be used in dance training and dance-making.

Dance is often accompanied by music, which is organized into clear, metric patterns. By understanding how to count music—by developing a sense of the rhythmic structure—you will be in a good position to sense how your movements should or could relate to the metric rhythms in the music. You will also have the option, when creating your own dances, to design your movement to mimic or be independent of the metric rhythms of the music.

Mechanical Rhythm

Mechanical rhythms are divisions of time that are created by machines and automatic devices. The ticking of a clock creates a mechanical rhythm. The clock never varies; it either ticks or is silent. The ringing pattern of a telephone creates a mechanical rhythm. When someone calls, the rings you hear are programmed to last for a certain time, and the intervals between rings are always the same. Mechanical rhythms are patterns that recur without any need for recuperation. Machinery in a factory produces an orchestra of different rhythms. It is the factory worker's job to keep up with the rhythm of the machine. The worker may get tired, but the machine keeps the same rhythm. Can you think of two other examples of mechanical rhythms?

It may help you to think of mechanical rhythms as rhythms devoid of breath, rest, or spirit. Humans can imitate mechanical action by eliminating breath, rest, or spirit from their execution of a task. For instance, if you were to

mime reading this book in a mechanical way, you might move your head in a sharp, rhythmic way and turn pages in the same manner. This would be very different from your natural reading rhythm, which would allow you to linger or speed up, depending on what was on a given page. Perhaps you have heard someone play a musical instrument mechanically. They may have accurately played each of the notes, but somehow the whole rendering was less than moving. There was no spirit in the recital. Look for this subtlety in dance performances. Do you ever have the sense that you are watching trained robots or dancing machines? Look for this in your own dancing. Are there times when you are just going through the motions in a mechanical manner? Are there times when you might be trying so hard to do a movement pattern that you lose the connection to your own breath and spirit as you move?

Using Time As a Choreographic Tool

"Beat," "tempo," and "rhythm" are all words useful for talking about the element of time in the context of dance. Variations in beat, tempo, and rhythm are all means of working with time as a choreographic tool. Going back to our definition of dance, recall that we identified four components that distinguish dance from other human activities. We noted that dance has function, intentional rhythm, is composed of one or more culturally patterned sequences, and displays extraordinary nonverbal movement. Two of these components are particularly pertinent to our discussion of the element of time as a choreographic tool.

Intentional Rhythm

An alluring aspect of many popular dances is how the dance fits the music so well. It can be very reassuring to an audience to be able to hear strong accents and see correspondingly strong movements or to hear a soft, lilting melody and see a correspondingly soft, pliant dancer move to the music. It was very common in the early days of ballet for the choreographer to attempt to make the music visual, that is, to make stage pictures that were analogous to the mood or story line of the music. The rhythmic structure that defined the movements came directly from the music.

Contemporary choreographers are looking at their work in a new light and are not necessarily allowing the music to dictate the timing of the movements. Even in ballet (and even in classical ballet!) choreographers are now working with rhythms that have to do with breath, emotion, or effort rather than simply following the rhythms and accents of the music.

Working With Music

Choreographing to music has its benefits. Music can be not only a source but also a direction for the statement you want to make with your dance. Consider the subject of love. There is no shortage of music inspired by this theme. Popular, classical, primitive, modern, literal and abstract love songs, symphonies, and other compositions exist to inspire the listener to feel the joy, pain, elation, sadness, and all other aspects of love. There is an infinite number of ways to dance about a subject like love. If you find a piece of music that really speaks to you, that touches or moves you or prompts memories of love, then you have a specific starting point in an otherwise vast sea of options. Once you have found your inspirational music and have begun to choreograph your dance, you need to keep a few questions in mind as you work.

How does the dance you are making *add* to the music? Unless you are using music with lyrics from another language, you can assume that the audience also understands the words; you will not add to the music by acting out the words. Does your movement go beyond the literal interpretation of the music?

What is the relationship between your dance and the music? You need to decide if your dance will follow the timing or complement the tone of the music, and if the music creates an atmosphere or a structure.

Also consider familiarity when choosing your music. You may have a favorite recording artist whose music you enjoy dancing to socially. This person's music would, at first, seem like a great choice for a dance composition. Think again. You and your peers have strong associations with that music—with movements that go with it and the emotional response it evokes. How are you going to make a dance that adds to those associations and goes beyond them into new ideas? There is also a good chance that when this popular piece of music is played, those who are familiar with it will be confused if you do not fulfill their expectations. These same considerations apply to the use of any popular music: classical, operatic, country and western, rap, house, or any other style. When working with familiar music, go back to these two questions: How does the dance add to the music, and what is the relationship of the dance to the music?

Working with music can define the framework for your dance—the speed of the movement, the build of the dance, the climax, the accents, and the tone of the piece. Is it dark and slow, or bright and slow? Gently sweeping or

INSIDE INSIGHT

Can you imagine the president of the United States feeling compelled to issue a statement about the appropriate balance of dance, music, and verse? As far back as the French court of Charles IX in 1570, the relationship of the elements of theater was a subject that warranted official comment. Charles IX founded the Academy of Poetry and Music (L'Académie de Poesie et Musique) to guide the moral and ethical development in his country. He believed that when music is well ordered, men are morally disciplined, but when music is disordered, men become immoral and corrupt.

In her book, *Ballet in Western Culture* (Boston: Allyn & Bacon, 1999, page 40), author Carol Lee tells us, "Instrumentalists were encouraged to compose music that would coincide with the rhythms in metrical verse. Following the same rule, the length of dance steps had to closely fit the duration of musical notes." Talk about intentional rhythm!

strongly aggressive? Music is also finite. Generally, when the music is over, so is the dance. You can use the music to solve three choreographic challenges: when to begin, when to build, and when to stop.

The way that you work with music will either be intentionally reassuring or intentionally disquieting. Suppose you were to work with a piece of music such as Pachelbel's "Canon in D Minor." Not only is this is a sweet, harmonious, comforting piece of music, it is also a very well-known piece; you would probably be correct in assuming that at least a few people watching your dance would be familiar with the music and have their own associations with it. Consider the effect if you were to choreograph one of the following subjects using this music:

➤ A love duet

➤ A dance about the motion of a river

➤ A boxing match

➤ A stamping dance

The dances about love or the river would be harmonious with the mood and the timing of the music; they would be reassuring to watch. Dances about a boxing match or a stamping ceremony would be counter to the music and, therefore, would be confounding to watch. Done well, a boxing dance done to lyrical, classical music might invite the audience to see the grace in boxing or to be moved by the juxtaposition of harmony and brutality. Done well, a stamping dance might be used to highlight the eccentricities of a misfit or the frustration of an energetic person made to operate in a serene, civilized environment.

Working with music still allows you to explore your own interests in rhythmic structure, and it still allows you to make decisions about the duration of your movements. If the music is going "ooomp paa paa, ooomp paa paa," you can either "ooomp" with it, or you can sustain your movement in a contrasting way. By making your movements either correspond to or contrast with the music's beat, tempo, and rhythm, your use of time will influence the audience's experience.

We have been focusing on music that is rooted in European standards of familiar harmony, melody, and rhythmic structure. There are, of course, myriad resources from other cultures that use time and tone differently. You would do well to investigate some of the rhythmically complex folk music of the world, the tonally diverse classical music of other cultures, and the sound fields being created by contemporary musicians. Work with music that is predictable to you. It can make life simple. But also leave yourself open to music that is new to you. As we will see in the next section, music from other cultures can be a good starting point for dances that either comment on your culture or investigate established cultural patterns.

Culturally Patterned Sequences

Folk dances use time in specific and often complex ways. Social dances typically use time in simple ways. Whether or not you are a folk dancer or even a social dancer, you have still absorbed aspects of your culture's sense of time, and you might even be conscious of culturally patterned movement sequences that relate to time. For example, have you ever noticed how people seem to have internal timers that go off while standing in a line? At first, there is respect for personal space, and those in line maintain a certain distance from one another. Then, regardless of whether the front person moves or not, the back part of the line moves forward, and the line starts to compress. This is that cultural sense of time in action. This behavior is not necessarily evident in other cultures.

As a choreographer you will draw from your personal cultural experiences, either replicating familiar and comfortable patterns or exploring and exposing new, challenging patterns. Your sense of tempo, beat, and rhythm is affected by the cultural patterns to which you have been exposed. For example, most of you have probably heard the loud, ultra-low bass notes of modern hip-hop and rap music emanating from cars with high-powered stereo systems. While previously restricted to a few specific cultures, this rhythm is now pervasive and can be heard regularly throughout the United States. Note how often you hear this rhythm on the street during the next week.

INSIDE INSIGHT
Choreographer Merce Cunningham and his longtime collaborator and composer, John Cage, asserted that music and dance could be separate entities, that no relationship necessarily exists between the two. Often Cunningham's dancers would perform even though they had never heard the music to which they were dancing. This innovation was a radical departure from centuries of dance history in which all concert dances were choreographed to music. Cunningham's contribution to the choreographic process changed the course of dance history and challenged choreographers to work with the element of time with a new kind of integrity.

Attending to the element of time in choreography involves developing an awareness of tempo and beat—speed and pulse. Attention also goes to the nature of the patterns that the beats make—organic, metric, and mechanical rhythms. Finally, culturally determined assumptions about duration, repetition, and balance need to be taken into account when assessing whether the use of time is appropriate for the function the dance is intended to serve.

We are exposed to mechanical rhythms every day, but we may not be aware of these sounds as rhythms both because we can identify the source of the sound and because the regularity of the rhythms makes them blend into a general background of sound. We may not notice the effect that these rhythms have on us. As a dance student and a choreographer, you should become aware of your responses to mechanical rhythms. Do the next Try This Experiment to get a sense of the movement difference that results from working with the various kinds of rhythm we have discussed:

Try This Experiment

~ Sit or stand where you have enough room to extend both of your arms in all directions. Allow your arms to rest by your sides as you focus on your breath.

~ Gradually allow your arms to float up as you inhale and to return to your sides as you exhale. The longer you inhale, the higher up your arms will float, and the longer it will take to let them float back down.

~ Repeat this movement phrase four or five times, getting a sense of how your movement is connected to your breath.

~ Find a piece of music that is performed by human musicians rather than by a drum machine or computer. Try to find a meter that has a tempo similar to your breath rhythm.

~ Repeat the same movement phrase, this time working with the music's metric rhythm. You now have a sense of how music is counted.

~ Finally, find a mechanical rhythm in your environment. Repeat your movement phrase by raising and lowering your arms only on the beats dictated by the sound. If you cannot find a sound that works for you, use a clock, and move in rhythm with the second hand.

Can you sense the difference in the movements based on these different kinds of rhythms? No one rhythm is better or worse than another. Each is useful for different purposes.

Think About It

1. Unless you are in a sensory-deprivation chamber, you are going to be surrounded by rhythms that have choreographic potential. Observe a tree in a light wind, and note the rhythms that are created by the leaves and the branches, maybe even the landing and departing birds and squirrels. Weave these into a repeating 4-count rhythmic pattern. Sit quietly in a room, and integrate all the mechanical rhythms you can hear in the building—clocks, heating systems, doors, and bells. Again, weave these into a 4-count rhythmic pattern. If you were to perform these as the basis of a dance set to one of Bach's Brandenburg concertos, would you be working with metric, organic, or mechanical rhythm?

2. Using five movement words, create four variations in time so that one repetition is even, one is uneven, one goes with a selection of music, and one goes against the same music. Keep the sequence of the words the same; simply vary the timing. For instance, if your sequence was a step, hop, leap, bounce, and swing, your first two repetitions might be done in silence. In the first repetition, each movement takes the same amount of time—an uneven rhythm. In the second repetition the movement is done to an uneven rhythm. The next two repetitions are dictated by music. The music may have accents and pauses that the movements mimic in the third repetition. In the sequence in the fourth repetition the rhythm doesn't match the music.

3. Take a popular song, one you and your friends like for dancing and listening. Experiment with making changes in the dance you usually do to this song by varying the timing of the movements. You are playing with some familiar movements, so at first this will seem awkward. Remember, it is just an experiment. Who knows? You might just invent a new dance!

4. Many define music as "sound organized in time." What does that definition have in common with the definition of dance we are using in this book? If music is sound organized in time, can any organized sounds be music? By that same principle, can any organized movements be dance? Why or why not?

Your Turn to Dance

Accent

1. Working without music at first, start by standing still and counting phrases of 8 counts, getting the sense of the tempo you've chosen and the duration of the phrase.

2. Next, accent the first count with an isolation and hold that new shape for the remaining 7 counts. Try to surprise yourself with the impulse of each isolation. Remember, the isolation can be gentle or strong.

3. Next, accent the first count with an isolation, then take the remaining 7 counts to change the rest of the shape in a sustained movement.

4. Next, play with whether you are accenting with an isolation or a whole body change. Play with whether you are using the remaining 7 counts to change the whole shape or only an isolated part.

5. Finally, add another accent but vary its location in the phrase. Do not feel that you need to have a secondary accent in each 8-count phrase.

What have you discovered by doing this exploration? Without music, what could this piece be about? Take that insight and decide how the piece should begin. Does it call for an entrance or does it start onstage? What develops as the piece evolves? In the end, what news has the piece offered? How has your manipulation of the element of time been effectively used?

Timing Is Everything

This dance explores the effect of changing the speed of movement. You will quickly become aware of the integration of all the elements as discussed at the beginning of the chapter. A quick, slashing movement is no longer a slash when you change the element of time. You will also encounter challenges of acceleration and deceleration.

1. First set for yourself a road map. The map will end at the same spot on which you began. Pick five spots in your performing space and go from spot to spot. Take care that they are not equidistant—each part of the path should be a different length.

2. Assign a different activity on the path to each of your spots. For example, turn, twist the upper body, or raise your arms. You decide. But once you decide, stick with that gesture- or posture-change sequence.

3. Assign yourself 5 counts to move along the longest path, then 4 on the next longest, 3 on the next, and so on. In other words, depending on your map, your sequence might be a phrase that is 4 then 1 then 5 then 2 then 3 counts—a mixed-meter phrase.

4. Give yourself a consistent pulse and coordinate the duration of the gesture with that of the allotted path.

5. For your final challenge, shift the count structure by one pathway—maybe you are now allowed only 1 count to cover the entire (previously 5-count) path.

6. Perform the two versions back to back. Which one works best first?

What might this dance be about? If you were to go on with it, how would you develop it?

Space

*A*wareness of space—what you can do in it and with it—is critical to the study of dance. Dance is an art form that transforms space. A bare stage can become a beach, a ballroom, a busy street, a sculpture garden, or an infinite number of other spaces. In dance you can even create spaces that are fantastic, symbolic, or surreal.

Dancing bodies create relationships with each other and with the space. We have an intuition about space and about relationships in space and we bring those to the act of watching and interpreting dance. In fact, it is those intuitions that are called into play (in all senses of that word) when we contemplate relationships in space.

Your use of space indicates what forces are acting on your body. Moving on one spot, moving as if being pushed or pulled through space, moving from low to high, and moving on a straight or curving path—all of these choices will indicate which forces you choose to show acting on your body. Where is your focus as you move? How does your size change or not change as you move? Is the space between you and the other dancers appropriate for the material?

In order to create the magical transformations of space that dance can achieve, it will help you to be aware of the components of spatial design. In addition, it will be useful to consider how you use space in your daily affairs—the different spaces you maintain between yourself and the rest of the world. This interpersonal spatial awareness will be applicable to your dance training, dance-making, and dance appreciation.

In this chapter we will consider six components of spatial design: level, shape, direction, dimension, perspective, and focus. We will also investigate the four interpersonal spaces with which we all structure our lives: intimate, personal, social, and distant. By understanding the principles that govern the use of space, you will be in a better position to deal most effectively with this element of dance.

Level

If you were asked to make an opening shape for a dance (to arrange yourself in a still position that had some interest), what level would you be most likely to assume? Would you crouch low to the floor? Would you lie down on your back? Would you stand on your toes? All of these choices have to do with your level, which may be high, middle, or low.

Level indicates your position relative to the ground. Low is assumed to be below the level of the knee, middle level is from the knee to the top of the head, and high is above the head. These are not rules to be checked with a yardstick; they are general orientations for discussing level.

Some people are quite comfortable on the ground, some are happier crouching, and others prefer standing still or jumping. How low is low, and how high is high, will depend on your personal preferences and abilities. Obviously, if your work involves extreme level changes—going from very low to very high—you will be required to exert more effort than someone whose work stays at a low or middle level.

Movement at a low level often implies being rooted, grounded. A body lying onstage is a form that has submitted to the pull of gravity. You might see rest, death, sleep, or simply a horizontal shape. Rising up to a crouch, a crawl, or any version of low support still indicates an overall relationship to gravity where gravity is winning. The form is more down than up. There is still a strong sense of being rooted, of being able to use the body's center of gravity with great power. In the middle level the body has more options for movement, quick direction changes, and speed. The high level shows an escape from gravity; it defies its pull by leaving the ground with leaps and jumps. In Western cultures this level is typically used to express joy and ethereal transformation (figure 7.1).

FIGURE 7.1   The high level shows a desire to escape the bonds of gravity.

Shape

Shape refers to the form your body makes in space. Whether bent, stretched, curved, or twisted, the shape your body makes indicates the nature of the forces acting on it.

A person stretched out on a couch makes a horizontal shape; a basketball player makes a vertical shape when jumping for the ball at the start of a game. Although each of those shapes indicates something about the person's relationship to gravity, neither one qualifies as dance. Recall that dance deliberately structures the display of the forces acting on a body. Those forces are made evident through your body's shape. Force will be perceived as perpendicular to the line of the torso. Consider examples from stage combat to understand why shape is so important. If you were to mime being punched in the stomach, the shape of your back would curve to show that force affecting you from the front. If you were to mime being hit in the side of the face, you would twist your spine and stagger backward. The shape of the body telegraphs the force to the audience. A skilled actor uses the torso to reinforce the drama. Likewise, in dance the shape of the torso directs the line of force, which is reinforced by the shaping of the arms, legs, and head.

Shape is often a starting point for composition students. Working with contrasts, such as open and closed, wide and narrow, curved and straight, not only challenges creativity but also brings an awareness of shape as a rich, simple resource. Picture a dancer standing on two feet, holding her arms wide, and looking up. Slowly her arms bend, her head drops, and she becomes a closed shape as she sinks toward the floor. Just before she gets all the way low, she shoots one arm up and draws herself back up and open to her original position. Just by using the contrast of open and closed, a dance is made. Just by focusing on shape, the dancer can make evident the forces acting on her body.

Let us use this same dance to look at the concept of symmetry. A shape that is balanced from side to side is said to be symmetrical. This concept of balance is important in dance because the shape of the body will inform the viewer of the forces acting on it. At the beginning of the imaginary dance described, the dancer was standing on two feet with arms raised high. This would be a symmetrical shape. If one side of the shape is a mirror image of the other side, you have a symmetrical shape. But suppose, as another dancer performs the same routine, one of his arms is bent, and he is slightly curved to one side. This would produce an asymmetrical shape; it is unbalanced, and it implies that the dancer is struggling with the forces acting on his body.

Symmetry can be created with the shape of one body or several bodies. Two people leaning on each other, shoulder to shoulder, create a symmetrical ∧ shape. Such a shape connotes balance. How might you create an asymmetrical shape using two bodies? How does the apparent force change? Are asymmetrical shapes necessarily unbalanced?

Shape, as a component of spatial design, is an important dance resource. Attending to shape requires that you be aware of the forces you wish to show acting on your body—the pull of gravity, the use of momentum and centrifugal force, the real or abstract picture you wish to make, and the effort, or lack of it, you wish to show through your dance.

Try This Experiment

Collect shapes from nature and analyze them for symmetry or asymmetry. Use the outline of an object (such as a leaf, rock, branch, or feather) to define a floor pattern. You can explore the differences brought about by changing a movement's dimension using simple, everyday gestures. A wave, for instance, becomes something very different when the height of the gesture is changed or when the distance the arm travels forward and backward is changed. Choose another gesture and explore this aspect of dimension on your own.

Direction

So far we have addressed level, the position of the body relative to the floor, and shape, the contours that indicate which forces are acting on the body. Now it is time to look at moving the body forward, backward, sideways, and on a diagonal. These are the directions within which an infinite number of movement patterns are structured.

As a choreographer, the choices of direction you make in designing your floor pattern will enable you to reinforce the statement you wish to make. As a performer, your awareness of direction will allow you to execute the choreography clearly and completely. As a student, your attention to direction will help you discover the patterns of movements required in a technique class.

Let us consider another sequence of movements in terms of direction:

> Imagine an empty stage. Imagine a dancer entering. The dancer takes four steps, then drops suddenly to the floor. He slowly stretches out on his stomach, looking past his hands. He pulls himself forward using only his hands, then slowly draws in his legs. Gradually he rises to a crouch then, folding his arms over his head, he runs in a zigzag pattern offstage.

Where did he start? Where did you imagine him to *go*? How big or how small did he become? Did he use a lot of space? Was he going to something or escaping from something? What kind of pattern did he make?

What space did that short description suggest to you? Could you imagine the dancer in a smoke-filled room or as a person on a battlefield?

Let us make a few changes here. Suppose another dancer staggers onto an empty stage. Right away, simply by changing the direction of her entrance from a straight path to a zigzag path, we have a completely different dance! Let us also say that she changes level during those four steps. By incorporating her level change with the stagger, we have also set the dance on a new course. Now let us say that she rolls over on her back, raises her face to the sky, and, as if drawn to the stars, stands and ambles off slowly looking up at the stars. Well, that is it for the battlefield setting, is it not? Likewise, this would not be a piece about someone in personal danger. We have entirely redefined that space because of these changes in direction.

Floor Pattern

If you had ink on the bottoms of your feet, and you got up and moved through your dance space, your ink-stained feet would create a pattern on the floor. This is called a *floor pattern*. The space between your footprints might show that you went into the air, or that you took short, quick steps. A turn might show up as a smudge. A slide would make a long, straight line.

Your floor pattern is the design you make by moving through your performing space. The patterns you form will show the audience the statement you wish to make with your movement. In our previous example, the dancer's path might be a straight one, indicating some kind of draw or urgency. Then again, the dancer could stagger indirectly, fall down, and grope around in a new direction; he could also run off in yet another direction, indicating something very different.

A floor plan shows the journey the dancer will take. When you dance you outline a journey that has a beginning, middle, and end. There are three kinds of journeys:

1. Journeys that end where they began

2. Journeys that end somewhere new

3. Journeys that do not have an end, but by implication seem to continue (for example, dances with a fade-to-black ending)

Your floor pattern will indicate which of these journeys is important to your dance and what happens along the way. Motion forward traditionally implies presentation, progress, and growth. Motion backward traditionally implies retreat, regress, weakening. Motion sideways traditionally indicates shifting, vacillating. Motion on a diagonal traditionally demonstrates gradual growth or retreat. The traditional aspect of each assumption is important to bear in mind because it is possible to work with these directions without hoping to conjure any of these dramatic overtones. However, as we will explore further when we discuss perspective, there are some physical facts about these directions that lend themselves to these implications.

INSIDE INSIGHT

As the dances of the Renaissance courts became more and more elaborate, and as the need to perform these dances with ease and grace became more and more important in achieving and maintaining one's status in court, efficient sideways movement was a matter of great importance. In 1588-1589, Thoinot Arbeau wrote *Orchésographie*, a how-to manual of social dance forms—forms that were being absorbed into theatrical productions as well. It was Arbeau who formally introduced the value of turnout (the outward rotation of the legs resulting in the heels being closer to the midline of the body than are the toes) in moving sideways. It also proved a valuable way for men to show off their diamond shoe buckles and their delicate ankle bows as they danced!

Direct Versus Indirect Patterns

When defining the space by choosing the direction of your movements, you are working with three options:

1. You can move in a straight line.
2. You can move in a curved line.
3. You can move on one spot.

Contained within those three options is an infinite number of possible variations. Where do you begin? Onstage? Offstage? What is the first part of your journey? One long, straight line that goes from one side of the stage to another? A series of very short, straight lines that connect at right angles to each other (making an overall zigzag)? One line that goes only to the center, connected to another line that exits in another direction?

Spatial design has use in the classroom when you are trying to learn a movement pattern. Look to see what parts of the pattern involve direct or indirect movement. Spatial design is also useful for choreographing your own work. Direct motion connotes a different sense of control, purpose, and direction than indirect motion connotes. Indirect patterns could imply stealth, insecurity, indecision, even indifference. Direct patterns can imply that the forces acting on the body are stronger on the going-to side than on the going-from side, whatever those forces might be. Finally, direct versus indirect motion can be an interesting way to look at everyday motion—the floor patterns you make as you move through spaces, such as the grocery store, mall, library, even your own home.

Dimension

No matter how big or how small, dimension is the relative size of the body, or the space the body occupies onstage. Dimension is one more clue about what kinds of forces are acting on the dancer. It is the difference between waving at someone by raising your hand to your chest and moving your fingers or throwing your arm up high and waving wildly.

You can look at the contrasts between big and small in terms of height, width, and depth. Just as your perception of level will be relative, so too your perception of dimension will be relative to other spatial clues. If there are five dancers moving in leaps and bounds all over the stage and a sixth dancer walks slowly, the contrast between the dimension used by the walking dancer and the leaping dancers creates interest. You could also create interesting contrasts of force by having five dancers walk slowly and making the sixth dancer leap and bound, moving through more stages of height, width, and depth.

Dimension requires variety in order to be effective. Without contrasts in these three aspects, one force prevails and can easily lose magical power. It is like listening to someone who speaks in a monotone; you can be loud and monotonous or soft and monotonous. Keep an eye out for ways to shade your definition of force by manipulating dimension. The magical use of dimension to shape space will help define the who, what, when, and where of your dancing.

Perspective

A sculptor creates three-dimensional shapes with an interest in each possible view angle. Most likely, the sculptor is also aware of the difference that distance makes on the appreciation of the work and strives to find a setting for the final product that puts it in its best advantage. The sculptor's challenge is similar to the challenge of the choreographer, with one notable difference—movement. When appreciating sculpture, the audience gets to move. When appreciating dance, the audience generally stays put, and the dancers do the moving. As soon as the dancers start moving, they create new stage pictures for the fixed audience to view. Bodies become larger or smaller depending on whether they move toward or away from the audience. The space looks balanced or unbalanced depending on how the dancers are arranged. Dancers appear intimate or remote depending on where they are placed. The sculptor works with level, shape, and dimension but rarely has to deal with the spatial component of direction. As soon as that aspect is introduced, you need to acknowledge that perspective is going to play an important role in the magical transformation of the performing space (figure 7.2, a and b).

In *The Art of Making Dances*, modern dance pioneer Doris Humphrey discusses the magic of the stage space (see figure 7.3). She talks about areas of a performing space where, according to her, a dancer will be perceived as most or least powerful. She bases these opinions on the facts of perspective.

A person standing far away is a small image that gets larger as that person approaches the viewer; thus, when you're onstage, the farther away you stand from the audience, the smaller you appear. The farther away you get, the harder it is for an audience to pick up details and small gestures. At a distance, the audience is more likely to identify you as a shape (open, closed, pointy, balanced, or rounded) than as a person.

Since you become larger as you move toward the audience, the audience has an easier time picking up the details of gestures, movements that occur close to the body, and facial clues. As a choreographer, you can choose to use simple facts of perspective to set up a mood or situation.

INSIDE INSIGHT

During the Renaissance, artists began exploring different kinds of perspective—a painted or constructed setting that gives the illusion of depth. Audiences were aware that an illusion was being created and were delighted by the trick of the eye. The eye was carried to a "vanishing point" in the background, usually a point higher than the ground in the foreground.

On stage this translated into a "raked stage," which was a stage where the back of the stage was higher than the front. Thus a person standing in the back of the stage was "upstage" and a person in the front was "downstage." We still use these terms today.

FIGURE 7.2 Concerts in Western societies are usually performed with (a) the audience on one side. In other cultures dance is often performed with (b) the audience in the round.

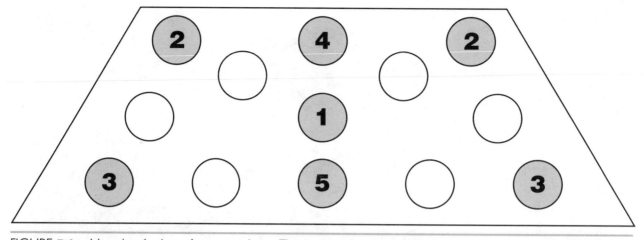

FIGURE 7.3   Humphrey's chart of stage weighting. The numbered circles are the strongest areas on stage with 1 being the strongest; the other circles are the weakest areas.

Adapted from *The Art of Making Dances* by Doris Humphrey. Copyright © 1959, 1987 by Charles F. Woodford and Barbara Pollack.

Look at figure 7.4 and consider where you might place yourself onstage for the best effect in the circumstances suggested. Let us suppose you want to appear afraid, and you have designed a rounded shape that is low to the ground. Would you place yourself in the center of the stage, downstage near the audience, or upstage in a corner near the back wall? (If you believe your answer depends on what the dance is about, you are beginning to understand the importance of spatial design!) Look at the stage from the perspective, or point of view, of the audience (box A) and the perspective of the dancer (box B).

Where would you put yourself if

➤ you want to appear to be afraid;

➤ you want to appear as large as possible;

➤ you want to appear as small as possible;

➤ you want to appear powerful;

➤ you want to share something very personal; or

➤ you want to show something spiritual?

Did you find it was easier to place yourself onstage as a dancer looking out or as an audience member looking in? Neither approach is correct or incorrect. It is helpful to be able to read a floor plan from both perspectives because not all choreographers will orient themselves the same way. However, when the terms "stage left" and "stage right" are used,

they refer to the *performer's* left and right as he faces the audience (box B). Given a preference, most dancers would start movement using the right side of the body, moving to the right.

Looking at the stage from the perspective that makes the most sense to you, draw your own stage space on a separate piece of paper.

Try to picture the floor pattern you would make or the path you would take to most effectively show the following circumstances:

➤ Start out weak and gradually become stronger.

➤ Start out confident and gradually become confused.

➤ Start out proud and gradually become embarrassed.

➤ Start out young and gradually become old.

Each of these progressions could probably be accomplished without moving through space at all but, instead, by using a combination of dancing and acting skills. Likewise, a floor pattern that takes the dancer diagonally from upstage to downstage does not necessarily *mean* anything. However, facts of perspective and the conventions of the theater can contribute to the meaning of movement if the movement is designed to utilize these two factors.

On your own paper, draw two empty stages, one from the perspective of the audience, with

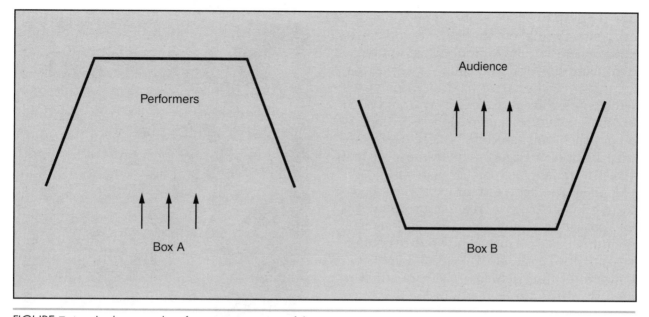

FIGURE 7.4   Audience and performer perspectives of the stage.

the open side to the bottom, and one from the perspective of a dancer, with the open side to the top. On one stage draw a simple floor pattern. This could even be a letter or a number. Then reproduce that pattern from the other perspective. Go back to your first stage and add a second dancer's pattern. Then reproduce that second pattern on your other stage. (Psst! Sometimes, if you're stuck for movement this simple reversing exercise can get you going again!)

Focus

Although the face can be used without emotional reference, it is nevertheless one more clue to an audience about the nature of the forces to which you are reacting as you dance. The direction of your gaze can be another important source of information to an audience who is trying to determine which forces you are presenting.

If you look in the same direction as you travel, you indicate that you are responding to a different kind of force than if you look in a direction other than that of your travel. You can easily feel this difference by walking across a room and keeping your focus front, then returning across the room looking behind you.

Focus can be intimate, personal, social, or distant, depending on what you want to reveal in your movement. It is also possible to have a completely neutral face as you perform. It is up to you to decide what is most appropriate.

People have a special kind of focus when they are in a private space. It is an inward focus—a look you have when you are deep in thought or when you do not feel the need to relate to other people. It is an expression you might have when you are deeply troubled or touched. As a performer you can communicate this sense of space using your focus—the same focus that you use when you walk down the street deep in thought and the same focus that comes over you when some event has moved you and left you speechless.

You show a different kind of focus when relating to a close friend. You tend to stand nearer to each other than you would to a stranger; you might make softer and direct eye contact, and the muscles in your face tend to be more relaxed and responsive. As a performer you can communicate this sense of space using your focus—the same focus that you use with a friend near you.

Yet another kind of focus is used in social circumstances. You could call this your public face. This is the classroom look, the grocery-store look, the look you have when walking down a dark street at night. You make enough eye contact with those strangers around you to know where they are without engaging anyone in conversation or relationship. As we will discuss further in the next section, this focus is used with people three to six feet away from you. It involves both direct and peripheral vision. As a performer you can communicate this sense of space using your focus—the same focus that you use walking in a mall by yourself.

Finally, you have distant focus. This is the focus of celestial contemplation, also known as the "spaced-out" look. Your mind is elsewhere, not intimate or personal, and you are pondering universal thoughts. This focus comes over dancers for three reasons: They are afraid to look forward into the faces of the audience, they are truly overwhelmed by the force of the movement and its power and are having a spiritual experience, or the distant focus has been specifically requested by the choreographer. Any one of these is valid. The second option will probably read most genuinely, but the first has carried many a nervous dancer through performances.

Developing Interpersonal Spatial Awareness

Let us look more closely at the ways you intuitively use spatial awareness in your own life. Edward Hall, in *The Hidden Dimension* (New York: Doubleday, [1990], c1966), focuses on the animal basis of our human spatial awareness. It is a fascinating study that discusses how we are able to share the spaces we occupy in daily life, how we acknowledge each other's boundaries. These unwritten rules vary from person to person and culture to culture (figure 7.5). The distance between bodies onstage may have very different significance to different people. For instance, some would find a dance using contact improvisation to be lewd and appalling because the dancers are in close physical contact. Others find the dancers' remarkable abilities to share weight and show an immediate response awe inspiring.

FIGURE 7.5　What are the "rules" of personal space on this train? What are the rules about focus? How about hands?

This is a good example of how to understand the use of interpersonal spatial awareness when making choreographic choices. When learning to work skillfully with spatial design, you would be wise to consider some of the basic, human intuitions that apply to interpersonal spatial awareness.

Hall describes more than 10 distances that can be discriminated by humans in interaction. For our purposes we will generalize four separate distances and use the same terminology that we used when discussing the importance of focus: intimate, personal, social, and distant.

Intimate

This is the distance from your skin to about 12 inches away from your body; it is the distance maintained when comforting and protecting.

There is a high possibility of physical contact when two people are this close. It is impossible to see the whole body of the other person; therefore, each person relies less on vision than on smell and sense of body heat to judge position.

When we see two bodies in this proximity we intuitively sense the possibilities inherent with this kind of distance. This is not to say that any particular relationship is implied, but it does make it hard for an audience member to believe that two dancers standing or moving in this spatial relationship are unaware of the intimate nature of their positions. As a choreographer you can choose to develop this tension by never allowing the dancers to look at or touch each other, or you can give in to the obvious and acknowledge the intuitively intimate nature of their spatial relationship.

Personal

This is the distance from about 12 inches to 3 feet—about an arm's length—from your body. At this distance there is less likelihood of physical contact, but it is still possible. People in this spatial relationship can rely more on vision, but they still need to move their heads in order to see the whole body of the other person. Smell and heat are no longer good indicators of the other person's position.

Two or more bodies in this proximity can work from all three senses—kinesthetic, visual, and aural—to maintain ensemble (dance together). Their presentation implies accord on the simplest level.

Social

This is the distance from 3 feet to about 10 feet from your body. No physical contact is expected at this distance. It is possible to look in another person's direction and view that person's whole body without having to move your eyes or head. One of the most interesting things that Hall points out is the "mandatory recognition distance" at 8 feet; that is, at that distance you are socially obliged to acknowledge that another person is near (page 126). Dancers who maintain this distance onstage

can be assumed to acknowledge this social convention; it goes against basic intuition to expect that two or more dancers moving 8 feet or closer to each other are unaware of each other. What might be the effect achieved by requiring dancers moving in this proximity to avoid acknowledging each other?

Distant

Hall refers to this as "general" space, but for the sake of continuity we will define 10 feet as "distant" space. At this distance the head appears small, facial expressions are less likely to be effective, and posture becomes a more telling resource. Small gestures, such as wringing hands and shrugging shoulders, are less important. In terms of staging, the whole body has space around it, and, if the audience is about 15 or more feet away, it can see the whole stage space and perceive patterns and relationships of whole bodies. This is particularly important to beginning choreographers who may be showing their work in the context of a studio where it is not possible for the audience to be far enough away to see the entire stage. We would not intuitively assume that two people who are at least 10 feet apart have any knowledge of each other; it is possible to achieve a split focus at this distance and beyond.

Applying Spatial Awareness to Dance

We have looked at six components of spatial design: level, shape, direction, dimension, perspective, and focus, and we have explored ways to use these components as tools for learning movement and creating effective choreography. We have discussed the application of spatial awareness in daily living and have explored some of the conventions that address our need to share space with others in society. Intercultural study of spatial use reveals fascinating differences in the use of level, shape, direction, dimension, perspective, and focus. For instance, it is not uncommon in many religions for the leader (the priest, the minister, the shaman) to be in an elevated position, even if this means that everyone else has to be on their knees. The shape of the body is changed by the convention that stipulates that the head be bowed. The amount of space a Japanese subway rider is entitled to occupy is very little compared even to a rush-hour subway rider in New York City. In Tokyo there are mass transit officials who pack people on the trains. How we use space in daily life is certainly an interesting subject for thought. Let us take a final look at how you might apply your growing awareness of space to your dance study.

As a Student

Now that you know about the six components of spatial design, think about how much space you need to move comfortably. In improvisational work, does it bug you to have someone right next to you? Which level is most interesting or most comfortable for you to work in? Are you a low-level, floor person; a high-level, airy person; or a middle-level, move-ahead person? When it comes time to move through space, which dimension are you likely to work with? Do you prefer to work close, within an arm's reach, or do you want greater use of your limbs? Are you a forward, sideward, backward, or diagonal mover? Do you prefer straight or curving pathways? And where is your focus apt to be as you dance?

When you are required to learn other people's movement, pay attention to the way you structure your use of space. Do you normally stand in the back of the class so you can disappear, or is this a good place for you to follow the maximum number of people rather than rely on your own sense of the demonstrated movement? Are you in the front of the class so you can see the demonstration most easily? Is this a good place for you to check out your own progress without having someone else's body obscuring your view of the mirror? Are you most comfortable in the front of the line so that you can control the space in front of you?

All of these questions encourage you to investigate the ways that you use space as

you move in your class work. Think too about your personal, spatial preferences and the effect that various spaces have on your daily habits. For instance, if your workspace is very limited, the work itself might start to become drudgery simply because of the context. If you are a person who enjoys close interaction with other people but you work in a warehouse, you might sense that something is missing from your work.

As a Choreographer

Now that you have an increased awareness of how you might design your use of space, choreography will be even more exciting. Experimenting with the visual effects of level variations, the sculpting of space by creating shapes, the calm of symmetry and the dynamism of asymmetry, the power of focus, and the potential of dimension and range will offer you starting points for your work and ways to hone your final product.

Think, too, about choreography going beyond the studio and stage walls and into your daily life. Your use of space in social settings may not be mapped out by a floor plan, but, given a little attention, it might reveal aspects of your nature that would not have occurred to you otherwise. Movements at a party, for instance, include some of our discussion about pathways and journeys. When you arrive, do you stay by the door? Do you proceed to the center of the action? Do you head straight for the food? Do you lurk about on the edges of the space or move in among people? Do you excuse yourself to go to the rest room just because you need your own space for a few minutes? If you are at a party where there is social dancing, where do you begin your dance? Do you create the space you need or respond to the space that is available? Your awareness of the aspects of spatial design has direct application to your study of dance and to your creation of dances, but it also extends to a general awareness of your interaction with other people and places in your daily life.

Think About It

1. Think about the spaces that you occupy during the day. What range of movements do those spaces allow? This is a three-part exercise.

   a. Go to a fast-food restaurant and observe the movements of the servers. Write down the sequences of as many of their movements as you can in five minutes of observation (turn, reach, grab, step, stuff, push, and so on). While you are there, write down your estimate of the dimensions of the space that the servers have to work in.

   b. Go to a sporting event or practice and observe the movements of the athletes. Write down the sequences of as many of their movements as you can in five minutes of observation. While you are there, write down your estimate of the dimensions of the space they have to work in.

   c. In your dance space, combine the two sequences. Perform the athlete's sequence in the imagined dimensions of the server and vice versa. Make a sequence of alternating ranges using one word from each list. Work with a partner to show a contrast in range. Make up your own dimension and range dance using the sequence material you collected. What would be the best accompaniment for your dance?

2. Some choreographers deliberately choose dancers whose physical dimensions are similar. Why would same-size dancers be desirable to a choreographer? Why would it be desirable to work with bodies of different heights, weights, and shapes?

3. How is perspective used in advertising? How are you, the consumer, meant to be manipulated by the way an image moves across your television screen? (Car commercials are particularly catchy this way.)

4. With another dancer, explore the four interpersonal distances to develop a duet. One strategy would be to have a movement conversation—take turns moving and responding—at each of the four distances, and then choose the most interesting moments from each position. Another strategy to start from would be to devise a sequence of five or six movements and explore the effects of the different distances on your sequence.

Your Turn to Dance

Pattern Play

1. Draw a square on a sheet of paper. In this square, draw one floor pattern that starts in one place and ends in the same place. On the same square, draw another pattern that starts in one place and ends somewhere else. Finally, draw a third pattern that does not have an end. Look at your patterns and decide what relationship (if any) these three figures might have to each other and what forces might be made evident by manipulating the timing of their patterns.

2. Make yourself another imaginary stage space by drawing a large rectangle on a sheet of paper. Create a floor pattern that incorporates long, straight pathways with short, curving pathways. Indicate on this continuous path places where the dancer will move on one spot rather than through space.

3. On a third piece of paper, draw another floor pattern that incorporates long, curving pathways with short, straight pathways. Indicate on this continuous path places where the dancer will move on one spot rather than through space. Could the two patterns be performed as a duet?

After drawing all three possibilities, choose one of the three floor plans to develop into a dance. Some considerations:

~ Does the floor pattern become less or more evident as the movement becomes more and more designed? In answering this question you will decide what relationship the movement has to the space.

~ Experiment with giving the dancer license to do what she wants on the path you've defined, or choreograph the movement but not the time element in the path. Give the dancer license to change any spatial aspect except the pathway and see what comes up. Add to that the license to change any aspect of time.

Shape Up

1. In pairs, A and B, person A makes a shape, any shape. When the shape is settled the person says the word "one" to indicate he is set. Then B considers that shape and makes one that relates to it; it could be a mirror image, a reverse, an opposite, or an extension. When B has settled on a solution, she says, "Two." That's A's signal to step away and consider how he might create a new shape in relation to the one B is offering. When A has created such a shape, he says, "Three." Continue to 10. The key here is to work quickly. The less shopping around each partner does, the more successful the pair will be.

2. After going through step one, stop and process; then start over, but this time don't use the verbal cues. You are continuing to create new forms. You are also moving directly from one shape into the next responsive shape. No wandering around making up your mind. After 10 exchanges stop and process.

3. Repeat the trading but this time move the duet through space. Play with times of stillness and times of fluid transitions. The trick here is to be clear about who is leading and who is following, so move carefully enough that you are truly reacting to the shape being offered to you—make sure the shape you made is a response and not just a familiar or favorite shape. Again, try to move as directly as possible to the next shape, like filings being drawn by a magnet.

4. This exercise can be further complicated
   ~ by allowing one member of the duet to work solo while the other member holds a still shape.
   ~ by both dancers disbanding and rejoining in a new shape.

Effort

"Art is a lie that makes us realize the truth."

—Pablo Picasso

In dance, the body is both lie and truth. In social dances, the conventions of the dance are contrived to allow the participants to both say and not say how they feel about each other. Half strangers gyrating in close proximity, line dancers moving precisely as they stand shoulder to shoulder, tango dancers woven together into a single four-legged unit are telling each other the truth: "For the moment, we belong." That truth is communicated through the shapes the participants make in time and space. The conjunction of physical shape in time and space is defined here as effort. In traditional dances—dances that once held or still hold the community's belief in the magic of movement—participants affirm the importance and power of their shared history. That truth is communicated by the shapes the participants make in time and space. In concert dance the use of effort and shape goes one level deeper because the dancer's body is not complying with a set code but is using the body to make a new statement.

Your task as a dancer or choreographer is to find a way to demonstrate, through physical effort, the forces that are acting on the body. This effort is a combination of your physical, mental, and emotional powers, and the effort you display as you dance helps the audience understand the material you present. Are you trying to look like you are floating? If so, the effort you exert is different from the effort required to show that you are stuck or constrained.

When we use the word "effort" in a non-dance context, we usually mean some outward display of force or willpower. Think about what you would look like if you were pretending to lift a heavy suitcase. Think about how you would show the difficulty in resisting the temptation of a chocolate chip cookie. How would you show the difference between shoveling dry leaves and wet snow? You, as an actor or a dancer, could create these imaginary circumstances by showing different degrees of effort.

When a teacher criticizes you by saying that you did not put enough effort into your work, that teacher means that some part of your *inner impulse* to do the work is missing. Maybe it is sloppy, maybe you did not put much thought into it, or maybe you had not found a reason to care about the project. Think of an assignment you have recently completed that you *did* put a lot of effort into and another assignment that you put very little effort into completing. What is the difference between the physical, mental, or emotional power you brought to each? When we talk about putting more effort into something, we are talking about approaching a task with more gusto, interest, or care. We are talking about applying physical, mental, or emotional power.

Finding the Inner Impulse

In this chapter we will take an inside-out look at effort. Rather than viewing effort as a quality that is added to ordinary movement, we are going to see effort as action that comes from an inner impulse. We will look at effort as "the inner impulse from which movement originates." These are the words of Rudolf Laban (*The Mastery of Movement*. London: MacDonald & Evans, 1960, page 19), a man who spent his life studying the relationship between the inner motivation and the outer display of movement. Effort is the combination of muscular, mental, and emotional power in action.

What inner impulse moves a lion when it's stalking its prey? What inner impulse moves a puppy to chase a ball? What inner impulse moves an ant to follow the other ants that are collecting food? Effort in dance concerns the skill of discovering and presenting the muscular, mental, and emotional state that shows the inner impulse, or essence, of the dancer's subject.

In chapter 1 we spoke of some simple and recurring inner impulses when we discussed the need to balance tensions in the body by shifting weight, changing posture, and changing breath patterns. The impulse to sigh, for example, causes a softening in the chest and a change in one's general physical-tension patterns. The impulse to tense when someone stands too close for comfort is another example.

Suppose you are leaving a restaurant, and you suddenly realize that you have left your wallet on the table. The impulse to turn and rush back likely overtakes you. In this case, you will probably move through the restaurant with a different kind of effort than you did when you originally entered. Or suppose it is a cold, wintry day and a patch of sun shines on your living-room floor. You might be moved to rest in that spot and to enjoy a few minutes of warmth and calm. These are examples of action motivated by inner impulse. These are efforts.

INSIDE INSIGHT

In discussions about the elements of dance, you find that time and space are regularly named as two of the three elements of dance. But when it comes to the third element, you will find different names being used. You will likely encounter the word "energy." Perhaps "quality" or "force" will also be used. All of these words are right.

Use the word that makes the most sense to you, the one that allows you to think of the widest possible range of options. As a dancer or choreographer, your choices for controlling the flow of effort, force, or energy that you apply to movement are infinite. Your task is to explore that range according to your physical, social, and emotional needs and capabilities.

There Is Effort in Every Human Movement

There is some amount of effort in every human movement. The simple act of sitting upright in a chair requires some effort. Even while you sleep you exhibit muscular, mental, and emotional activity. The effort you use to block a net shot in a volleyball game depends on the size of your opponent. The effort you use to get to a ringing telephone depends on who you think might be calling.

Effort is the trigger that sparks human movement. We often think of effort as the "how" of movement, but now let us consider effort as the "why" of movement. If you needed to carry a child from a burning building, that effort would be very different than if you were to carry the same child to bed. Same weight, different reason. If you needed to leap across a stream in order to continue a hike, that effort would be different than if you were to leap the same distance onstage. Same weight, different reason. Even an action as simple as standing up when your name is called is a different kind of effort in the classroom than it is in the dentist's office. Same weight, different reason.

There is effort in every human movement, but only humans use effort deliberately. When you watch a dog digging a hole, it is clear that the dog is not trying to make it look as if the task were harder or easier than it really is. When you watch an ant dragging a bug twice its size, you do not get the sense that the ant is trying to make it appear that the bug is really very light. A leaf cannot change the way it falls so that it appears to be heavier than it is. Humans are different. We can use effort to create illusions. We can control and modify our natural human efforts (the inner impulse) to survive and communicate. We use our muscular, mental, and emotional powers to dance.

Forces That Affect Movement

The study of physics is all about forces. For our purposes, we will consider five of these forces, the ones that we work with most often and most deliberately in dance: gravity, momentum, resistance, inertia, and centrifugal forces. Dancers who understand and can skillfully manipulate these forces create the effort patterns that make their dances most effective.

Gravity

You are an expert on gravity. You deal with gravity every moment of your life. Depending on your goal, the effect of gravity on your body can require much effort or no effort at all (figure 8.1). A basketball player has to use much effort to be able to hang in the air to make a shot. A dancer will use a different kind of effort to balance on one leg. A child swinging a hula hoop uses a different kind of energy to keep that hoop from succumbing to gravity. In order to get a baseball to home plate the outfielder uses a different kind of effort to overcome the force of gravity on the ball. Effort is *very* different for an astronaut.

In order to resist one force there must be force in the opposite direction.

This truth is so obvious that we do not even think about it. But in our study of dance and the effort it takes to move, this simple truth needs more consideration. Remember, we have said that effort is the combination of muscular, mental, and emotional powers. Read this law again, and think about effort in those three ways.

The secret! In order to resist one force there must be force in the other direction. Those people who do amazing and enviable physical acts—like balancing on their toes, leaping to make net shots, and all sorts of other human tricks—have figured this out! In order to resist one force there must be force in the other direction.

FIGURE 8.1   What kind of effort is necessary to overcome gravity in these sports? What about in dance?

Dancers live with gravity in a different way than most people do in their everyday lives. To understand how to use that force to your advantage and, likewise, to learn to resist that force with different kinds of effort is knowledge that enables you to be as expressive and as exact as you need to be. For instance, if you wished to express a feeling of complete helplessness, gravity would be very useful. If you wished to express a feeling of power, gravity again would be very useful by enabling you to show strength through resistance. If you wished to express a feeling of weightlessness, you would have to work very hard to pretend that there was no gravity.

Momentum

Momentum is a property of a moving body that determines the length of time required to bring it to rest when that body is experiencing a constant force. The constant force is the power provided by the dancer—the power renewing a locomotor movement, the power sustaining any axial movement, and the power to start and to stop moving.

It is as simple as this: If you had a friend lift your completely relaxed arm, then release it so that it would swing by your side from front to back, eventually it would stop swinging and come to rest perpendicular to the floor. If you wished to sustain this swinging motion you, the dancer, would have to provide force, in the form of muscular contractions, to keep your arm swinging. There are an infinite number of variations on how you might keep your arm swinging. You might recreate the illusion of the arm being lifted by unseen forces and suddenly released again. You might draw the arm along your side, reach to the front, and release into the swing. You might continuously provide just enough lift to keep the arm from coming to rest. These and other variations are examples of the inner impulse that reveals the nature of the forces being marshaled to overcome the ordinary physics that would lead to a predictable display of energy. Without a display of unusual, special, or concerted effort, the body in question would not do anything extraordinary.

Resistance

Paired with the idea of momentum is the concept of resistance. Imagine a marble sitting at one end of a smooth-floored gymnasium. Imagine what happens when you give the marble a flick with your finger. It will roll in a straight line and gradually slow down. Eventually it will stop rolling. The same experiment would obviously have different results at the beach because the sand would make it harder for the marble to roll. In the gymnasium the marble encountered very little resistance, so it could roll easily. The sand provided the marble with a great deal of resistance, so it stopped rolling much sooner.

Weight equals resistance; the heavier the object, the greater its resistance to levity. For dancers, the more weight you use in your movement, the more resistance you will create, and the more you will be able to take advantage of gravity and of other forces related to your movement.

Try This Experiment

To understand this physically, go through the experiment twice, the first time imagining that your head is a heavy, sand-filled bag; the second time, a light, helium-filled balloon. Sit with your back long, so that your head is balanced over your shoulders. Imagine a slight impulse or gentle nudge that causes your head to fall toward your chest. Feel the differences between the heavy and light versions? The sandbag image enables you to work with gravity, momentum, and resistance, whereas the helium-balloon image probably did not.

Resistance isn't necessarily a bad thing. In movement, resistance also equals potential. As you brush your foot along the floor in a tendu, the resistance that the floor provides is energy accumulating in the gesture. That's why the tension in the tendu is so important to the success of the dégagé. When the foot is released or leaves the floor, the potential energy accumulated makes the leg rise more easily than if the foot is placed, then lifted. Same thing when you use your demi-plié in jumps. The more you go down, the higher you'll go up. Weight equals resistance and resistance equals potential.

Inertia

A body in front of the television remains in front of the television until disturbed by another force. Or, loosely translated into the law of inertia, a body at rest remains at rest until disturbed by an outside force. Our thoughts about inertia take us back to earlier thoughts concerning the inner impulse. Effort exists when the inner impulse brings us to action.

We must remember choice when thinking about inertia and human movement. A stone will rest on a path until it is moved by something or some force. The stone itself does not choose to move. Let us say that a strong rainstorm comes along and washes the stone to another resting place. The stone does not move as if washed by the rain; it *is* washed by the rain.

When we move—overcome inertia—in our daily lives, it is by choice or by reflex. The effort we use to move shows which kind of force has disturbed our resting bodies. Our movement choices fall into two categories:

1. Moving because
2. Moving "as if"

Only humans move as if overcoming inertia due to some force other than a real force. Think about it. Can you imagine a turtle crawling along and suddenly choosing to move as if it were on ice? Can you imagine a cow deciding to walk as if it needed milking? We are talking about effort and what that effort communicates. Only humans choose to move, to overcome inertia, in order to convey a particular effect.

Try This Experiment

Take a simple head gesture as an example. Start from a sitting position, back long, head balanced easily on top of the spine. Allow your head to follow as you twist your upper body to the right. If you twist as far as you possibly can, your head will move as well. Your head moves because of the movement in the back. Return to your resting position and experiment with the effects you can achieve by moving as if your head were not affected by the twist in the back.

The successional movement explored in the experiment makes use of inertia and can therefore look very relaxed and organic. Successional movement is that in which one part of the body initiates movement in the next joint. For instance, if you are standing tall with your weight evenly distributed on both feet, and you were to begin your descent to the floor by bending the top vertebra forward and allowing that motion to pull the next vertebra into the same curve, then the next and the next, you would eventually be standing while hanging forward at the waist. To return to vertical using successional movement, you would start from the base of your spine and uncurl vertebra by vertebra. With practice, successional spinal movements can appear to be the result of one impulse.

Try This Experiment

Do this experiment with a partner. Momentum is a force that can be used to reduce the amount of effort a dancer puts into moving. You can experiment with a friend to discover some of the freedom that momentum provides. Stand easily, knees relaxed, ready to be propelled in any direction. Your friend will gently provide a push to some part of your body (as you did by flicking the marble). See what kinds of movement come from following that line of force to its conclusion. Have your friend experiment with different amounts of force. Try to discover which kinds of effort are required to follow each line of force. Change roles and observe the effect of the use of momentum by your partner.

Centrifugal Force

Centrifugal force propels a mass away from a rotating center. Perhaps you have gone on one of those spinning contraptions popular at amusement parks—the ride that spins around and picks up speed until the floor drops away and everyone is pinned to the wall by virtue of centrifugal force. Centrifugal force is of great use for dancers since it enables motion to occur in the limbs and periphery without using customary effort. For instance, turning quickly and continuously causes the arms to rise in proportion to the speed of the turn. The arms, if relaxed, will float up effortlessly to shoulder height. If you have the balance to be able to hop and turn at the same time, you will find that your leg in the air will float up toward waist height, depending on the speed of your turn. You can use centrifugal force to escape the pull of gravity!

Effort That Reflects These Forces

Part of dance's magic is the opportunity to create an illusion of force, effort, or energy. A ballet dancer balancing on pointe creates the illusion that gravity has no effect on the body. A dancer can sail through the air without apparent effort, or show great effort to jump a few inches. The choice of which kind of force to show and how to make it evident is in the power of the dancer and choreographer. We mortals cannot escape the laws of physics, but we can work skillfully and magically to manipulate an audience's perception of these laws.

There are four fields you can manipulate to create the illusion of force or a lack of force:

time ~ space ~ weight ~ flow

Effort is the combination of these four fields.

Look at a leap and consider the possibilities each of these fields provides for manipulating the illusion of force in this simple action.

A long time in the air creates the illusion of a gravity-free creature. A short time in the air suggests more resistance, possibly more weight, less momentum, more inertia, and less assistance of centrifugal force. A very high leap suggests that the dancer is more free of the pull of gravity than one where the elevation is slight. However, long, low leaps indicate a lack of resistance in a different plane—the horizontal versus the vertical. Long, low leaps

indicate that the dancer has the assistance of momentum and is able to apply weight to propel forward. When we consider the flow of a movement, we are assessing the overall integration of all of the forces that act upon a body—gravity, resistance, momentum, inertia, and centrifugal force. A dancer who comes to a grinding halt between leaps breaks the flow of movement. To break this flow the dancer might appear to give in to gravity, be overcome by resistance, or completely lose momentum. The combination of these four fields provides the dancer with the means to make evident an infinite variety of forces acting on the body.

Each of these fields represents a continuum. When we looked at the use of time as an element we identified speed and duration as two aspects open to manipulation. Beat, tempo, and rhythm are manipulations of speed and duration, right? In terms of effort, time is on a continuum with "fast" at one end and "slow" at the other. When we looked at the use of space as an element, we identified six aspects open to manipulation: level, shape, direction, dimension, perspective, and focus. Combining level, shape, and dimension in terms of effort, space is on a continuum with "small" at one end and "large" at the other. Combining direction, perspective, and focus in terms of effort, flow is on a continuum with "direct" at one end and "indirect" at the other. Weight, we've said, equals resistance. We can think about resistance on a continuum of strong to light. The effort with which a movement is realized is the result of the degree to which it is:

Time (Fast or Slow) + Space (Small or Large) + Weight (Strong or Light) + Flow (Direct or Indirect)

Time, as discussed in chapter 6, can be measured and described in different ways. Movements could be discussed as fast, slow, or something between those two speeds. How is effort a product of time in conjunction with space, weight, and flow? Consider several time-related words and the effort implied by each one.

Arrange the words "quick," "gradual," "sluggish," "leisurely," "sudden," and "brisk" on the following scale according to their implied speed:

Slow _____Fast

Where would you place the word "endless"?

Time is a relative field of effort. In order to say one thing is quick, you need to have something less or more quick for a comparison.

Space is also a relative of effort. The direction that a movement takes in space will inform us about the kind of effort being used. As we discussed in chapter 6, a dancer who enters the stage moving in a direct line shows a different kind of effort than a dancer who enters the stage staggering forward. In *The Mastery of Movement*, Laban discussed direction and use of space in terms of direct and pliant (or flexible) movement. Words such as "poke," "jab," "punch," "thrust," and "pat" describe direct actions. Words such as "float," "wring," "glide," and "flick" describe what Laban would label flexible movements—movements that occur in a curved, rather than straight, line. What would you say is the difference between a poke and a punch? Both are direct movements; both are toward the fast end of the time line. How are these actions different?

The difference between a poke and a punch is weight—the amount of force involved with each one. Weight equals resistance. So, if weight equals resistance, then force, or, the amount of power used to overcome resistance, is going to be a factor when displaying effort. Strong force will result in a punch; light force will yield a poke. Use "strong" and "light" as the two ends of a line for force and weight. As we did with time, consider where several words that describe movement would fit relative to each other.

Arrange the words "slash," "dab," "glide," "wring," "float," and "thrust" on the following scale:

Light_____ Strong

The amount of weight or force used in each of these actions will both require and display a particular effort—a physical, mental, and emotional display.

If you see a mosquito light on your arm you'll either slap it quickly or slowly sneak up on it and then smack it, but you wouldn't wave your hand around and then be surprised when you missed the target. But if you are trying to clear smoke from near your face you'll wave your hand around to move the air as much as possible. That's an indirect use of force.

Looking at the following graph, consider where you would place yourself in terms of a preference for moving with either a direct or indirect style.

Direct _____Indirect

Toward which end would you rate your preference for movement styles you enjoy watching others perform?

You're familiar with the concept of range—how much extension is involved with movement. In considering range and effort we're asking, "How far and to what end?" Think about a driving range versus a putting green. The golfer has to work with very different efforts in each environment if the golf ball is going to go in the hole. The flow of the golfer's stroke is entirely different depending on the course. Likewise, the flow of movement will be affected by the need or opportunity to move through a full range of motion. Thinking about the technique classes you've had, do you prefer the section of the class that deals with small motor coordinations or do you prefer "living large"?

Small _____Large

Try This Experiment

Take one word on the continuum from each of the possible fields. For instance, Fast + Large + Direct + Strong. What are you doing if you move only your arm with that combination of fields? What's the name for the leg gesture that uses that combination? Is there one name for the action that is produced when your whole body flies through the air using this combination? Now it's your turn to experiment!

Integrating Inner and Outer Forces

Remember that there is effort in every human movement and that the display of effort makes evident the inner impulse in response to outer forces. Mastery of effort comes with being sensitive to that spark of inner impulse and being clever at manipulating the presentation of that spark in relation to the forces of gravity. The more we understand the interplay of these forces, the more we can use them to shape movement. To pull all of this together, consider a simple experiment initially involving only two actions: walking and standing still.

Try This Experiment

This experiment is an exploration of your options to deal with all the forces we have just considered: gravity, momentum, resistance, inertia, and centrifugal force. When you walk, you may walk anywhere for as long as you wish. You determine the speed and direction of your walking. You determine when you stop. When you have stopped, stand still until you wish to walk again. Now that you've worked with what was set forth as two simple tasks, do you agree that there were only two?

This experiment has to do with 1) feeling the pull of gravity on your vertical frame, 2) feeling the inner impulse to overcome inertia, 3) feeling the momentum of your falling body as you begin to move, 4) feeling the resistance of each step and the necessity to continue supplying force in order to continue moving, 5) feeling the lightness encountered in a swift turn, 6) feeling the inner impulse to come to rest again, and 7) lowering your center of gravity and increasing the resistance of your body in space so that you 8) came to a stillness. Physically, there is work to be done in terms of muscles firing, coordinating, balancing, and timing your locomotion and stillness.

Mentally, you make decisions about moving, directional changes, and speed changes. Emotionally, you become invested in any number of ways. Perhaps you feel silly doing this exercise, so you are a little tense. Perhaps you are bored doing this exercise, and so you are a little lax, not really being still, not really varying your speed or direction with ingenuity. Perhaps you are curious about your potential, and you are using this exercise to experiment with a variety of different movements, weights, and risks. Regardless of your approach, you will have some emotional response to moving with this focus. On completion, you will have a sense of the physical, mental, and emotional powers involved with the combination of these two simple tasks. Your own execution will have been a study of effort.

Now let us set up some physical, emotional, and mental challenges to discover effort. Use the following options—being still, turning, and the sequence of step-step-leap—to explore these three purely *physical* challenges:

1. Moving as fast as possible
2. Moving in curved lines
3. Moving as lightly as possible

Next work with three purely *emotional* challenges:

1. Motivated by fear
2. Motivated by confusion
3. Motivated by joy

Finally, work with three purely *mental* challenges:

1. Complete the sequence four times within 15 seconds.
2. Complete the sequence forming the letters *O* and *U*.
3. Imagine that you are a mosquito.

Can you feel that effort coming from within? Can you feel the forces of gravity, momentum, inertia, resistance, and centrifugal force as you work?

Your Best Effort

We have used the physical fact of life on earth—the forces of gravity—as a starting point for our discussion of effort. We have repeatedly stated that the display of effort includes not only muscular power but also mental and emotional power. As intelligent beings, we have the capacity to think, feel, and remember. We have the capacity to create from our experiences. We have the capacity to share our thoughts, feelings, and memories, and we have the capacity to hide them. We are capable of feeling one emotion and showing another. Dance is most successful when the dancer is totally present in body, mind, and spirit. When the effort shown is consistent with the physical, mental, and emotional intention, the dance makes sense. Consider a few ways that mental and emotional powers can affect the way we dance.

Mental Effort

Mental power is an important aspect of effort, which must be balanced by the other powers. Think of the contrast between a person digging a ditch and a person digging on an archaeological expedition. Each of these people will attend to a similar physical task in very different ways. Think of the contrast between the way a runner moves when training and the way he moves in a race. Applying this to dance, have you ever watched a performer who moved beautifully but seemed to be not quite involved with the dance? It is possible to think so much about the sequence or the steps that your mental power robs your muscular and emotional powers.

Overusing your mental powers affects your effort in other ways. For instance, your breathing will probably be restricted and your coordination may be off. A dancer's performance will be affected if the mental powers are out of balance with the muscular and emotional powers.

Try This Experiment

Try this movement sequence to see how over-intellectualizing can get in the way of a desired effort:

1. There is a total of seven steps. The first three steps travel forward, the next three turn in a circle, and the last step brings your feet together. The whole pattern moves in a straight line. Get up and try it.

2. Now repeat the pattern as you say the first seven letters of the alphabet, one letter per step.

3. Now repeat the pattern as you start with Z and recite the alphabet backwards.

How did your concentration on tangential tasks affect your performance?

Emotional Effort

Like mental power, emotional power can affect the effort a dancer feels and displays. Nervousness, self-confidence, fear, and joy certainly influence effort. We have the ability to use our imagination to create emotional states that suit our needs.

Children are very good at creating imaginary circumstances. That same skill is important in any creative activity, and it is particularly valuable to dancers. We can use that emotional power to create the transformations we call dance.

Try This Experiment

Sit comfortably, and allow your head to tilt and hang toward one shoulder. Now imagine that there is a string pulling the top of your head in a high, diagonal line. Feel that pull, and imagine that the string is suddenly cut. Return to your position with your head balanced on your spine. This time imagine that you are straining to overhear a conversation that is just out of earshot. Suddenly the speaker enters the room, and you want to look as if you are dozing. Finally, repeat this movement sequence without adding any imaginative circumstances. Can you feel a difference in the inner impulse of the three sequences? Can you sense a difference in the outward display of the three sequences?

Sometimes audiences have a hard time understanding a dance that has no particular dramatic intention but is simply a series of movements designed to be visually appealing. The effort shown by dancers in such dances is, nevertheless, a combination of their muscular, mental, and emotional states. The inner impulses that drive the dancers can be disconcerting precisely because they are not emotionally based. For example, a dancer has to execute a complicated leap and has some trepidation about landing it well. The dancer's concentration may come across as dramatic intensity when in fact it's very focused concentration. On the other hand, think about a time you may have seen a dancer with a smile pasted on her face. Did you wonder what she was smiling about when there was nothing noticeably happy about the dance?

Effort Is Telling and Compelling

Of all the things that make dancing so exciting and intriguing to watch and do, the way the dancer uses effort is ultimately the most compelling. An impressive extension of the leg is all the more incredible when it appears effortless. The riff of a tap dancer is more amazing when it seems impossible that a human being could transfer his weight that quickly—but he did! The plunge to the floor is even more awesome when the dancer, unharmed, gets up and falls again and again. From the delicate capers of the Renaissance aristocracy to the mattress-hauling moments of the Judson Dance Theater to the acro-ballet tricks of dance competitions, what we're looking at is the effort of a human being that informs us of our potential. Controlling or lacking control, giving in to gravity or transcending gravity, and falling and recovering are all metaphors for the human condition played out through the dancer's manipulation of effort. We each have our strengths and preferences when it comes to taking personal risks with movements. We have movement challenges we can throw ourselves into easily and others we just don't enjoy as much or seek out. Do you know what *your* strengths and preferences are? We will look at this more closely in chapter 9, "Body Intelligence," but what concerns us here is how the effort we bring to a task shapes our success in having that task be a satisfying one.

INSIDE INSIGHT

Simone Forti (1935–) spent time observing animal behavior and used her observations as a basis for several dances in which she applied the animals' uses of gravity, inertia, momentum, and impulse to her own movements. The following is an excerpt from her written observations, *Animal Stories* (found in *Terpsichore in Sneakers* by Sally Banes, Boston, MA: Houghton Mifflin, 1980):

~ Brown bear walk: Front limb steps and whole side contracts to pull back limb into place. Boom, boo-boom. Boom, boo-boom. Boom, boo-boom.

~ Giraffe walk: Back limb steps, crowds front limb which steps ahead. Boom-boom. Boom-boom.

In the 1930s Josephine Rathbone, a researcher at Columbia University, identified four distinct patterns of neuromuscular tension: assisting, resisting, posturing, and perseveration. (Someone who can't help nodding her head repeatedly is perseverating.) Since the 1960s Elizabeth Wetzig has been exploring the effects of these patterns on styles of creativity and communication and has formulated the Wetzig Coordination Patterns. Her work is based on the premise that there are four basic patterns of coordination—thrust, shape, swing, and hang. We each use all four patterns but we have a dominant, or "home," pattern, which, in combination with one other pattern, makes up our particular style. According to Wetzig, these are not just muscular patterns, they are modes of behavior—"a window to the mind's work" —through which one can, among other things, achieve insight into intelligence, talent, and learning styles. The kind of effort we are most comfortable in using is part of who we are. Which of those four patterns most appeal to you? Do you like moving in a thrusting, go-for-it, forceful way? Or are you more likely to move in a sculptural, composed, put-together way? There's a different kind of effort with each of those, yes? They're not mutually exclusive but they are different. They spring from or are evidence of a different nuance of inner impulse we considered earlier.

What are your personal preferences in shaping movement? Do you prefer movements that are direct, powerful, and make clear patterns, or might you be more at home with recognized shapes, symmetrical positions, or positions that have an established ideal form? Or maybe your favorite home pattern is rocking, swinging, balancing with momentum, playing with inertia? Or perhaps you like movements and shapes that are the product of a release of energy, like the stall at the apex of a swing?

Think About It

1. How do you open yourself up to the discovery of your inner impulse? When you need to create movement, do you put yourself in a place of discovery or are you more inclined to repeat familiar patterns in order to get to an inner impulse?

2. One of the most famous quotes attributed to Martha Graham is "The body never lies." Imagine a conversation between Graham and Picasso in which they discuss the idea of art, truth, and representation. Are their points of view different? If not, how do they agree? If so, with whom would you side?

3. When you are balancing in an arabesque the fields of effort combine as follows: Time—slow to a point of stillness; space—on one point; weight—light, lifting out of the floor; flow—free. How do these fields combine when you are falling into a lunge? How do they combine when you do a grand battement? How do they combine when you circle your hips?

4. Of the five forces that affect movement, which interests you most as you create?

5. How are you best able to bring your mind and body into a harmonious effort when you are a) learning or b) performing new movement?

Your Turn to Dance

Field Work

Take a combination you've been working on in class and rework it using the field of tension, or "flow." For instance, if your sequence had three grand battements in it, how could you perform each one with a different sense of flow? Go through the sequence focusing on one field at a time.

1. First play with the element of time (speed, duration). When is a shape a shape and when is it a transitional form?

2. Next explore what happens when you change the space of the movements slightly or dramatically.

3. Play with the lightness or heaviness of the movement and your choices to acknowledge or resist that weight. How do you create lightness? Do you create heaviness or merely acknowledge it?

4. Finally, play with the field of flow by experimenting with how one gesture combines with the next. What happens if you change that swing into a suspension or that balance into a moment at the apex of a swing? What if you stop a swing in the middle and hold that moment?

Take a Hike

1. Draw a fairly simple path that starts one place and ends in another. Your path will include a curving and a straight portion.

2. Walk your path so that you are familiar with the way you've designed the space. If you don't like it the way it is, change it. On this first pass you have no agenda.

3. On your second pass imagine yourself going through different environments. Focus your effort on the ground and on how your foundation is changing. Eliminate any unnecessary miming with the upper body that detracts from the sensations you are exploring through your feet and legs. Some options might be mud, deep water, waves coming on shore, hot sand, hot coals, broken glass, a newly waxed floor, boggy grass.

4. Repeat your dance, this time attending to the subtleties of shifting from one environment and one pattern into another. Note: Dramatically, it would be more obvious to appear to be surprised by a new environment, but for this exploration, please work on investigating the way one pattern can shift into another.

5. A further potentially interesting complication is to tell a story about a walk you remember taking as a child. Don't try to match the environment of the story with the movement. In other words, if you were walking on the beach in the story but your dance begins with an image of sliding on ice, don't change the ice to sand in your movement. The juxtaposition of contrasting elements will add more to the performance than mime would.

Part III

The Sense
of Movement

Body Intelligence

S tudents are drawn to dance for a variety of reasons. Some want to get in shape, learn exciting movements, or become more coordinated. Some are drawn to dance because they like moving—they like being physical—and they think that dance might be satisfying. Others come because they are dissatisfied with the way they look or move, and they hope that dance classes will improve their control over their bodies. The process of dance training can be a tricky balancing act between trying to change the way you are and trying to enjoy the way you are.

As you struggle to duplicate new patterns in technique class or rack your brain for a unique, inventive composition idea, you may curse your inability to both imitate and create. Setting your mind against your body ("Why can't I remember those steps?" or "I wish I could think up moves of my own!") is not the answer. A more productive approach involves discovering how your body works with your brain as a thinking partner. This understanding will give you insight into your strengths as a dancer and your preferences as a choreographer; it may stimulate a more balanced mind–body relationship.

The physical reactions, reflexes, and habits that are stored in your muscles as well as your mind make up your body intelligence. This chapter is devoted to a clearer understanding of the role body intelligence plays in dance and in daily life.

Examining Intelligence

What makes someone intelligent? What names come to mind when asked, "Who have been the most intelligent people in all history?" Names such as Albert Einstein, Socrates, Leonardo da Vinci, Madame Curie, Isaac Newton, and Michelangelo might occur to you. How about Yogi Berra? If asked to narrow your list to only one name, you might well protest that the task is impossible because each of these people showed a different kind of intelligence. In order to get a little closer to your own definition of intelligence, try the exploration in figure 9.1.

Intelligence is usually defined as an ability to learn from experience. Normally, intelligence is associated with brains, with the ability to make mental associations so that information makes sense. Notice that the expression "makes sense" suggests a mind–body process rather than a strictly mental one.

People have different styles of learning and perceiving and therefore differ in their intelligence. In general, when we consider someone to be intelligent, we observe that person to be capable of

➤ organizing abstract ideas to apply to concrete situations,

➤ anticipating and predicting causes and effects, and

➤ synthesizing information from many sources (figure 9.2).

With only slight adaptation, these criteria can be applied to the concept of body intelligence. A person who is physically coordinated and responsive is capable of

➤ mobilizing appropriate muscles with appropriate force;

➤ anticipating or sensing cause and effect; and

➤ synthesizing information from many sources, including sensory, emotional, and cultural.

What Is Intelligence?

1. Make a list of five people you know personally whom you consider to be intelligent.

2. Following each name, briefly indicate how his or her intelligence shows. For example:

   My brother—Understands abstract mathematical concepts

   My mother—Has a huge vocabulary, speaks four languages

   Diana—Learns dance steps immediately

3. Finally, think of three examples of your own intelligence. For example:

   I am able to plan ahead, can fix my own car, and can survive in the woods.

4. How would you define intelligence?

FIGURE 9.1   By answering these questions, you'll be able to develop your own definition of intelligence.

FIGURE 9.2   "How can you think and hit at the same time?" —Yogi Berra

Just as a person can memorize a series of mathematical formulas and still not be able to solve a problem, so it is possible for a dancer to memorize a series of steps and still not be able to dance the whole phrase. Without an understanding of the relationships in a math problem, it is difficult to manipulate the figures. Similarly, without a sense of the relationships of the steps in a dance sequence, it is difficult to create a whole that is more than its parts.

Body Intelligence

A mechanic who is rebuilding an engine has to know what parts go where as well as how to assemble them correctly. This information can be found in books, but only experience will teach the mechanic just how tight is "tight" or how a well-timed engine should sound. This is analogous to body intelligence.

Try This Experiment

1. Either sitting or standing in a comfortable position, think back to an experience you had that made you very angry—a time when you were wronged. Try to bring the person or people involved clearly into your mind. Imagine them in front of you now, telling you that what happened was all your fault.

2. Now become aware of any changes that have occurred in your body. Did your jaw clench? Did you find a tightness in your chest? Did your breath become uneven?

3. Shake off that memory and return to a relaxed, comfortable state. This time think back to an experience you had that brought you great pleasure—a time when something wonderful happened because of you. Try to bring those circumstances clearly into your mind.

4. Again, become aware of changes that have occurred in your body. Did you sigh? Did a smile come to your face? Did your chest soften or expand?

Working in the first emotion—anger—produces an outer change in the shape of the body, but that change comes not from trying to look like someone who is angry, but from a muscular recollection of a physical or emotional experience. This is an example of what we will call body intelligence.

The concept of body intelligence goes beyond recall of a particular pattern, skill, or sensation. *Body intelligence* is the ability to coordinate these four components of human action:

pattern ~ skill ~ sensation ~ emotion

In chapter 1 we discussed the fact that we are always moving and balancing tensions in the body. Those subconscious actions have patterns, require different kinds of skills (such as balancing or tracking tension), are a response to sensation (such as discovery or discomfort), and have an emotional base (such as excitement, impatience, or fear). Consider the response of nail biting. Let us say that when you become anxious you sometimes bite your nails. A pattern. But a skill? Yes, when you consider that by biting your nails you succeed in displacing your anxiety. A sensation? Clearly, but the sensation is not just the feel of fingernail between teeth. That oral response is a coping mechanism that goes back to infant coping mechanisms like thumb sucking. It's a way of feeding back sensation to control and comfort yourself. This isn't a conscious process. If you have such a habit—of nail biting or tapping or clearing your throat or rocking—you'll know that even though you are using sensation to calm or cope, you don't consciously attend to the sensation. Let us say that you also cross your arms over your chest. Another pattern. But a skill? Yes, when you consider that by assuming this posture you not only feel safer but you also communicate to the rest of the world that you feel threatened. Body intelligence is the ability to coordinate pattern, skill, sensation, and emotion into action.

In sports, body intelligence is used by the athlete to achieve a particular goal, such as timing a jump to catch a ball or tucking quickly in a dive. In drama, body intelligence is used by the actor to develop a character. Where does this character carry tension? How does the character stand? Walk? Sit down? Is the character clumsy, nervous, or self-conscious?

In dance, body intelligence is used . . . . How would you finish the sentence?

Try This Experiment

Pick a sport. Consider the four components of body intelligence and how they are a part of the sport you chose. For example:

Sport: Soccer

Pattern: Step-step-kick

Skill: Controlling the ball

Sensation: Sensing when to pass, how hard to kick

Emotion: Risk, excitement, competition, danger

Now, what about dance?

Pattern:

Skill:

Sensation:

Emotion:

According to psychologist Howard Gardner, humans have multiple intelligences. In *Frames of Mind: The Theory of Multiple Intelligences* (New York: Basic Books, 1983), he lists musical, logical-mathematical, body, and linguistic intelligence as being distinct. As we will see in chapter 9, many factors contribute to excellence in math, languages, or sports. There are differences among those who are envied for being the best in some field. Your basic sports enthusiast may be pretty good in all sports but particularly good at one.

Likewise, all dancers have their strengths based on their own body intelligences. You may be a dancer who quickly perceives a pattern but has difficulty making your body execute that pattern. You may be a dancer who can copy any movement but has a hard time making sense of the sequence. You may be a dancer who enjoys the thrill of leaping and flying but cannot find another speed in yourself to use for slow, sustained movements. Some dancers prefer to be balanced and upright while others prefer to be off-center and unstable. How did these preferences develop? How did you come to sense what feels right for your body (figure 9.3)?

FIGURE 9.3   How would your life be different if you had had this experience as a child? How would your dance be different?

Development of Body Intelligence

One of the ongoing debates in developmental psychology concerns nature versus nurture—the debate whether intelligence is inherited or the result of one's environment and circumstances. Which side do you favor?

If we reconsider the three criteria of body intelligence posited earlier in the chapter, a strong case could be made stating that body intelligence is developed from an individual's inherited nature as well as environment. On further investigation, we will also discover that the way a person has adapted to changing physical, mental, and social requirements has an effect on the evolution of a unique body intelligence.

Inherited Factors

Even before we are born, we are moving—stretching, kicking, tensing, and reacting to new physical developments (figure 9.4). Even before arms are fully formed, a fetus pushes and probes at the wall of the womb. By the time an infant arrives in the world and is separated from the mother, he is already equipped with patterns and skills, such as grasping and sucking. These and other skills necessary for survival—breathing, swallowing, and communicating—are instinctive.

We arrive in the world with our own genetic coding, which influences our individual development of body intelligence. Although most human survival no longer depends on running, throwing, and digging, our experience of those activities as children does inform us, through body intelligence, about our capabilities as adults. Let us look at some of the genetically determined factors at work and their influence on the development of body intelligence.

People come in all different heights, widths, and weights. The proportions of your body will make some activities easier for you and others more difficult. It's just plain physics. For instance, long legs are an advantage for long-distance runners, but they can be a dis-

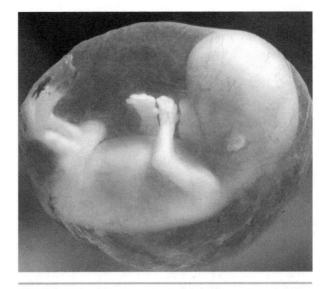

FIGURE 9.4 Our first dance experiences begin earlier than you might expect.

advantage in running sports that require quick changes of direction. The muscle-bound build of a boxer or weight lifter might be a disadvantage in other sports that depend on strength and flexibility.

As you read about body types, keep two important facts in mind. First, anyone, regardless of shape, size, weight, height, or physical impairment, can dance and can make dances. Different cultures value some physical characteristics over others. Different people value some physical characteristics over others. Contrary to what the media might have you believe, there is no ideal body. The second important fact to bear in mind is this: If you don't make your dance, it cannot be made. There are aspects of your discrete physical constitution, your life experience in your body, and your unique potential that completely qualify you for the dance you make. This chapter helps you explore factors that contribute to making you the mover you are—but ultimately, who's driving this bus? You are!

Your body type is an important, inherited factor that will influence the development of your body intelligence. In general, bodies can be divided into three builds: endomorphic, mesomorphic, and ectomorphic. In fact, very few individuals are true to any one of these classifications. Still, the system of classification is useful for discussing the kinds of activities that are more naturally suited to one body type or another. These three types are described by William Sheldon, Stanley Stevens, and William Tucker in *The Varieties of Human Physique: An Introduction to Constitutional Psychology* (Darien, CT: Hafner, 1970) as follows (see also Sheldon's *The Atlas of Men: A Guide for Somatotyping the Adult Male at All Ages* [New York: Harper, 1954]).

➤ *Endomorph*—Appears to be round, soft, and weighty. The limbs are short, bones are thick, and the center of gravity is low. The chest and hips are broad, with fatty deposits on the abdomen, chest, arms, and hips. The neck is short, and the head is large. This body is suited for activities in which weight and padding would be advantageous, such as playing contact sports or operating heavy equipment.

➤ *Mesomorph*—Appears to be sturdy, muscular, and rectangular. The bones are thick, the torso is somewhat longer than that of the endomorph, the neck is longer, and the head is smaller. The mesomorph does not carry excess fat in the buttocks and hips. Because this body is endowed with large muscles and evenly proportioned limbs, most physical activities can be accomplished with relative ease and coordination. Of the three body types, mesomorphs are most inclined to regular, rhythmic activities.

➤ *Ectomorph*—Appears to be long, slender, and frail. The bones are small and muscles are thin. The limbs are long, but the torso is short, thus the center of gravity for this body is higher than for others. The ectomorph does not carry fatty tissue and is narrow in the hips and chest. Because of the light body mass, activities that involve air time, such as running, leaping, and diving, are more easily accomplished by this body.

Which body type describes you most closely? Which type of activities are easiest for you?

Environmental Factors

The person you have become and the person you are in the process of becoming are products of all you have done. Some part of that person developed even before you were able to speak and rationally organize your thoughts. Your early physical contact with your parents and siblings had an effect on your feelings about physical contact and your physical sense. How much were you held as an infant? Did your parents comfort you with touch or voice? How were you protected from danger as a child? Were you contained? ("Don't go off the porch!") Restrained? ("Back in the playpen with you!") Were you verbally guided away from hazards? ("Be careful, there's glass over there!") How did you develop the skills to stay alive? How

---

INSIDE INSIGHT

In *The Code of Terpsichore,* published in 1830, Dancing Master Carlo Blasis [blahZEE] asserts that there are three distinct types of dancers, each suited by their physique to different roles in performance. The *danseur noble* must be stately, elegant, and "of noble carriage." Dancers of middle height (our mesomorphs) would be cast in "satiric" roles. They were the *demi-caractère* dancers. The shortest, stockiest, sturdiest dancers would be cast as the *danseur comique*. Although Blasis attempts to describe their work with respect, there is a sense of condescension in the way that he values the role of the villagers. See what you think:

> To offer a true picture of pastoral life, the dancer, in his performance, must copy and mimic the steps, attitudes, simplicity of manner and sometimes even the frolicsome and rude motions of the villager, who, inspired by the sound of his rustic instruments, and animated by the society and liveliness of his cherished companion, or beloved mistress, gives his whole soul up, without restraint, to the pleasures of dancing.

Do you think these stereotypes still exist in Western concert dance?

was your physical curiosity encouraged or dampened?

The environments in which you have lived also have had an effect on the kind of body intelligence you have developed. People raised in an urban environment will probably carry and conduct themselves differently than those raised in a rural setting. In the United States, East Coast people seem to be different from West Coast people, Southerners seem to be different from Northerners, and Americans seem to be identifiable all over the world. As a child you were exposed to textures, temperatures, comforts, and dangers that are part of the way you see the world. These variables have influenced your body intelligence—your ability to pattern, sense, develop appropriate skills, and respond to your experience (figure 9.5).

INSIDE INSIGHT

Sometimes called "the mother of modern dance," Isadora Duncan was indeed an innovator (see photo). She was certainly a product of her time—which included the Russian Revolution, World War I, and a family that was suspicious of traditional social structure—but she was not alone in eschewing the practices of "acceptable concert dance." Other women, such as Loie Fuller, Ruth St. Denis, and Mary Wigman, made significant contributions that influenced this form that was to become modern dance. Research into their biographies will lead you to discover how their sense of dance is a product of their accumulated body intelligence.

What dance comes uniquely from your experiences?

FIGURE 9.5 Many of our adult activities are shaped by childhood experiences.

Adaptive Development

The point of this chapter is to provide you with a base of understanding so that you can build on your strengths and positively approach aspects you would like to change.

Refined motor responses develop in two ways: through imitation and through adaptation.

We have instinctive motor responses that are necessary for survival—swallowing, sucking, breathing—and we have others that usually develop soon after birth—grasping and tracking (that is, following sounds, objects, and possibly scents). We are not given specific instructions in any of these skills, but we come to master them by trial and error, gradually learning to suck and swallow without choking or getting the hiccups, to grasp with appropriate effort, and to follow and even anticipate the origin or path of sights, sounds, and scents. We learn to refine these instinctive motor responses largely through adaptation.

Some adaptations take place as the result of an injury or an illness. See the next Try This Experiment on adaptation:

Try This Experiment

Pretend that you have twisted your ankle, and walk as if you are favoring that joint. What adaptations do you make to relieve the ankle from bearing weight? Does your opposite arm swing more than it otherwise would? Does your upper body make a circle as you walk? Is there constant tension in the front of your foot? What else do you notice about your adaptations?

If you have been even slightly active in the course of growing up, you have probably suffered slightly from pulled muscles, broken bones, cuts, scrapes, bruises, and combinations of these products of living a little bit dangerously. You have survived, but you may well carry with you scar tissue, weakened limbs, or bad memories—both mental and muscular. Whether you are one of the mind-over-matter types (who claim to be unaffected by pain) or one who gives in completely to any kind of stress, you still carry the physical memory of the adaptations necessitated by your injury.

Other necessities besides injury and illness cause an adaptive change in your body intelligence. The necessities of circumstances and customs furnish you with new patterns and skills to master new sensory and emotional responses. You walk a little differently when you approach a meeting with someone you deem more powerful than you, do you not? You may wear different clothes to some appointments than you would ordinarily wear—different shoes (which affect your walk), different garments (which affect how you sit or stand). Behaviors that are unacceptable in one circumstance may be expected in another. You adapt. For example, we generally avoid walking or standing close to strangers; however, if you were to move to Tokyo, you would probably become accustomed to this kind of closeness. Your development of refined motor responses—the way you act, react, and move—is partly a product of the circumstances and experiences you have unintentionally encountered.

Your development of refined motor responses is also a product of conscious and sometimes unconscious decisions to mold your behavior—to train, to receive instruction, to model yourself after some ideal. Through instruction by imitation, repetition, and correction you acquire new skills, modify old patterns, and experience new sensations and emotions. Most commonly, we think of training being directed by a teacher or a coach. The example and opinion of these people serve as inspiration to our own development.

When you make a decision to take a dance or gymnastics class, you choose to take direction from a teacher when learning to imitate the positions, timing, and basics of the form. When you make a decision to go out for a sport, you put yourself in the hands of the coach who gives you pointers on how to be a better player. But there are other people we use privately to coach our day-to-day activities. Certainly we are coached by our families in the acceptable ways to stand, sit, walk, and respond to others. Our friends coach us in movements, postures, and even personal timing that they find acceptable. Finally, we refine our behavior according to the advice of complete strangers that is available through the media. Advertisers are grateful for our ready acceptance of these coaches and our eager interest in imitating the models they have designed.

We see, then, that while some aspects of the development of body intelligence come from inherited factors beyond your control, many of the finer points of who you have become arise from your environment. Without a clear recognition of both the goals of your training and your strengths and weaknesses, which makes your training *sensible,* your pursuit of imitation can very well be frustrating. It is critical that you learn a process of imitation that enables you to develop in *all* four components of body intelligence—pattern, skill, sensation, and emotion—in order to be able to integrate your mental, physical, and emotional selves.

Body Intelligence and Dance

Dance is a physical activity with physical limits. These limits will vary from dancer to dancer. Your training will involve extending your physical limits—a process that has its rewards and frustrations. Questions that recur in the training process are: How far am I willing to push my own limits? What am I trying to be like or look like? Why are some movements so difficult and some so easy for me? Why can I remember some steps and not others? The answers to these questions will come from an examination of your body intelligence. Finding the line between straining and extending your physical limits, recognizing the difference between affecting and absorbing someone else's style, and sensing the distinction between duplicating and recreating a sequence of movement are all challenges of dance training.

Style: Finding the Dance in You

Originally, a *stylus* was a special stick used for making impressions on wax tablets. Today we still use a derivative of the word—"style"—to describe the kind of impression made on us by another person, place, or thing. For instance,

you may describe someone's home as decorated in a modern style—meaning you were impressed with the use of glass, shiny metal, or unconventionally shaped furniture.

You might describe one teacher as having a relaxed style based on the way you are addressed as students and the kinds of rules you are expected to follow in the class. Another teacher may impress you as having a more conventional style. Remember, style is an instrument used to make an impression. Just as a room can be transformed to a different style, so can a person transform by adopting different styles for different occasions; that is, by selecting different tools, such as choice of words, clothing, posture, or attitude.

When we refer to style in dance we are still talking about the impression a dancer makes with movement. So, where does style come from? In dance, *style* is a product of your efforts and your essence. The style you have as a dancer will come from the physical training you have had and the person you are. Your style will be the integration of the patterns, skills, sensations, and emotions you confront (or invite!) as a dancer.

Style is imbedded in the coordination patterns that are most comfortable to each individual. In chapter 8, we looked into the concept, introduced by Wetzig and her colleagues, that every individual has a "home pattern" or combination of patterns, and it is that home base that manifests in an individual's style. What's your style in life? How might that affect your discovery of your style in dance? Explore your own body intelligence by answering the questions in figure 9.6.

Beginning dancers struggle to simply stand up while also remembering to keep the tummy in, tail down, shoulders dropped, sternum lifted, ribs relaxed, legs straight, and to *breathe!* But eventually, as the sensation of useful alignment becomes second nature and the special demands of your chosen technique (such as a turned-out or parallel base) become more familiar, you will find that you have, in fact, evolved into your own style.

This evolution can easily have both positive and negative aspects. For instance, if you are drawn to the lightness and elegance of ballet, you might approach the tasks in class with an

What Is Your Body Intelligence?

1. If asked to create a straight path across your dance space without walking, which would you most likely do?

    a. skip

    b. take giant leaps

    c. crawl

    d. _____

2. The assignment is step-step-(event). Which would you most likely choose?

    a. step-step-turn

    b. step-step-balance

    c. step-step-leap

    d. step-step-_____

    Your choice will be conditioned by the space in which you are working. Which space did you select from your imagination?

3. Do you generally use your arms when making up movements, or do you "add the arms" once you have gotten the feet organized?

4. When shaping movement, do you work from image (how you look) or from feeling?

5. If someone asked you to demonstrate how you dance, what would you show?

6. Which part or aspect of your body

    is your best attribute?

    is strongest?

    is most injury prone?

    are you most comfortable with?

    are you least comfortable with?

    do people notice first?

    do people use to describe you?

    holds your tension?

FIGURE 9.6   What do the answers to the questions tell you about your own body intelligence or style?

image of yourself floating and balancing easily. This will help. You might also be seduced by tilted heads, spread fingers, and occasionally drooping hands and miss the foundation of these affectations. This will not help. All style and no substance.

Perhaps you are drawn to the sensual, beat-driven power of theatrical jazz. The music and the pace appeal to you, and you have a host of popular video, movie, and advertising images that describe not only how you should look but also all the great things that will happen to you once you master that look. Again, the positive and the negative. The good news is that you

may discover a new power in your movement style. The bad news is that you may, once again, hit the all-style-no-substance dilemma.

Finally, modern dance may seem to be a good place to discover and develop your style because you can do anything you want in modern dance, right? Not quite. There is certainly room for personal interpretation and invention in most modern dance techniques, but no technique is without its differentiating substance. Later in this text we will look at some of these differences, but for now our point is that regardless of the technique you study, you will always have two jobs:

1. To discover the essence of the technique
2. To discover your essence within that technique

Then you have style.

Integrity: Finding the Dancer You Are

Your development as a dancer (and as a person) depends on your integrity. The more you are able to appreciate and work with your unique gifts and talents, the more you will have to offer as a dancer and as a person. If you generally work with outer, other-body goals, your chances of being present for your own transformations are coincidental. Maintaining your integrity, in both class work and choreographic work, requires that you continually evaluate how you move and what you are moved by in terms of images, sensations, and motivations. Comparisons and some competition are inevitable in an art form that deals with transforming the same basic material: the human body. Still, you will be ahead of the game if you can use such comparisons to add to your body intelligence.

In this chapter we have discussed differences in the development of body intelligence. How does that information fit in your development as a dancer? It may be true that "*her* legs are so long and thin; *my* legs will never look like that." But unless you are contemplating major surgery, forget her legs. The point is, what about *your* legs?

Your duty as a dancer is to reveal, through the magic of movement, a spark of the soul. Your soul. Your awareness and application of the principles of body intelligence and your dedication to discovering your own unique potential as a dancer will lead you to that magic.

Think About It

1. Describe the difference between personality and style. (Think of someone whose style you could easily describe. Would you use the same words to describe that person's personality?)

2. Consider ways that you deliberately adopt a style that is different from your regular nature. What are the circumstances that lead you to this? Analyze this adopted behavior in terms of the four components of body intelligence.
   a. What is the pattern? (Shuffling my feet.)
   b. What is the skill? (Successfully imitating the walk of a laid-back rock star.)
   c. What is the sensation? (Comfortable for a little while, then my neck starts to hurt.)
   d. What is the emotion? (When I walk like this person I feel more acceptable and more comfortable socially.)

3. Early in this chapter you saw a quote from one of the most important men in baseball history. What did Yogi Berra mean when he asked, "How can you think and hit at the same time?" What does this have to do with dance?

4. The book *The Varieties of the Human Physique* describes the three different body types. It was first published in 1940 and was reissued in 1970. Do you think those types are still viable categories? Why or why not?

5. If you were a tree, what kind of tree would you be? If you were an animal, what kind of animal would you be? How do each of these choices reflect your body intelligence?

6. What is the earliest dance combination you can remember learning? (This may be from this year's class or from an earlier time in your life.) How well can you repeat the combination today? Polish that performance and identify three adjectives that you associate with the memory (such as cute, nervous, or petrified).

Your Turn to Dance

Chameleon Dances

Develop a short movement phrase (8 counts should be sufficient). Perform the phrase in the style of the person you think is the best dancer in your class. Perform the phrase in the style of a person in your family. Perform the phrase as an audition. Perform the phrase as a gift.

Confounding Dances

Create a dance in which you address one of the following issues:

~ A body type issue: by modifying the way your body appears

~ A pattern issue: by identifying one of your favorite movements and building your entire dance around that

~ A sensation issue: by posing a physical problem such as working blindfolded, or balancing on one leg the entire dance, or wearing a straitjacket.

Your Sense of Style

What is the sense of movement? There are several ways to answer that question. You could answer by discussing what you see as the point or purpose of movement or what you see as the sensations generated by moving. You could answer by discussing how you interpret someone else's movements or by categorizing movement into similar groups or styles. You might even use the phrase "sense of movement" to describe something that appears to be moving but is in fact still, as in, "The way the model's hair appears to be blowing creates a sense of movement in the photograph."

The words "style," "type," or "genre" are generally used to describe our sense of movements with specific qualities that fit a pattern. But what are those patterns? In chapter 1 we learned that one of the defining characteristics that distinguishes dance from other physical activities is that dance uses culturally patterned sequences of movement that are rooted in a people's history and memory. We use patterns to help us place new information in the context of what we've already experienced. In the case of dance, patterns are helpful as we try to master new movement or remember steps or sequences we've done before. Patterns help us analyze dances and talk about what we see. We look at patterns when we look at history. This chapter, which looks at styles of dance as conjunctions of patterns, asks you to consider how looking for movement patterns rather than generic labels might enrich your sense of movement.

Patterns Make Sense

When we looked at the element of time in chapter 6, we considered beat and pulse and the act of sensing time. We sense time by identifying patterns—of accents, of recurring units, of repetition. When we sense movement we are also sensing patterns. These patterns are our individual and cultural codes. They are the ways we communicate both intentionally and unintentionally—consciously and subconsciously.

If you were raised in New York City, your way of walking down the street is part of your nature. You maintain a neutral focus, avert your eyes when passing close to a stranger, and keep to yourself. But if you are a tourist visiting New York from a small town, you may be shocked or even a little frightened by these conventions. These are not patterns you are familiar with. You might be even more shocked when a person steps into a subway train and addresses everyone on the train and you find that you're the only one paying attention to him. Where you come from, when someone speaks to you, you do that person the courtesy of listening. After a few days in the city and a few more subway rides, you too recognize a pattern. A man steps on the subway and speaks to the passengers and you don't pay him any mind either. You can tell from his voice, posture, focus and *from the way he is* what he wants—and by your posture, focus, and body language you communicate your response. Europeans will comment that Americans seem almost goofy to them, so willing are we to engage with strangers and make friendly conversation. The Japanese will comment that Americans distinguish themselves as being rude and selfish by speaking too loudly in public and being unaware of others. These patterns, these ways of being, are both individual and cultural codes. To discuss a sense of movement is to discuss patterns.

What Are We Looking at Here?

We're looking at patterns of perceiving, emoting, relating, and valuing. They are patterns of attack, response, balance, and organization. The neat labels that come from history are not so neat any more. A style of dance is an umbrella that describes the patterns of movement attack, weight use, and shape, and the nature of the body's center.

What distinguishes modern dance from ballet? The stock answer is: the use of the torso and the importance of verticality. But wait! Don't ballet dancers bend their torsos? And isn't verticality important in modern dance too? Let's take an easier distinction, the difference between ballet and jazz. Simple. Jazz uses different music and jazz uses isolations. Hold on. What's the difference between a grand battement done to Liszt and the same movement done to Jennifer Lopez? And don't ballet dancers use isolations? Okay, let's make it reeeall simple: Surely we can distinguish ballet from tap, right? It's the shoes! But what about those dance-makers who have deliberately used the percussive potential of pointe shoes as a choreographic element, creating ballets in which the dancers tap with their pointe shoes? Aaaaa!!!

What's in a Name?

In referring to a style of dance you refer to the conjunction of patterns associated with a history, culture, and a set of conventions and values. A "style" of dance is the whole sense of movement, the body and the mind, the spirit and the flesh if you will, working in synthesis. Labels such as "modern dance" or "jazz" or "folk dance" or "ethnic dance" have minimal value as labels of style. At best, they roughly describe what the dance is *not*, but they do not clearly describe what the dance actually *is*.

"Modern dance" was a label used in the early part of the 20th century to describe a form of concert dance that was not vaudeville, not classical ballet, and not concert dance of the Romantic style. "Jazz dance" was a label that associated a movement style with a new style of music; but that label still didn't tell us what the form looked like or whether it was a social dance or a concert form. It indicated that it was not ballet and not modern dance. "Folk dance" is a label that tells us the dance is part of a culture's heritage, and therefore we can expect that it has a social and ritual function. Could classical ballet be considered a folk form? Possibly, but intuition tells us that folk dances have to do with the folk of a culture, not with its dominant class. So the style suggested by the label tells us not what it *is* but what it is *not.*

Finally, there's ethnic dance—an "us versus them" label if there ever was one! In writing about how we sense our natural and built environments, Lucy Lippard, art critic, commented that to contemporary urban and suburbanites, "Nature is where we are not." The term "ethnic dance" is the dance equivalent of that comment. Broadly put, ethnic dance is what people of other ethnic groups dance. Bharata natyam is a highly developed movement tradition that has been evolving in Indian culture since the second century BC (figure 10.1). It is the classical dance of Indian culture. Yet you will hear it referred to as ethnic dance! Therefore, from an Indian perspective, ballet is an ethnic dance. The use of the label "ethnic dance" does not give us useful information about the style of the movement; it merely describes the cultural bias of the speaker. In order to use the word "style" in an enlightened way we need to be able to discuss the experiential quality of the movement.

Toward a New Vocabulary of Style

Innovations in dance traditions come when an individual is compelled by experience to find a more fulfilling form—when what has worked before no longer yields the same satisfaction.

FIGURE 10.1   Bharata natyam is a dance style that is practiced all over India.

So looking at the concept of style, we must also consider how that style is a product of its own time and, to some extent, its own culture. In this world of easy access to images, sounds, media, and reference material, what used to belong to one group, civilization, or culture can now easily and anonymously be co-opted by an individual or a group. The world is becoming less diverse as we share more news, information, and, one hopes, insight. As we move toward homogeneity, labels mean less. What's "modern" about modern dance? Is ballet an ethnic dance? Do all Africans do "African dance"? Is there such a thing as a jazz ballet? Who are the "folk" who folk dance? Can a person "do a little Butoh"? We need a new vocabulary for discussing style.

Try This Experiment:

Stand in a parallel position near a support—a wall, a chair, a desk—and extend your leg to the front (tendu). You are going to experiment with different ways to lift the leg in the forward plane.

Using the image of a helium balloon attached to your ankle, keep your leg fully extended as the balloon gently and easily lifts the leg. As you feel the quadriceps grip, try to renew the image of your leg suspended and floating.

Next, bring to mind the picture of a perfect 90-degree front extension. Before actually lifting the leg, really see that image in your mind—extended supporting leg, long back, supported abdominal muscles, the gesture leg long and absolutely parallel to the ground. Then, when you have that image in your sense memory, lift the leg and hold it there, renewing the position with your sense of that perfect shape.

You may want to change to the other leg for the last two parts of this exploration.

Rather than standing and going through a tendu, allow yourself to take a step forward as you brush up to that same 90-degree extension. Once you arrive, renew the position by continuing to sense that forward momentum you used to lift the leg.

Last, let the leg swing forward and back, gradually gaining height; as you reach your full extension, see how long you can renew that position by continuing to feel the force from the swing fading into a falling leg.

In the experiment, which one of these was a grand battement? Which one was a forward kick? What's in a name? Which one was modern dance? Which one was ballet? Which one was jazz? Which one was expressive? Which one was meaningless? Which one felt most at home to you?

Eastern Versus Western Style

There are literally hundreds of different systems or theories one might use to analyze, identify, and expand the qualitative movement patterns characteristic of an individual or a group. Each of these systems, theories, and therapies looks at the whole organism—the whole person—from a slightly different organization. You are probably at least a little familiar with some of the Eastern traditions such as yoga, chi gung, ayurveda, and tai chi. These and many of the other Eastern movement practices are ancient systems that have evolved as effective ways to bring the body and mind into harmony. What distinguishes these styles from historically Western styles?

Try This Experiment

This experiment was first introduced by Leah Mann of Lelavision, a Seattle-based performance group. Whether or not you've ever studied a form of yoga, stand up right now and do a fake yoga pose. If you actually know some real yoga poses, don't do them now. Make up a new one. Now try tai chi. Whether you've ever taken a tai chi class or not, fake your way through some tai chi movement. Again, if you really do know this form, don't do the real deal; instead make up movement sequences that don't really exist. Finally, it's Bruce Lee time—fake karate!

In the "fake it" experiment, how did you know what to do? If there had been a blind person in the room, how would you have described the movements you were making and faking? You could fake them because you recognize aspects of their characteristic coordinations. You could imitate their style. They are slow or fast, direct or indirect, contorted or symmetrical. You were probably aware that in order to imitate these styles of movement, a different attitude had to be imitated or activated as well. Would that have been part of your description?

The Western movement traditions are only recently starting to rebound from the historical separation of mind and body. For years, Western systems that analyzed patterns of coordination focused only on the outside form and ignored the relationship between the patterns of the mind and the patterns of the body. The past 75 years have been a period of exciting exploration of the relationship of body and mind.

Body—Mind Comes West

While the yogis were off in the East standing on their heads, balancing on their hands, and having out-of-body experiences, Westerners were prancing around trying to figure out what it meant to look right. OK, that's a little simplistic; but it is true that we had to lose the corsets (men wore them too!) and whalebones before the idea of breath and organic movement could be explored. Once we Westerners started to rediscover the body, we could start to explore the relationship of body and mind.

One of the earliest and most broadly referenced systems used to explore those relationships is Laban Movement Analysis. Laban's work was briefly mentioned in chapter 8, but we will go into more detail here. Rudolf Laban (1879-1958) was a choreographer, dancer, scientist, philosopher, and teacher in Europe. He was a keen observer of all kinds of movement, including but not limited to dance. His goal was to create not only a means of recording movement but also a system for observing movement. He wanted to design a system that could record not only the steps but the quality of the movement as well. Was it light and quick? Light and slow? Heavy and quick? Heavy becoming light and slow?

Try This Experiment

Explore these four qualities: light, heavy, quick, slow. Rest one wrist on the edge of the desk or arm rest, then move your arm off that surface in a manner that is 1) light and quick, 2) light and slow, 3) heavy and quick, and 4) heavy becoming light and slow. Now get four different scraps of paper and draw a way to indicate each pattern without using words. See if someone else can tell which pattern goes with which of your drawings/notations.

Laban had not fully formulated his notation system when he was asked to lend his expertise, not as a soldier but as an efficiency expert, to the British war effort during World War II. With little time and fewer resources, the British were interested in making the best use of their factory workers' time and effort. Laban turned his attention to time and motion studies. He made suggestions about how the workers might make changes in their use of effort, or the quality of their movements. Just as you instinctively knew to change the quality of your arm movements when you switched from fake tai chi to fake karate, Laban recommended that the workers change the quality of some of their movements in order to move more efficiently.

A co-worker of Laban's investigated the relationship of shape and effort. What does shape have to do with effort? In an earlier chapter we looked at the aspects that affect the element of space and can be manipulated for aesthetic effect. Do you remember those? Level, dimension, direction, perspective, focus and . . . shape! Next time you drive through a fast-food place, notice the shape and arrangement of the space the server occupies at the pickup window. The space is organized so that a person of average height and weight can stand in one spot, easily and efficiently pluck all the condiments, grab the straws and napkins, and draw the sodas without having to change shape. In some places, leaning the hip on a mechanism opens the window. The equipment used most often is easiest to access. Attention to a well-designed workspace is not prompted by humanitarian interest. The restaurant chain is interested in getting the cars away from the window as quickly as possible throughout an employee's shift. The workspace is designed so that the shape of the body allows it to function with maximum efficiency and minimum tension. Combining the shape research with the effort studies resulted in a method then called "Effort/Shape," which described changes in movement quality.

Since Laban's pioneering notation system in the 1900s, systems have proliferated. Variously called "methods," "systems," or "approaches," they are organized ways to integrate form, function, attention, and emotion in the human being (see figure 10.2). While there are differences in focus and terminology, most systems share an interest in considering the human as a unity of body and mind (hence the now popular body–mind terminology). They agree that there is a correlation between a person's movement patterns and other behavior patterns, and they share the goal of expanding human potential by expanding movement options. Each of these systems for analyzing movement has different value in assessing and defining the style of a movement.

Each of these systems has value in helping us recognize a) the kinds of styles we easily appreciate watching, b) the styles we can learn with greatest ease, and c) the styles we might benefit from challenging ourselves to master. In this text we will focus on one, Wetzig's Coordination Patterns, to create a meaningful understanding of style. As we will see in the next chapter, by applying Wetzig's patterns of coordination we have a new vocabulary with which to analyze and discuss the sense of movement style, freeing us from labels that have lost their meaning and opening the door to the next wave of movement integration.

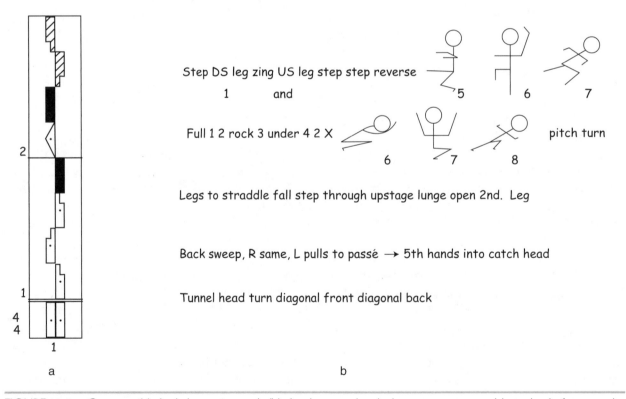

FIGURE 10.2   Compare (a) the Labanotation with (b) the drawings. In which circumstances would one kind of notation be more useful than the other?

Think About It

1. Look at the way you write down or draw your notes when you are making up dances. That is your "notation system." What does that tell you about the way you a) remember movement, b) represent movement, and c) "chunk" movement? What does your notation system tell you about your sense of movement?

2. Some other systems or approaches you might like to explore either online or in books are the Feldenkrais Method, Alexander Technique, Hakomi Therapy, Body–Mind Centering, and Bartenieff Fundamentals. Research one of these to discover the experiences that influenced the founder's interest in his particular niche. As we know, Laban was first interested in figuring out how the body could move most efficiently, but eventually the work was used to help people move with more ease and comfort. What can you discover about the ways the other systems developed?

3. How would you describe the differences among the following five dance styles: ballet, modern, jazz, folk, and hip-hop? Which words would distinguish one from another? First just do some associating, writing down whatever occurs to you. Then make a chart that lists the styles across the top with rows below for each of the elements of dance: time, space, effort, and shape. How are these styles distinct?

Dance styles					
Dance elements	Ballet	Modern	Jazz	Folk	Hip-hop
Time					
Space					
Effort					
Shape					

4. In the first edition of *Ballet & Modern Dance: A Concise History* (Princeton Books, 1986), Jack Anderson wrote, "No one has ever really liked the term 'modern dance.' Dancers, choreographers, and critics have found it awkward or confusing." Martha Graham herself referred to her dances as "ballets." What do you think would be a better name?

5. What's different about the style of modern dance created by the early moderns from the style we now call modern dance?

Your Turn to Dance

Playing With Style

Go back to your fake karate or tai chi experiment. You may combine both if you like. Play around with the fake movement, without using music, and pay special attention to how the breath informs (literally gives form to) your movement. Add stillness for attention and effect. When you have a sequence you like, try to lock in the muscle sense and then see how the piece feels and looks when done to classical ballet music. How do you retain the sense of the original study? Can movement set to one style be reset to another style? What changes in that case?

Experience or Habit?

The early moderns were keen on miming the arts of so-called primitive people. In *Modern Dance Forms* by Louis Horst and Carroll Russell (San Francisco: Impulse, 1961, page 59), the "primitive's directness" is qualified as "an ability to derive dance movement from life experience rather than from a sort of decorative habit." For this study, explore the dance that occurs when you derive movement from life experience.

Pick an experience that is pleasant and not psychologically complicated. Can you recall a simple physical success? Do you remember when you first learned to ride a bike? Do you remember reaching the top of a peak after a long, arduous climb? Have you ever crossed a river jumping from stone to stone? First, make a list of 10 simple physical successes you remember from your childhood or immediate past. Pick one to further explore based on how clearly you are able to identify the essence of that sensation. Remember, mime is imitation, not excavation. Pedaling an imaginary bicycle is mime (and probably not very good mime!), but figuring out a way to replicate that feeling of careening, barely in control, with your hair flying behind you in the wind—that's essence! As you work, eliminate any decorative habits that creep in. Make this a short final product (32 counts or thereabouts) but explore the line between experience and habit. Be prepared to discuss the style of your work.

Patterns of Coordination and Style

Why is it that some movements feel right to us and other movements feel unnatural? Why does some choreography come to us easily while other choreography makes us feel like we have two left feet? Most of us don't find the same natural ease with all styles of choreography. In creating choreography, we may sometimes feel that we are making the same dance over and over again. Both as students, eager to expand our movement capabilities, and as choreographers, eager to have the widest possible breadth of expression, we find value in deepening our strengths and pushing our limits. How can we find ways to honor what we do easily and also explore, with comfortable curiosity, ways of moving that come to us less naturally?

Style and Cultural Code

The answer to the question of how to explore movement that comes less naturally is somewhat complex. But to simplify the question, let's focus on how we think, feel, and move. Let us clearly understand that every person—in every local geographical area, in every state in the union, in every culture, and in every historical period—thinks, feels, and moves differently. Everyone belongs to certain groups of people or feels comfortable with certain kinds of people, often those who share a specific point of view about the world. These groups of people form our belief systems. These systems dictate which behaviors are acceptable (ways of thinking,

---
145

feeling, and moving) to the group. As we change our belief systems, we make room for any new acceptable behavior, and that in turn makes us feel comfortable within the new context. So, the ways in which we acquire new patterns of thinking, feeling, and moving are predicated on new experiences that become, however slowly, a natural way of behaving. Consequently, by observing how we think, feel, and move we can familiarize ourselves with a new way of behaving and isolate the differences between personal, group, and cultural behaviors. In this chapter we use observations about our personal preferences to help us consider what our patterns reveal about us and our culture.

From a personal perspective, we will search for movements that can be used to describe our own patterns of coordination. Remember, we are not merely looking for our favorite string of steps; we are considering how our movement preferences reflect, or do not reflect, a larger cultural context. For instance, how do your movement preferences differ from the minuet and the waltz? Would you say that the movements you see in contemporary social dance are different from those you see in the minuet or waltz? And what distinguishes the minuet from the waltz? Certainly, the sequence of steps is different in each of these styles of movement, but have we clearly understood the different body positions of the participants? One of the biggest shifts from the minuet to the waltz is that in the latter the partners turn to face each other in a closed position. How does this body position differ from how we perform today, for example, in a hip-hop-style dance? In its day, the waltz, in which the partners move together in a closed embrace, seemed scandalous. What would people from past times think of our gyrations today? What do these shifts in perceptions about movement tell us about thinking, feeling, and moving with respect to social norms or patterns? What is the difference between a waltz-ready society and a hip-hop-ready society?

Consider all the terminology, placements, positions, sequences, and combinations you have encountered in your dance technique classes up to this point. All these elements provide us with specific means to communicate and express our thoughts, feelings, and movement. But we would, in most contexts outside the world of dance, hesitate to inject these expressions into a social dance environment. Generally, classroom movement options are inappropriate and would look and feel silly

INSIDE INSIGHT

Pina Bausch, artistic director of Germany's Tanztheater Wuppertal, is a dancer who incorporates smell, taste, and repetition in her dances. Central to Bausch's work is the study of human relationships and repetition. Her style challenges the audience to contemplate the beauty in natural movement and gesture. By repeating a natural, apparently spontaneous gesture, such as brushing an arm, over and over again, a familiar pattern is highlighted as a choreographic element. In many of her pieces the stage is covered with leaves or dirt or peat or puddles of water. In those performances the audience can smell and even taste the air that is changed by the environment of the dance.

to us in the world of our social lives. There is a difference between the acceptable movements in the world of social dance and the world of dance performance. If we contrast the cultural patterns of those two worlds, we know it would seem weird to do a glissade-pirouette-assemblé at a party, just as we know it does not feel right to add pelvic isolations to a square dance. These movements are inappropriate because they do not fit the dances' contexts and they violate their specific cultural codes.

Each historical era and geography has its own cultural code, or ethos, which informs us about acceptable styles for each dance context and appropriate thoughts, feelings, and movements for a specific time. We discover these historical codes by studying cultural history, manners and modes of behavior, gesture, costumes and makeup, and the various institutions that dictate these codes (religion, politics, education, philosophy).

On a more personal level we derive specific behavioral codes from our family, friends, teachers, social and psychological contexts, and all the "-isms" and "-ologys" of our time. We each have codes we follow in constructing our style. When we're with close friends we've got one style; when we're in the presence of authority we fall into another style. We assemble these codes based on several pieces of information. The patterns we use to look good or blend or succeed are a compilation of our experiences, our conscious processing of those experiences, and our comfort zones.

Patterns of coordination can help us understand and intelligently discuss and describe movement style. This chapter makes the premise that such a description of style is as productive or more productive than using labels to describe movement styles. Think back to that minuet and waltz description. Those are named dances, dances that in fact have different forms depending on the location and the period of their performance or use. If a choreographer says, "Now let's try this in a minuet style," what might she actually mean? She might mean in a stately manner, or using mincing steps, or with a kind of self-conscious reserve. Using whatever you knew about the minuet, you would attempt to shape or shade

your movement according to that style. How would that stylistic shaping change if a choreographer said, "Now let's try that with more of a funk style"? In either case, you would try to adopt a different pattern of coordination that included physical and attitudinal change.

Coordination Patterns Help Us Discuss Style

The patterns of thrust, shape, swing, and hang, first introduced in chapter 8, are useful here because the coordination of these patterns gives us a way to consider style as a cultural projection and product. Each pattern is a mind–body connection that includes a quality and type of movement with a quality and type of thinking and feeling. We noted in the previous chapter that labels often mislead or hold little useful discrimination. Perhaps by looking at coordination patterns in dance we can find a way to discuss style that makes us less dependent on outdated labels.

Table 11.1 on p. 149 shows a condensed version of Elizabeth Wetzig's chart of the patterns and their manifestations. (Wetzig has an even more elaborate chart extending these patterns into music, garden style, and other realms. You can explore the full chart by going to www.symmetrical energyarts.com/weitzig_coord_chart.htm). Each line represents a different window through which one might look to recognize a pattern of coordination. Wetzig didn't provide a flow chart but rather a variety of ways that a person might manifest (or recognize) the patterns that are most comfortable or familiar to them.

Try This Experiment

You can guess at the outcomes of some of the experiments without physically doing the movement, but this one you have to actually, physically *do* to get the point. Here's your sequence:

Step forward on your left leg, extending the right behind you.

Swing the right leg through to the front, then bend the supporting left leg.

Step up onto that right leg as you make a one-quarter turn to face a new direction.

Keep your left leg unweighted.

Take the left leg back into a lunge.

Run three steps and stop in a crouch.

Start wiggling your head (like a bobble-head doll). Allow that wiggle to move into the neck, chest, and abdomen as you rise to standing.

Add your own finish.

Repeat the sequence several times, finding the timing, attack, and flow that feels right to you. You are looking for your particular style. You can play around with any portion of the sequence, but do so not in an attempt to be creative but to honor any intuition you have about appropriate use of momentum or accent.

When you are trying to integrate new information, how are you most likely to process your experience? What kinds of patterns do you look for? How do you experience patterns?

What was your experience of that sequence? Let's use only the first row of Table 11.1 to get some insight into your style.

Some of these aspects of preference may sound familiar to you if you think about the different ways of learning to dance that were first mentioned in chapter 2. There was the dive-right-in approach, which we can relate to a thrust way of encountering a new challenge. There was the technical approach, which relates to the shape way of encountering, and there was the creative movement approach, which relates to the swing and hang ways of encountering a new challenge. How did you encounter the challenge of learning the sequence of movements in the experiment?

1. Did you take a big, bold first step? Was power an interest or curiosity of yours? As you swung your leg through to the sit back, was there a sense of drive? Did you feel a sense of shooting up to the relevé? Did you drop into a strong, grounded lunge in preparation for the takeoff, then bam! Off like a shot? Or . . .

2. Did you sense as you stepped forward that the move is familiar as piqué arabesque? Did you "work the position," then brush through, with pelvis correctly aligned, to a low battement tendu? Then a strong push and quarter turn to another piqué, with your foot sur le cou-de-pied? Or . . .

3. Did you take that first step and play with the suspension, swing the leg through and see what happened? Oh! Too much momentum to stay in plié! Up you go to suspend . . . suspend . . . suspend . . . drop, rebound, and run, run, run, stop . . . Already found a rhythm? Or . . .

4. Did you step forward leaving your back leg trailing like a jet stream, allowing that movement to reach its natural conclusion (at which point the leg was allowed to fall with gravity and in so doing gathered new momentum, swinging through to the front)? As the moving leg lost its momentum, the shape became unstable and to keep from falling you stepped into the hang? Or . . .

5. Did you find yourself doing a combination of these movement styles?

Can you sense how each style is a valid but different way of moving? In each case, we're approaching the same sequence with a different style. In each case, we're looking at different ways to experience the same sequence. If you found that number 1 in the list most closely described your encounter, you used a thrust pattern. Movement style number 2 is more of a shape pattern; number 3 is more of a swing pattern, and number 4 is more of a hang pattern. None of these styles uses one pattern exclusively. Which patterns seemed most descriptive of your encounter?

It may help to think of a pattern of coordination in terms of a horoscope. What's your astrological sign? Do you think the traits associated with your sign are 100 percent accurate? Astrologers work with elaborate planetary charts to give their readings. They want to know the relationships of the planets. Your birth date identifies the primary astrological sign, but an astrologer also needs your exact birth time and location in order to do an accurate reading. Where were the

TABLE 11.1   PATTERNS OF COORDINATION

	Thrust	Shape	Swing	Hang
Most comfortable mode of encounter	Assertive, direct "doing," power, work	Formal, correct "placement," recognition	Valuing, interactive— "play," fun, teasing	Connecting, random, "being," energy flow
Learns best, communicates	Visually, with patterns	Aurally, with stories	Mixing visual, auditory, and kinesthetic	Kinetically, with movement essence
Movement design	Clear, diagonals, asymmetric	Measured, step by step, symmetric	Interplay, back and forth, antipodal	Figure 8, random, gyroscopic
Uses as primary relationship	Differentiate by contrasting	Differentiate by sorting	Associate by comparing	Associate by connecting
Primary type of functioning	Sensing	Thinking	Feeling	Intuition

other planets at that moment? In other words, what were the pulls and pushes operating? Have you ever read your horoscope and thought, Bingo! That is *so* me! Have you ever read your horoscope and thought, That is *so* bogus! Some days it happens to fit; some days it doesn't fit at all. In the same way that a horoscope (accurate or bogus) describes tendencies, so does a coordination pattern. And just as a personalized horoscope takes into account the movements of other planets and their influences, so too your patterns of coordination are pairs—coordinates, not just one line.

What's Your Home Base?

When we talk about patterns of coordination, let's make sure to note the importance of the word "coordination." In chapter 10 we defined style as "an integration of patterns, skills, sensations, and emotions." A style is the coordination of a dominant pattern with a subordinate one. The dominant pattern is the "home base" pattern, the one that feels most familiar, or comfortable, or correct. (To go back to the horoscope analogy, your dominant pattern is the equivalent of your sign.) This is the pattern that you are most apt to draw on when you learn new

things, meet new people, or when you are in your "encounter" mode or peak performance zone. This is not to say that you are a one-speed bicycle unable to encounter the world in any other way. Remember, "coordination" means you are going to draw on more than one pattern, but your home base is, by definition, the state in which you are most relaxed. The subordinate pattern supports or complements the dominant pattern. For example, you may be most comfortable logically categorizing movements while giving them silly, playful, made-up names. That would be an example of a shape/swing pattern. You go at the exercise in your home-base mode and then support it with a secondary pattern.

What can you observe about your style from the way you approached the memorizing and remembering—the way you created sense of the sequence? Wetzig gives us several different ways to find an applicable description of our patterns of coordination. Previously we asked how you encounter new movement. Try this question on for size: How did you design your movement in the experimental sequence?

What can you observe about your style from the way you designed your movement? See the second row of table 11.1.

Give yourself a good few minutes for this one. It will take that long for a pattern to emerge. Read through the whole experiment and then find a place to do the work. You're asked to focus on the patterns that you would *not* normally associate with your style in movement design. If you like making asymmetric shapes and designs and clear lines, try to find the most opposite manner you can.

Standing in one place, close your eyes and sense the impulse to move. See if you can begin to move in a way that is not your style. At first move only on one spot, but as you continue to explore, allow yourself to move through space. Now rest and consider how successful you were at getting out of your home base, at leaving your comfort zone and trying something different. Which pattern did you drift to as an opposite of your home-base pattern? Read back over the aspects of movement design and see if you recognize how your home base was blended with a secondary pattern.

How did you approach the previous experiment? Standing there with your eyes closed, when you felt that impulse to move, how did you process it as being a home base or an oppositional pattern? Did you process it logically? Intuitively? Can you find that mode of processing here? See the third row of table 11.1.

Going back to the extended sequence, you might ask yourself, "What was my most comfortable mode of encounter?" "How did I design that phrase?" Or you might wonder, "When I was working with that, was I mostly thinking or feeling or sensing or using my intuition?"

Thrust, shape, hang, and swing are patterns, not merely actions. In order to be "in thrust" you don't have to move around jabbing, poking, or punching at things. You don't have to be on a swing to be "in swing." You don't have to pretend to be a statue to be "in shape" or hang from a bungee cord to be "in hang." Thinking about the style you used in dancing the first sequence, you might have found that one of the "Did you?" questions that followed described your experience exactly. Or you might have thought, My style is mostly like

shape, but power was an important part for me too. So you'd be in shape/thrust.

Patterns of Coordination Integrate Body With Mind

Do you see how you are looking for a way to integrate not only your physical actions but also how those actions are tied to the way you think? Your choices in movement are part of complex personal patterning. When you marvel, "I would never have seen that connection," you are observing someone who patterns in a different way than you do.

Stand up and allow yourself to bounce softly as you swing your arms front to back. Rest. Now go back to that bounce, but this time as you bounce, circle your hips. Keep that hip circle going and put the swinging arms back in. For many people this is a tricky coordination. How did you do?

If you got the arm swing–hip circle coordination right off, how did you find it so quickly? Maybe your body recalled similar coordination from an African styles class. Or maybe you were very logical about the relationship of the arms to the pelvis, keeping the two separate. Or did you go into a feeling mode, getting a kick out of both the difficulty and the newness? Did you go into a different kind of feeling mode, sensing how the overall rhythm coordinated upper and lower body halves?

The application of patterns of coordination can help you pick up combinations more quickly, find the flow of a piece of choreography, discover where movement is initiated or motivated, find commonalities with patterns you already know, and discover ways to shade your performance. Let's say you are struggling in a jazz class, always one count behind and frustrated by the quick succession of isolations and shifts. What if you looked at the movement as being thrust based and tried to connect to that way of moving? Or, conversely, what if you enjoy moving quickly and sharply and you are asked to explore movement that is slow and flowing? If you relax and give yourself to exploring that pattern of coordination, you might find that you discover a new way of being.

In your choreography, you can apply your understanding of these patterns of coordination to move out of your habits and challenge yourself in new territories. You can also use these patterns to dig further into the patterns that are most comfortable to you and mine them for deeper insights. Let's say you are a shape-dominant mover and are most comfortable coordinating that with hang patterns. What would happen if you worked deeply to emphasize that coordination pattern, exploring how long or how easily you could "hang a shape"?

In your exploration of other dance traditions and genres, looking for patterns of coordination can help you discover which values and codes are implicit in the dance. Have those changed through time? What distinguishes an "outsider" from an "insider" in a dance form? How is your favorite social dance transformed when a parent tries to imitate it? Does someone from outside the culture imitate a Nigerian village dance as accurately as a native Nigerian? Are there some dances that simply *belong* to one cultural group? Why or why not? Using the patterns of coordination, you can more accurately describe the differences you see. By looking with more curiosity at what's underlying a dance, and by learning to describe its patterns of coordination, we learn about ourselves and others while we learn about dance.

Think About It

1. Think about your family. What patterns characterize your family? Try drawing a short family tree with people's patterns associated. Do you notice any overall pattern?

2. Which pattern would you say best describes the generation older than yours (sticking with your socioeconomic group)?

3. Assuming that you have been able to recognize home base in your technique class, did it come from the repetition of style your teacher offers or from your own predisposition to what feels comfortable?

Synonyms: Thrust, Shape, Hang, Swing

In this construction you'll go deeper into the patterns using synonyms of each word to explore the nuances of the words themselves and your interpretations. If done in one session, this is a long structure. You would probably profit more by exploring it in four different sessions with time to reflect and journal in between.

Thrust: Push, shove, drive, propel, plunge, force

Choose three of the six words offered. Take each of your three words, one at a time, and improvise with that one word for one minute. Do not mime; truly *experience* the physicality of the word. Stick with one movement idea and explore its complexity rather than changing the subject continually. In other words, if you start out by pushing your hand on your arm, investigate how "push" changes if you press on different places on your arm rather than jumping from arm to leg to wall to nose. Go with your first instinct. Develop that for one minute, then clear your head and go on to "shove." If thrust is not a home base for you, pay attention to what occurs to you as you work.

Shape: form, figure, outline, contour, line, curve, profile, structure

Again, choose three of the eight options listed and improvise for one minute with each, taking care to develop rather than shift from one idea to another. With this pattern, allow stillness to inform your exploration.

Swing: sway, rock, gather momentum, rebound, return, release, (swing)

The synonyms for swing are a little trickier than for thrust, shape, and hang. Why might that be? Choose three and explore as above. Remember, part of swing is playfulness, buoyancy, and lightness, so as you explore, try to do so with humor.

Hang: dangle, suspend, droop, weightless, postpone, delay

With hang, pay particular attention to the moment and potential in its active stillness, the moment when you are sustaining momentum but not moving through space. How long can you prolong that moment? Play also with the hang of sustained continuous movement.

When you have explored all four patterns, reflect on what you discovered about your home base. Finally, choose to share a structured improvisation based on either your home base pattern or a combination of home base and the pattern you found most challenging.

In the Garden

Wetzig, in her fully expanded chart, has correlated different kinds of gardens with different pattern types.

Thrust: Japanese garden—pebble beds, large rock accents
Shape: English garden—topiary trees and bushes, manicured beds
Swing: Monet's garden, or any cottage garden planted with variety, wild shapes, and surprises
Hang: Natural—wildflowers, wooded glade, or untended growth

Which of these appeals to you most? Read through the entire prompt, then go to work discovering this dance!

Collect images from magazines or books that show such landscapes. Surround yourself with these images and immerse yourself in the textures, light, contrasts, sense of space, scents, sounds, the feel of the ground underfoot, the potential proximity of other garden visitors. Imagine yourself in such a landscape.

When you feel you have fully absorbed the images, place yourself in a workspace or studio and stand in a neutral position with eyes closed. Bring those images to mind. "Look" around the corners of the garden in the images to imagine what might be there. Try for a 360-degree sense of the place where you are standing. You are going to make a dance in celebration of this garden— its beauty, its power, its origin, the hands that tend it, the nourishment it receives, the glory of this one spot on earth. Standing still, you will feel the impulse to move in response to your sense of this place. As that impulse wanes or runs its course, allow yourself to return to stillness, but attend to your shape so that your new stillness is the result of that first impulse rather than a return to a neutral position. You will begin to hear the correct music in your head, music that plays in or is compatible with this garden. As you hear this music (that you alone can hear) allow your dance to take on its own integrity. When you are done, make notes of your sensations, your images, and your sequences to attempt to reconstruct the dance another time.

Part IV

The Politics of Dancing

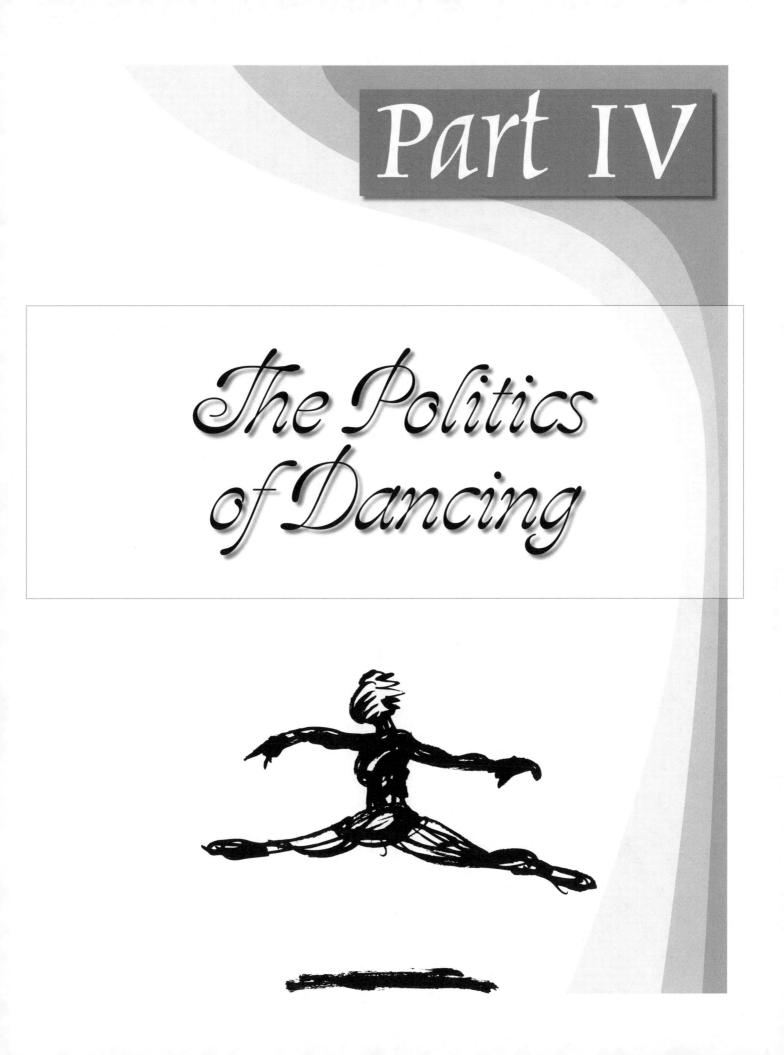

12

Making a Statement Through Dance

"The more original a discovery, the more obvious it seems afterwards."

Arthur Koestler (1905-83), Hungarian-born writer

"Freedom of speech and freedom of action are meaningless without freedom to think. And there is no freedom of thought without doubt."

Bergen Baldwin Evans (1904-78), American writer

We have examined the characteristics of dance, studied the elements of the art form, and considered ways that an individual's physical and perceptual strengths influence dance and choreographic choices. We are now prepared to integrate all of this information as we consider how to use dance to make a statement about the world and one's experience of it.

This text aims to enable you to access your unique brand of creativity and, by using the art of dance, share some aspect of yourself with others. Ideally, this process involves finding a way (or several ways) to integrate the physical, emotional, and spiritual aspects of yourself. When you find this integration, chances are you have created something original.

In this chapter we will focus on two things:

1. How to have an original thought
2. How to explore your original thought

You will find this chapter useful both in your dance class and in other activities that require you to think for yourself and be creative. Different activities require creative problem-solving strategies, and it is usually safe to assume that there are at least two ways to solve any problem—most of the time there are even more. This kind of thinking is central to our approach to making a statement by using dance. We will assume that there are as many dance solutions as there are choreographers and that each choreographer will bring wisdom and experience to the dance creation.

"Movement Resources I Have Known"

Whether you were asked to construct a short sequence or an evening-length work, at this point in your dance career you have probably had a chance to try your hand at some choreographic enterprise. Recall some of the resources you used to form your studies or dances. For the purposes of this text, "study" will refer to a short dance—complete with beginning, middle, and end—that presents an in-depth investigation of the movement possibilities of a narrowly defined topic. For instance, a study on rising and falling might include 20 ways to rise and fall. In the course of finding those ways, you might discover a dance about life and death, or success and failure, or some other contrast. Your rising-and-falling dance would still be considered a study—a string of movement options. A study is to a dance what a sketch is to a painting.

When you are asked to create a dance study, a sketch, a scientific abstract, or a synopsis of a play, you go through the same creative process of identifying all the resources that might help you put your ideas into perspective. In the composition work you have done to this point, you have drawn on a number of resources which you may or may not have consciously considered.

Technique

"Technique is just a means of arriving at a statement."

Jackson Pollock

Not all composition classes include the study of a particular dance style or technique. If imitation has been a part of your training, you will likely incorporate the movement skills that interest you as you continue exploring your newly developing physical skills. If imitation has not been stressed in your training, you will draw on styles of movement that you find familiar, comfortable, and acceptable. These are your techniques.

Regardless of which techniques you have been exposed to, you have no doubt found certain moves that feel good to you. You may have discovered a new height to your leaps, a new way to go to the floor, a new strength in some part of your body that enables you to do other movements that are new to you. Exercises and combinations learned in your technique classes can be a good starting point for dance studies, particularly if you work with material that you enjoy doing and feel you do well.

Suppose you are blessed with long hamstrings. Length and flexibility in these muscles make it relatively easy for you to do certain movements, such as high kicks and splits. Chances are your studies will have a lot of high kicks and a split or two—movements that are impressive, extraordinary, and happen to be easy for you to do. Recall from chapter 1 that one of the criteria that distinguish dance from other physical activities is that dance incorporates extraordinary movements. Without much physical or creative effort, you can whip out movements that are going to pass as dance and be impressive. This is not to imply that there is anything wrong with using your natural talents. In fact, quite the contrary; it is a good idea to work with your unique gifts and talents. Beware, however, of getting stuck in the habits of easy solutions. Sure, it is a pleasure to watch people move with confidence, but it gets boring quickly if a dancer can do only one thing, such as turn, do high kicks, or hold a leg extended. As you sample and draw from your techniques, bear in mind that as exciting as it is to see a dancer move with confidence, it is also exciting to see a person take risks.

As you apply the principles of technique in your composition work, be aware that technique is a beginning, a resource, a base. Technique does not speak. *You*, through your unique way of using technique, deliver the statement.

Media

As we discussed in the previous chapter on body intelligence, you are all that you have seen, heard, felt, smelled, tasted, and sensed.

The media have certainly tried to be a part of those experiences. Is television part of your life? Do you read the newspaper? Do you look through magazines? Do you listen to the radio or to recorded music? All of these resources—deliberate or otherwise—inform your dance studies.

New fashions in posture, dress, language, music, and recreation continually replace those that were once unacceptable; they suddenly become the new standard of acceptability. In general, what is familiar is what is acceptable. You and your classmates may have a familiar way of moving to your favorite songs. Images in magazines, on billboards, and on packages will reinforce a way of dressing, standing, walking, and relaxing. These are resources you use in creating your own compositions. Advertisers hope that these will be your standards of beauty, tension, and expression. Perhaps you have accepted these standards. Perhaps you have established your own.

Your standards will provide you with a sense of what is good, interesting, funny, or inspiring. As discussed in the section on technique, it can be a pleasure to watch a dancer move with confidence. Even if we have seen similar movements before, we enjoy seeing them again if the dancer presents them with new life. Likewise, if you can breathe new life into movement patterns that have become clichés, you can use the resources of the media in a creative, innovative way.

You can use a test—the "That's stupid!" test—to determine if you are locked into clichéd standards. Often, "That's stupid!"

is a way of saying, "That's different from what I'm familiar with." As you are able to appreciate different kinds of expression, the quick dismissal will give way to more specific observations.

Remember this test as you examine media resources for new dance patterns. Some sources that may already have been useful to you are movies and videos about dance history. Often these are the most direct sources available for understanding dances from other cultures. Through these resources we can see that many of the conventions we associate with contemporary dance did not apply to dance in earlier days. For instance, men used to be much more involved with dance than has been the case in modern Western culture. Consider, as well, that today's image of a ballerina is of a very thin, long-legged woman. But in the early days of ballet, ballerinas were not nearly as thin as they are required to be today. Likewise, modern dancers were strong and tended to be stouter; however, contemporary professional modern dancers tend to resemble the traditional ballerina image. Times change. The resources of the media can open our eyes to the possibilities of what has been and also give us a way to look objectively at what is.

When using the media as resources for original thought, bear in mind that in this art form an original thought involves the integration of mind, body, and soul. Sure—steal the moves that appeal to you from a commercial or a program, but take care to invest your own mind, body, and soul as you work with and re-create this material.

Other Students

Another great movement resource you may have used in your dance compositions is the talent of your peers. As you have no doubt discovered, working with other people has advantages and disadvantages. Different choreographers work with the movement resources of other dancers in various ways. As a dancer you will soon discover that you feel more comfortable working with certain kinds of processes than with others. When you are wearing the choreographer's hat, it can be helpful to maintain some perspective on the expectations you have of the dancers working with you. Consider a few of the more common categories into which choreographers can be classified.

The Dictator

Some choreographers simply relish the opportunity to be in charge and have their ideas heard. It seems that the opportunity to direct is as important or more important than the opportunity to create. On the bright side, this kind of choreographer usually has a clear vision of the way things should be. She is not interested in entertaining other people's ideas, so the rehearsal process does not involve a lot of discussion and democratic weighing of options. It means that if you as a dancer do not think much of the choreography, you keep your ideas to yourself and find a way to do what is asked. The dictator-choreographer is a good person to work with if you enjoy being directed and molded. She can help you discover new options that you would probably not have chosen if you were working on your own. This is not a good person to work with if you enjoy having input in the creative process.

The Visionary

Some choreographers require seemingly impossible tasks in the name of art. They can see the dance in their heads and recognize opportunities for stunning and spectacular human feats as they direct their dancers. In general, these choreographers do take into account the skills of the individual dancer and always keep one eye open for idiosyncrasies that could be transformed into spectacle or special effect. They ask for the impossible, and they often get it! These choreographers forget that the human body is governed by the laws of gravity and energy, and they push those laws to the limits. They are great people to work with if you are the sort of person who enjoys taking risks and being pushed to explore the outer limits of your endurance, balance, and flexibility. This can be exhilarating!

The Sponge

Some choreographers use dancers as if they were puddles of ideas waiting to be mopped up and put in a glass. With a few vague ideas, they begin with a "Try this; no this—no this . . ." approach, basically letting the dancers do the creating. In fact, this is a very common method of working. The unfortunate aspect is that the dancers are rarely credited with having generated most of the movement material. This kind of choreographer is good to work with if you enjoy contributing your ideas and trying out variations that are suggested by an outside eye but are less comfortable with making aesthetic decisions yourself. If you have respect for a choreographer's artistic vision and are proud to have played a part in contributing to that vision, this is a good choreographer for you to seek out.

The Collaborator

Collaboration is a long, sometimes tedious and often frustrating process. It involves listening and compromising, respecting other ideas, and letting go of the notion of personal ownership of an artistic product. In true collaboration all ideas are weighed equally and, through consensus, either trashed or incorporated into the final project. There is no director, no individual who holds ultimate artistic control. This is a good process to pursue if you are a person who enjoys having your opinions and solutions reflected in the final product. This is not a good process if you are in a hurry to get something done or if you are the kind of person who "keeps score" and might feel cheated if your work is not reflected as much as others'. A little voice should go off in your head when you hear someone say they'd like to collaborate with you. Find out what the terms are before you commit, only to discover your collaborator is really a sponge or a dictator!

The Amalgamated Choreographer

You will find aspects of each of these types in most choreographers, yourself included. When learning to work with others, both as a choreographer and as a participant in other people's work, it can be helpful to recognize which styles and power structures work best for you so that you can be clear in your dealings with others and make the most of your time together. If you need other people's input in order to have an original thought, it will speed your process if you communicate that. If, on the other hand, you need your dancers' patient and diligent effort to realize your vision, this too needs to be understood.

None of these choreographic styles is wrong or right. Choreography is an individual matter. To create your own dances, be aware of your own style and choose to work with choreographers and dancers who will help you grow. Perhaps, in order to break your movement habits, you will ally yourself with someone who insists on a specific execution of movement. Perhaps, in order to challenge your inventiveness, you will choose to work with someone who gives dancers more responsibility. By paying close attention (not judgment, but attention!) to the way other students work and move, yet another valuable resource for composition will be open to you.

"Composition Strategies I Have Known"

You have your resources, and you have your assignment. Now what?

You jump in with both feet. You draw your floor plan, or you create your 4 shapes (or 40 shapes, depending on the assignment), or you create your sequence of times, or you begin wherever you can imagine beginning. Often your teacher will supply you with a flowchart that breaks the creative process into bite-sized chunks. Here is an example of a process that uses an ordinary gesture, such as a handshake or a wave, as the basis of a short dance.

1. Choose a gesture.
2. Make it faster or slower than normal.
3. Make it travel.
4. Make it change level twice.
5. Create a short, patterned phrase of movement from these experiments.
6. Teach your pattern to another person.
7. Do your patterns, but maintain contact with a partner.

To help you get started, your teacher may have provided you with an order to follow—a form—while building your dance study. In the beginning, these directions can be very helpful in leading you to a finished product. But in real life, there is no recipe for creativity. Creative works come from a motivated commitment to say something. Following someone else's recipe may help you discover that you have something to say, but the product will be different if you can find a way to identify your original thoughts.

How about taking direction from your peers? By now you have had a chance to work with lots of different groups. You have probably discovered that in some groups there were too many ideas and in other groups no ideas seemed worth pursuing. What makes one group work and not another? Think back to some of your group work, to a particularly successful group experience.

➤ Whose ideas were used?
➤ What process was used to make those decisions?
➤ How did you feel about having your ideas accepted, rejected, or altered?
➤ Overall, do you prefer working with a group, a partner, or on your own?

Now think back to a group experience that was less fruitful.

➤ What killed people's creativity?
➤ Would better communication skills have helped?
➤ Would better listening skills have helped?
➤ Were there assumptions operating in the group that cut off full experimentation?
➤ Did everyone bring a generosity of spirit to the group?

Written planning may have been useful to you. As mentioned previously, it can be helpful to draw out your floor plan, both to see if you have become stuck in one place onstage and to make a map for later reference. Another strategy for organizing your thoughts may have been to write out a shorthand description of the important events of your study.

Two dancers, A and B:

1. A and B begin crouched together.
2. A rises and runs to the back (upstage).
3. B rolls to the side.
4. A falls and rolls toward B.
5. B tries to rise but only gets halfway up.
6. A clings to B, pulls B back to the floor.
7. A and B end crouched together again.

This method can also be useful for providing an overall look at what the dance is about. In addition, by playing with the language in such a description, you can often discover or create a fresh, new dance! Try filling in the blanks in a way that creates a dance that is different from the first example.

Two dancers, A and B:

1. A and B begin _____ together.
2. A _____ and runs to the back (upstage).
3. B _____ to _____.
4. A falls and _____ B.
5. B tries to _____ but only _____.
6. A_____ B and _____ B_____.
7. A and B end _____.

Last but not least is the strategy known as "the deadline." The dance project is due, so you make some decisions, trot out the same old movements, string them together, and do your best to perform what you remember. (This is the generic solo. Just as your supermarket carries things like detergent and cleanser with no particular brand, you can create a dance that has no particular brand.) You know it is not your best work, but . . . well . . . you just ran out of time to create something special.

If you have ever found yourself out of time and still unprepared, the rest of this chapter is for you. If you have ever been disappointed with the dances you have presented, read on. The art and process of making a statement through dance is similar to the art and process of any synthesis of thought or materials. There is play involved, and there is discipline. There is adventure in exploring many options, and there is patience required to redefine the focus

of the statement you wish to make. We have reviewed some of the resources, processes, and strategies you have probably used, consciously or subconsciously, when preparing your dance compositions. Having an original dance thought is not too different from writing an essay or creating a painting.

Getting Started

Composition in any art is rarely a linear process. More often you will begin, change your mind, start somewhere else, collect more information (thoughts, images, sounds), add, subtract, and so on. This process of beginning can go on as long as time and patience allow. One choreographer might brood over a piece for two or three years. Another might have only 45 minutes to stage a work, so decisions need to be made quickly. Your creative schedule will depend on how and when you will be evaluated.

We have all had some experience with the creative process used in writing, so consider that as a model for the process of creating in dance. In writing, there are six stages of composition:

1. Prewrite
2. Make notes
3. Draft
4. Rewrite
5. Polish
6. Publish (hand in!)

The prewrite stage is like shopping. Let us say you know you are going to need a new jacket in the next couple of months. Gradually you become very aware of jackets. You find yourself looking at the jackets strangers wear or you are mysteriously drawn to the jacket department of any clothing store you pass. The world becomes a sea of jackets. In this shopping stage, you tune yourself to news and information about your subject. You make yourself receptive. You talk to people. You do not necessarily *buy (write)* anything. You dream. You simply collect. In dance, the prewrite stage is the time to use all your senses to take in any and all information about your field of interest. Study other people; look at animals and insects;

look for accidental patterns, lines, coincidences. Close your eyes and sense. Experiment and improvise without a plan; do it just for fun.

Next comes the time for taking notes. This is the stage where your personality starts to play a part in the creative process. What do *you* find interesting? What connections do *you* make with your life and your subject? Someone says something interesting, and you write it down or ask for a reference. You go to the library and read through books, magazines, or whatever resources will give you that spark, central theme, or focus. This is the stage where you allow the material to grab *you*. In dance, the note-taking stage is the time for writing, collecting pictures, gathering music, clothing, and related things that have to do with your subject.

When your notebook is full, your pockets stuffed with scraps of ideas, and your workspace cluttered with related materials, you will feel close to having something to say. You begin to draft. In dance, this is the stage where you begin to set movement patterns that are close to feeling right.

In writing, some people begin by making an outline. Others might begin by modeling their writing after the pattern of another author. (But remember, the writing process actually began long before!) This is often the most difficult stage of the creative process because, in spite of all the resources that have been gathered, people *still* lack the confidence to recognize what they find interesting about a subject.

In dance the problem is often the same. Young choreographers come to the studio forgetting that the process of choreography began on the street, in their daydreams, the checkout line, the library, and their classes; they need those resources to begin their first choreographic draft. In any creative process, it is a mistake to attempt to leap straight from the assignment to the final product. That would be like expecting to pour a jigsaw puzzle out of the box directly into its completed form. What fun would *that* be?

After you create your rough draft, you breathe a sigh of relief and set your work aside so that you can return to it with fresh eyes a little later. Your rewrite stage may include getting feedback from friends or family. Or perhaps you feel confident enough in your abilities to rework your composition on your own—cutting out the fat or adding necessary examples. Add another check to make sure that all your spelling is right, the punctuation is in order, and the overall appearance is kind to the reader, and it is ready to hand in!

In dance you might ask a friend to watch a rehearsal and give you feedback, or you might even teach your work to another dancer to see if he can make it say what you want it to. If you are lucky enough to have access to a video camera, you can tape your work and do your own editing. In dance, feedback and review are *critical* to the creative process. As a performing art, dance is meant to be shared. Critical feedback is therefore a vital part of the choreographic process. Unlike shopping for and eventually buying a jacket, in dance, you are never stuck with something that no longer fits or feels fashionable. The creative process is ongoing, fed by your new ideas and the reactions and ideas of your audiences.

INSIDE INSIGHT

Is all art meant to be shared? If you make a dance and perform it in your backyard and no one watches you, is it still "art"? Of course it is! In the "artist's loop" there is a connection from artist to audience through the content of the work. The audience, through its encounter with the work, gains insight into the mind of the artist; the artist, through the content of the work, offers her insight to the audience and so on. This process can start at every corner of the triangle.

Let us look for similarities in the creative process used in painting. First the painter collects and stores images, shapes, colors, contrasts, textures, and relationships. She talks about what she plans to do and receives feedback. She makes notes and sketches; she looks back at her earlier work and at the ways other artists have treated the same subject. She must also prepare her canvas. How big will the surface be? What shape will the surface be? What kind of surface will be appropriate? Then she begins. She paints, erases, overpaints; she leaves it in the corner for a while; she looks at it every day and talks to it; she allows a few close friends a peek. Then she works on it some more, and, eventually, she feels that she has captured all that the piece was meant to contain. She has made her statement. A few more touches, and it is ready to be framed!

Six Stages of the Creative Process

When we described the creative process for writing and painting we assumed that a subject or field of interest had already been identified. We referred to collecting images almost as if they could be found scattered about like leaves or stones. In a sense, they can be. Your motivation for a dance can come from many sources: an assignment, a piece of music, a dream, a feeling, an event witnessed or experienced. In fact, any aspect of life that has motivated you is fair game for treatment in dance. Later we will discuss the ways in which some subjects may be more suitable than others, but for now, let us keep focusing only on process and make a direct comparison of the writing process to that of dance composition.

Writing	Dance
1. Prewrite	1. Collect
2. Make notes	2. Note and improvise
3. Draft	3. Choose and develop movement material
4. Rewrite	4. Rework material
5. Polish	5. Rehearse and refine
6. Publish	6. Perform

Collecting

Choose a general concept, such as love, and try to experience it in every sense—sight, smell, sound, touch, and so on. In the movie *Tap*, the main character explains to a crowd the process his famous father used to invent new tap steps: "He took the sounds from the street," he says, and he has the crowd listen to the rhythms of the passing cars, the pumps, the whistles, and, in short, city life. You may not pick up the beat quite as quickly as the cast of the movie, but the point remains valid. You can begin by using your senses and all three perceptual modes to collect all kinds of great material that is *yours*—unique to you and original.

Noting and Improvising

Begin to make notes, draw pictures, collect samples, record dreams, and generally catalog the relevant images you discover (figure 12.1). As your collection of notes, pictures, samples, dreams, and other relevant images builds, allow yourself a time and place to improvise with these images.

Begin to clarify the gift you hope to make with your work.

The process of clarifying can be difficult. The challenge here is to define the problem, not the solution. Perhaps the problem has already been defined for you. For instance, your assignment is to make a dance using curved and straight pathways. That is a perfectly valid problem, but probably not one you can get too excited about, unless you create *your own* problem to make things interesting (both for you and your audience). Here are some examples of how you might use your sense inventory to explore the assignment:

1. *Sight*—Trace the outline of a tree's branches in winter, and let that be your floor plan.

2. *Sound*—In an urban setting, time the intervals between the honking of horns or the passing of cars; let the length of those intervals determine how long you will move in a straight

4. *Touch*—Collect five objects. Put them in a sack. If you are right-handed, then hold a pen in your left hand (vice versa for lefties). Close your eyes. With the hand you usually use for writing, pick one of the objects from the sack. Using your other hand, draw a line of texture based on whatever you have pulled from the bag. Make one continuous line—your straight and curving-path dance.

5. *Smell*—Which path would you take to someone wearing a lovely perfume? Which path would you take to discover who had stepped in something a bit stinky? Which path would you take to determine the source of a burning odor? (Remember, this is a study about pathways, not about leading with your nose!)

6. *Kinesthetic*—What is it like to move through a crowd to reach a friend? What kind of pathway do you follow on a walk in the woods? Which path would you take to the cafeteria?

7. *Vestibular*—Close your eyes, spin around about 10 times, and try to walk in a straight line (keeping your eyes closed). Close your eyes

FIGURE 12.1   Collecting images and making notes are part of the creative process.

and try to go from your bedroom to your front door, being aware of your path and how you are moving on it. No hands! Devise a movement phrase, such as swing-swing-suspend-drop. Do this phrase with your eyes closed, and allow yourself to move through space. Record the pathways generated by your different momentums.

At this stage of the creative process, you do not need to know exactly what you are going to say. You need only to be open to many different

path and when you will change to a contrasting curve. In a rural setting, you might use the rhythm of wood being chopped or the bark of a dog.

3. *Taste*—Soft foods turn to mush. (How could a pathway be made to dissolve?) Chewy foods require indirect effort. (Maybe a zigzag pattern?) A mouthful of peas pop and explode as they are chewed. A pizza has to be dragged and pulled apart.

aspects of your subject, to discover what you have to offer and what makes you enthusiastic. You are not shopping for an answer; you are shopping for a problem.

You are looking for an aspect of the world you wonder about.

The problem you identify—the focus you select—will be your working focus. This may or may not be your final focus, but it will provide you with a place to start refining your thoughts and drafting what you would like to say. When you have defined at least two interesting problems, you are ready to move on to drafting one or more solutions.

Choosing and Developing Your Focus

"Any great work of art revives and readapts time and space, and the measure of its success is the extent to which it makes you an inhabitant of that world—the extent to which it invites you in and lets you breathe its strange, special air."

Leonard Bernstein (1918-90)

Now we get to the question of form and intent. What, exactly, do you want your dance to *do* to the audience? Or, in the words of Leonard Bernstein, what "strange, special air" shall we breathe? Let us say (and hope) that you have done your research; you have established that there is something in the world that you would like to comment on, and now you must decide: What is the function I would like this piece to serve? What is the focus of this piece? The answers to these questions will lead you to the most appropriate structure of your material.

➤ Is there a *specific message* you would like to deliver?

Drugs are bad for you.

A dog is my best friend.

A bear can kill you.

➤ Is there a *feeling* you would like to deliver?

When I am in love, I feel like I can fly.

I wish I could help.

I will never be picked for anything.

➤ Is there an *opinion* or a *realization* you want to share?

People are like animals in the way they treat each other.

A person can have many friends but still be alone.

Events outside our control shape our lives.

Your choice of structure will depend on the function you would like your piece to serve. The same is true in written and painted communication.

Suppose you have an assignment to read an article and write a paper on it. If the function of your paper is to show the teacher that you read the article, then you rephrase the opening paragraph, pull out a few quotes from the middle, and rephrase the closing paragraphs. You take the information in the article, report it in your own words, and hand it in without adding new information. This level of response does indicate to the teacher that you have read the article. It does not give the teacher any idea about how you felt about the subject, what else you might know about it, or what kinds of experiences you can add to the author's point of view. To go to this second level requires a little more thought and investment on your part. At this deeper level, you would identify relationships that you had discovered in your reading. Perhaps you have found another article on the same subject, and you can make comparisons. Perhaps you have direct experience with the subject, and you include your own observations. The first kind of report is an example of a response on a literal level. The second, in-depth response would be called an interpretive response. There is one more level to go: the evaluative response. At this level, you would quickly establish the author's point of view and then spend most of your time explaining the effect the article had on you. Suppose it is an article about Vietnam veterans returning to their homes. You might be moved to write a poem or a story of your own. You might find a veteran to interview. You might make a collage of images and slogans from that time. In short, you use the information in the assigned article as a jumping-off point for creating your own opinion. You have an original thought, and you make an original statement based on your experience.

These three levels are sometimes described in this way:

1. *Literal*—Restating what is there
2. *Interpretive*—Restating what is there *and* pointing out relationships you observe
3. *Evaluative*—Restating what is there *and* creating new relationships not already suggested

In painting you also find three ways of interpreting a subject. A painter may copy an image as closely as possible (figure 12.2), change some aspect of the subject for a particular effect (figure 12.3), or create a completely new form to go with a unique point of view about the subject (figure 12.4).

None of these three approaches is any better—or even any more sophisticated—than another. The choice of structure depends on what the artist wants to accomplish. The form will follow the function. If a painter wants us to appreciate the beauty of a particular landscape, then a painting that is as accurate as possible will best serve the purpose. If a painter wants to communicate passion or desperation, then the source material may not even be represented! We may only see colors, lines, and unidentified forms.

Now back to dance. What names would you use to describe these three approaches to forming a dance statement? Look at the following list of words, and choose the three words that best describe the solutions one might use to solve a dance problem:

Imitate	Copy	Report	Duplicate
Express	Infer	Interpret	Figure
Invent	Evaluate	Abstract	Imply

Keeping the three levels of solutions in our minds, let's apply them to the creative process. Suppose your class is studying how to use different movement qualities to achieve a desired choreographic effect.

FIGURE 12.2 Here the painting is almost an exact copy of the original image.

FIGURE 12.3 We can still recognize the original subject, but the landscape has been changed for effect.

FIGURE 12.4 The painter has created a new form rather than re-creating an object.

*Your assignment: Create a solo based on
two contrasting movement qualities.*

Where do you begin? With the first stage of creating: collecting. You open yourself up to the world of qualities. You tune in to the qualities of everyday things around you. Trees, rocks, dogs, buzzers, songs, fabrics, candies, crowds, and buildings are all source material for a study on qualities. Rough, heavy, furry, piercing, tender, soft, energizing, jarring, and majestic are all qualities (and there will be thousands more!) that come directly from your life.

Your next step is to make notes. Movements, feelings, thrills, fears, comfort, pain, and sensations are all saved for future reference and development. Now narrow your focus: Identify the most important or most interesting aspects of your exploration of quality.

Let us say you choose the contrast between tight and loose. Who knows why? It might be that the contrast kept jumping out at you during your collection process. Go back through your notes, back through your sense and perception inventories to rediscover all that you already know about these qualities in your life.

Next apply the three levels of solutions discussed previously to determine what you want your study to accomplish. Until you have experimented with all three structures, it will be hard to decide which is most appropriate. Here are some examples of how you might define a tight–loose dance problem within each of the structures:

1. Imitate
   - ➤ I want to present the different tension patterns I have observed in people at school—how they hold themselves, walk, stand, and so on. I will imitate these people and collect them into one dance.
   - ➤ I want to present the importance of balancing tension in the body while practicing technique. I will imitate a dance student who is completely tense and will make my point by letting one body part become loose, then tense again when another body part becomes loose. In the end, I will be a loose heap on the floor.
   - ➤ I want to present the range of going from completely loose to completely tight. I will imitate water gradually freezing solid.

2. Interpret
   - ➤ I want the audience to sense the limitations of tension and relaxation. My dance will be a straight line across the floor, and each step will either be completely tight or completely loose; progress will be difficult.

3. Invent
   - ➤ I want the audience to see that tight does not necessarily mean strong, and loose does not necessarily mean floppy or weak. I will design movements to show that tight, taken to its extreme, becomes weak, and looseness, taken to its extreme, becomes very strong.
   - ➤ I want the audience to draw its own conclusions about these two extremes. I will present a series of duets where one dancer is very loose and the partner is very tight. Then I will reverse their roles and repeat the entire dance.

Refining and Redefining Your Focus

"Creativity is allowing yourself to make mistakes. Art is knowing which ones to keep."

Scott Adams, American cartoonist

The final stage of getting started occurs when you can look at all your exploratory material and say, "This is it!"

"This is the subject I feel most compelled to present."

"This will be a gift from me to the world."

"This is my original thought."

In the reworking stage, be prepared to do some major housecleaning. That is, look at the material you have created and decide if it hangs together as a whole and if aspects need to be modified or eliminated. This stage is a bit like spring cleaning—it's a good time to throw out things you do not use, put a shine on things you truly love, and store things that no longer belong where they have been.

Sometimes the reworking stage loops you right back to the beginning of the creative process; sometimes it requires little more than a few small modifications.

Rehearsing

Rehearsal. It seems that people either love it or hate it. If what you love about the choreographic process is the magic of the discovery of a dance, then repeating and refining the actual steps and sequences can seem mundane. If you are the sort who endures the creative process in order to be able to enjoy working with the completed sequences, then rehearsal is the icing on the cake for you.

In the immortal words of musician and philosopher John Cage, "If you find something boring, do it again." The rehearsal stage can be an exciting and immensely satisfying part of the creative process, and yes, it can be very creative. This is the time when the soul of the performer can expand into the material that has been formed.

Getting started can last as long as time and patience allow. As you become more skilled at collecting and as you develop your powers of perception, you will probably discover that dance subjects and problems come to you often. Having an idea will no longer be a problem, but selecting among many dance-worthy ideas may prove challenging!

In the next chapter we will discuss forming your dance problem into a well-developed piece. When making your choice among your possible focuses, consider a few final questions:

Is your problem a dance problem? In *The Art of Making Dances*, Doris Humphrey opened her chapter on theme with these words:

> No matter what the subject, the first test to apply is one word—action. Does the theme have inherently the motivation for movement? At all times we must be aware that the dance art is unique in its medium of movement (along with mime, a sister art). Unique, too, is its power to evoke emotion within its vocabulary, to arouse the kinetic sense, to speak of the subtleties of the body and soul. But the language has definite limitations and should not be forced to communicate beyond its range, which is, again, that part of experience which can be expressed in physical action. (page 34)

You can also apply the test of description. Can you describe, using words, the substance of your piece? Do you find that your description fails to capture the essence of your focus? In short, if a song, poem, painting, or essay can be used to *fully* capture the essence of your thought, then write a song, poem, essay, or paint the picture. If you are using any of these sources as a springboard for your ideas (as is often the case with music), *be sure* that your work adds to the art that already exists. Acting out the words to a song might be useful if the song is being played for people who speak a different language or for people who are deaf, but in most cases it is not necessary.

There are three important questions to ask yourself before developing your thought into a piece:

1. Have you identified a dance problem?
2. Can the problem be best solved in the medium of dance?
3. Are you bringing new information to light?

If all your answers are positive, move on to the dance!

Think About It

1. What, for you, is the most frustrating part about making dances? What is the most pleasurable part?

2. What would you say is the part of your dance class that you do best? Are you good at balancing? Good at turning? Do you feel your arms move smoothly? Do you do well in movement across the floor? How do you see that (or those) strengths reflected in your composition work?

   a. Now consider the part of class that you dread.

   b. Think about parallels these preferences have in other parts of your life. In general, do you prefer a fast or slow pace? Do you prefer situations where you are in control, or do you prefer situations where there might be surprises?

   c. Think about the type of choreographer you are most inclined to work with.

3. The next time you attend a social function where there is social dancing, stand back and observe the kinds of movement most people are making when they dance. Where did these movements come from? Consider the fact that two years ago people moved in a different way. Imagine how people would have danced on this kind of occasion 50 years ago, or 100 years ago. Why do these dances change, and how do people know to change their dancing? What role does the media play in popularizing a way of dancing? Could you (yes, *you!*) invent a new social dance?

4. On which subjects do you feel qualified to make a statement? For instance, you are probably clear about your dietary preferences. You can talk about what you like and do not like to eat. But what about big ideas? What kind of statement can you make about justice or peace or kindness? Which insights are yours alone?

5. "Originality is nothing but judicious imitation. The most original writers borrowed one from another." Voltaire (1694-1778), French philosopher and writer

   What is "original" about your originality?

6. Does a dance have to "say" something? What do we mean when we say that a work of art has a message or makes a statement?

Your Turn to Dance

Just Say "Yes"

Sometimes the burden of originality locks up rather than releases our best work. In this dance, first make a list of the craziest dance ideas you can imagine. Challenge yourself to keep going farther and farther out, if for no other reason than to sense what kinds of boundaries you operate within. For instance, what about a dance in which the dancers stand on containers of frozen orange juice? Yes, eventually the containers will break and there will be sticky frozen concentrate on the stage. That poses some problems, but who said art had to be convenient?

~ What are two physically crazy ideas for dances?

~ What are two emotionally crazy ideas for dances?

~ What are two of the wildest costume ideas you have?

~ What are two ridiculous props you could work with?

~ What are two wild ways you could include an audience?

Judicious Imitation

Rather than burdening yourself with being original, follow Voltaire's premise (see question 5 on page 168) and use someone else's movement that you feel good about. Boldly steal the clichés you love best and arrange them in a sequence that feels good.

1. What kind of statement have you just made?

2. What can you do to take that statement to the next level of interpretation?

3. If most of the clichés came from one teacher or source, think about how that person would respond to your arrangement. Would they be flattered? Surprised? In your imagination, ask them to tell you what to do next. Do it.

4. Thinking back to number 1 , finish this study by making a second phrase that in some way comments on your first.

13

Composition

Composition is the process of creating form by bringing related pieces together. Purpose guides the process of composition. For instance, a mechanic could take all the pieces of an engine and assemble them either so that they have an interesting look or so that they create a functioning engine. Both compositions are valid; they just have different purposes. We would call one a sculpture and the other an engine, and we would have different expectations for each composition (figure 13.1).

Like a mechanic or a sculptor, a choreographer brings together related movements to compose dances. The form that this composition takes depends on the purpose the choreographer intends to fulfill with the dance. Whether these mechanical, sculptural, or choreographic forms are successful in conveying the ideas that the composers had in mind depends on their understanding of the three primary considerations of composition: function, materials, and audience.

Function

The mechanic trying to rebuild an engine that will power a car safely and quietly has to know how an engine works, the order in which to assemble the pieces, which pieces can be used again, and which need to be replaced. A good mechanic also is sensitive to the interests of the car owner (the audience) and needs to find out whether the owner wants to spend the money necessary to create a new engine or would prefer to get by as cheaply as possible.

FIGURE 13.1 The sculptor has made a new purpose for these cars.

The sculptor using engine parts to create art does not need to know how an engine works, but he does need to decide what the purpose of this collection of engine parts should be. A funny-looking, engine-shaped sculpture? A frightening, engine-like sculpture? A sculpture that bears no resemblance to an engine at all? Once those decisions have been made, the sculptor works with the available pieces in any order, using the pieces he likes and leaving out others. A piece that might normally belong inside a working engine might work better *for an aesthetic purpose* on the outside.

The sculptor's composition also may be guided by the intended audience. Will this be seen from all sides? Will people be able to climb or sit on it? Should it fit in someone's living room? Should it fit on someone's coffee table? If the mechanic regularly ignores the interests of the audience—the customers—he probably will go out of business. On the other hand, the sculptor could choose to be the only audience for the work and simply create for the pleasure of composition.

The choreographer uses life experiences to create dances in much the same way that both the sculptor and the mechanic compose their products. By developing training and skills using the tools of the trade, and by applying the principles of form and function (what it is supposed to look like and what it is supposed to do), the choreographer becomes engaged in the process of composition.

A dance can serve several functions: tell a story, showcase a particular skill, express an insight, entertain, arouse, explore, and an infinite list of others. All are valid functions for a dance.

Materials

The materials of dance must come from the choreographer's experience. Perceptions, sensations, feelings, and ideas all add up to a perspective that one wishes to share with the world. Along with having something to say, a choreographer will benefit from developing physical skills that allow the widest possible range of movement choices. In addition, it helps to have a basic understanding of some of the theories of composition. Just as the mechanic needs to understand the theories associated with the workings of an internal-combustion engine and how its parts are supposed to fit together, likewise a choreographer needs to understand some basic composition theories.

Audience

Finally, the choreographer needs to consider the audience that will, hopefully, be touched by the dance. Like the mechanic and the sculptor, the choreographer needs to be clear about the interests of the audiences likely to view the work. The choreographer also needs to decide how important it is that an audience precisely understands the work. If the mechanic's audiences (the customers) do not understand what they have paid for, they are not likely to come back with their business. If the sculptor's work fails to attract audiences that understand the work, he will not be recognized by enough

people to become famous. Even though he may still enjoy the creative process, he must accept recognition from only a small audience.

If a choreographer's audiences do not understand what the dance is trying to say, they are likely not to seek out the work again. The choreographer may enjoy making dances anyway and be satisfied with pleasing a more select audience (figure 13.2). If an audience has never seen any dance before, its members are likely to react to a very sensual dance the only way they know how—to draw from their experiences of other public performances of sensuality. An attempt at humor may fall flat if the viewers have not seen enough dance to understand why it is humorous. Similarly, an audience, regardless of its sophistication, will quickly become bored by choreography that lacks content, direction, or craft. Stepping back and asking yourself, "What do I want the audience to see?" can be a helpful way to direct your work and evaluate its success.

As we explore the process of composition we will look at principles that apply to creating not only good dances but also effective speeches, insightful lab reports, and compelling writing

FIGURE 13.2 The choreographer may be satisfied with pleasing a more select audience.

assignments. Without going too far out on a limb, you could even make a case for applying the principles of composition to some of your personal relationships. What we are aiming at here is the development of your abilities to communicate your perceptions, sensations, feelings, and ideas as effectively as possible. Whether this means you build engines, sculptures, or dances does not matter. To this process of composition there is an art.

Arranger or Composer?

In the flower-delivery business there are books that customers can look at to choose which arrangement to send to a loved one across the country. You can go into a shop in Cleveland, Ohio, point to a picture, pay the bill, and know that that exact arrangement can and will be created by a florist in Topeka, Kansas. The designs you choose from have proven to be very popular over the years, so the floral industry has standardized them. Is the florist who gets the order in Topeka an arranger or a composer?

A man is cleaning out his basement and decides that in order to make his job more fun, he will nail, glue, tie, or somehow attach together the things that he decides are now junk and make a table. Old boards, pieces of plastic, empty jugs, odd lengths of rope, dried-up paint cans, broken tools, and a dead lawn mower are attached as they are discovered. The product is about 6 feet wide, 4 feet tall, and has very

few level surfaces on which anything could be placed. Nevertheless, he set out to make a table, so that is what he calls his final product. Is this table maker an arranger or a composer?

A dance student has paid close attention in technique class and has learned to execute many exciting movements and sequences presented by the teacher. She is a good dancer because she picks up steps quickly and imitates them very accurately. Making up dances comes fairly easily to her because she has mastered so many exciting sequences; she simply strings several of these together and voilà! A dance! Is this dancer an arranger or a composer?

How do these roles of arranger and composer differ? This question particularly plagues beginning composition students because they tend to feel insecure about their ability to create anything original. As we discussed in the previous chapter, original thought is something that emerges when you trust your own experience and bring some aspect of yourself to your creative efforts. Have you ever found yourself in a creative void, rejecting a movement or sequence because it has been done a million times? Have you ever been frustrated because you felt you are nothing but an arranger and you want to be a composer?

This chapter aims to get you over the chasm between arranging and composing, to provide you with the tools to shape your work and be able to use the materials of dance to compose in a personally satisfying way. These materials are not new; they have been reworked for centuries. It is not your job to discover the elements of dance,

INSIDE INSIGHT

Marcel Duchamp (1887-1968) challenged conventions of the artist as arranger or composer by submitting that mere choice was equivalent to creation. His "ready-made" sculptures were simply common objects placed in an art museum. In 1917 he exhibited a piece titled *Fountain*. The fountain was a porcelain urinal that was placed on a pedestal. It remains one of the more popular exhibits in the Tate Museum in London. If you were to put a frame around a tree and call it "art," would you be a composer or an arranger?

nor is it necessary to reinvent the art form. A composer, sculptor, musician, or mechanic is simply responsible for integrating life experiences through composition.

The Discovery of Form

Someone offers you a hand in greeting, and you respond by extending your own. But in an emergency, when someone extends his hand to you in desperation, you first respond by bracing your entire body and *then* extending your own hand. The form of your response to the world is based on your life experience. Think back to the primary considerations of composition we discussed at the beginning of this chapter—function, materials, audience—and to how those three considerations are automatically part of your ability to respond to both of these situations.

From the Latin *integer,* meaning "whole" or "entire," comes the verb "integrate," which means to form into a whole, to unite with something else. Your ability to integrate is based on your unique way of being "response-able." As a choreographer you feel, perceive, and sense, and in integrating those responses you discover your own form.

Have you ever had an experience you looked back on and thought, "I can't believe I *did* that!" Well, whatever it was that you did was an act of forming, of responding to and integrating your life experience. Your discovery of that form may have filled you with pride, embarrassment, or excitement, but regardless of how you later evaluated your experience, the point is that you *discovered* a form of response, which most likely came to you in that particular moment. That is what the discovery of form in choreography is about. The discovery happens in the doing, in the moment, when you are trying one thing and something else happens that relates to something else, reminds you of something else, or turns into something else.

We began this chapter by identifying three primary considerations in composing—function, materials, and audience. We then pointed out that there is a difference between arranging and composing. Composing requires an active response to your world using what you know and what you suspect. From this active, response-able, integrating position, you will discover a form that makes visual, auditory, and kinesthetic sense. This discovery of form is the beginning of the creative process. From this beginning the choreographer continues by exploring other aspects of the form. What

INSIDE INSIGHT

Wynton Marsalis, a famous musician, once kidded a young student about being "hip," saying that to be hip was to have a limited number of responses to a maximum number of circumstances. He was pointing out that if a musician is going to make music that comes from the soul, he has to dig into the soul to find it.

emerges in that process of exploration are the important ideas or, in the case of dance, the movements that will define it.

Theme

A theme is a composition structure, a unifying idea. Parties have themes: The Roaring '20s, The 1950s. Conventions have themes: The Asphalt Pavers' Annual Meeting, The National Organization of Women Convention. Courses have themes: Contemporary African Politics, Western Attitudes Toward Death and Dying. You know what a theme is, but you may not have considered it in terms of choreography. When we refer to a *theme* in choreography, we mean something more specific than the basic idea, mood, or general heading. In choreography,

A theme is a sequence of movements that are recognizable as a sequence.

In choreography, a theme is not announced as it is with parties, conventions, and courses. The title may hint at the mood (solitude), the period (ragtime), or the content (*Swan Lake*) of the dance, but it does not reveal a theme. The theme is established as the dance unfolds, through repetition and contrast. When the same sequence occurs over and over, the audience members are able to recognize the movement and look at subtle differences in its presentation; they understand what idea is being developed through the dance.

Building on a theme is a bit like displaying a crystal. You choose which facets of the crystal are most interesting to look at or will produce the most interesting patterns in the light. When you hold a crystal up to the light, you make rainbows, dots, sparkles, or streamers. You choose the kind of patterns you want to make by the way you choose to display the crystal.

A dance can be composed of a single repeating sequence that recurs throughout the work, or of several related sequences that show different facets of the same concept. As an example, let us make up a short movement theme:

step close step hop-turn shake

There are five actions. One way you might establish this sequence as a theme is to begin your dance by having five dancers enter solo, each identically performing this sequence. Or you could have each one do the sequence but vary the timing. Or you could have them enter as a group and split off as solos. Or you could . . . . What else could you do to begin a dance by introducing this theme?

What do you remember from earlier chapters that you could apply to this process of thematic development? How about varying aspects of the time, space, or effort involved with the theme? How about using a pattern found in nature, the rhythm of a poem, or the code of your phone number?

As long as the elements of the sequence remain in the same order, you are still working with the same theme. Note also that this theme is defined strictly by a series of movements, not by a mood, a costume, or a particular sentiment. All those aspects of a dance are certainly valid, but they are outside the realm of the theme as it is defined here.

Motif

To return to the dance we have been building, let us suppose the first five dancers make their solo entrances identically repeating the phrase, then a sixth dancer enters by stepping onstage and tossing the head to the side. The other dancers pick up this head toss and use it to signal each other and indicate disapproval and condemnation. The dance ends with one of the dancers being rejected and killed by the others. Not the loveliest scenario, but certainly a valid dance outline. Throughout, the dancers might or might not stick strictly to the movement theme we defined. The important element for the audience to keep track of is the head toss and how it evolves. The head toss is a *motif*.

A motif is the movement (or movements) that an audience will remember as characteristic to your piece: arms together and shoulders up, poking hands, swooping stage crosses, and so on.

A theme is varied. A motif is developed.

Think of someone you know who has a distinctive personal mannerism. Maybe this person overuses the word "like," or frequently says "y'know." Think of someone you know whom you could characterize with a single phrase or gesture. That is a motif.

Now think of someone you know who has a habit that you could adopt to characterize this person. Maybe she is usually late and wastes a lot of time making excuses. Maybe she is sensitive to dirt and regularly washes, fusses, and cleans up before sitting down. If there is a pattern of behavior that would characterize her, that pattern would better be referred to as a theme than a motif.

The only reason to think about the difference between a theme and a motif is that it can be helpful to know what you expect the audience to pick up so that they understand your work. The more you can identify what is important, the easier it will be for an audience to understand.

Principles of Composition

There are seven principles of composition that guide the creation of a dance. But remember, these same principles are going to apply to creating other kinds of compositions too. Various critics and art reviewers may compose their lists differently, but the following seven principles will serve as a useful reference:

1. Contrast
2. Repetition
3. Transition
4. Variation
5. Development
6. Climax
7. Resolution

Contrast

"juxtaposition of . . . color, tone, or emotion in a work of art"

Merriam Webster's Collegiate Dictionary, Eleventh Edition

Contrast is a diversity of color, emotion, or tone. It is the green of the leaves that makes the yellow of the daffodil especially bright. Contrast intensifies experiences.

In order to keep your dance from becoming monotonous, the audience needs a break—in speed of the movement, intensity, level, direction (or draw), and quality. Have you ever had a teacher who spoke in a monotone? If so, you may remember the difficulty you had staying awake in that class. The same thing goes for dances. Without the principle of contrast, your work will put your audience to sleep.

Sharp movements seem sharper when juxtaposed with soft or sustained movements.

INSIDE INSIGHT

Contrast can be a good starting place if you are stuck for a way to begin a composition assignment. Pick any set of opposites to use as a basis for improvisation and you will probably discover some intersting material. Here is a preliminary list:

open–close
high–low
fast–slow
here–there
fight–flight
in–out
hard–soft
hot–cold
horizontal–vertical

Small gestures become more intimate when contrasted with large movements. Leaps seem even higher when they begin or end at a low level. Explore this principle of contrast for yourself by trying an experiment.

Try This Experiment

Think of a color and a simple, repeating movement that you can do in association with that color. Find two other movements that occur on different levels and are also associated with that color. Perform them in a series. (If you are sitting in a library and do not want to risk being thrown out for dancing in the stacks, you can still experiment with this by using only your hands!) Call that series A.

To make series B, go through the same process but with a different color, one that most radically contrasts with your first choice. Find a simple, repeating movement, then add two other related movements to this B sequence. Perform your contrasting statements as A B A. How does the feel of your composition change if you rearrange the sequence as A1 B1 A2 B2 A3 B3? Which do you prefer?

Did you think about function and audience in your experiment? As simple as these compositions are, what might be the function of each? (What does each say?) Could you vary that function by varying the time, space, or effort involved? What would the members of an audience need to see to make that contrast as effective as possible? Would they need to be very close? Would they need to be able to see your face? How would the work change if it were performed on a football field? If performed by 30 people at the same time? Contrasts can evolve. They can involve shading a movement or a phrase just enough so that there is a perceptible difference from the previous effort or intention. Black-and-white contrasts can be effective, and so can black, gray, and white. There is neither a formula nor a limit to one's method of creating contrast.

Let us go back to the experiment and rework your A phrase so that all three parts evolve rather than slam into your B phrase. Instead of making all three A moves as hard as possible

and all three B moves as soft as possible, find a way to go from hard to soft more gradually so that the contrast is still there but is more subtle. Reevaluate your work. Does one method of contrast make more sense than the other? Does another method now occur to you?

Repetition

"You got to give your audience something to hang onto."

John Coltrane

Your movement idea can be developed, varied, reversed, slowed down, sped up, stood on its head, and completely distorted, but as long as the members of the audience have some clue about what you, the choreographer, have identified as important, they will be able to sense what your work is about. One way to emphasize the things that are important is to repeat them. By repeating a sequence, a phrase, a floor pattern, or even one simple gesture, you give the audience clues to what ties your dance together. Let us look at how *repetition* is used to assist audiences of other presentations.

The standard three-part recipe for speech writing is (1) tell your listeners what you are going to say, (2) say what you are going to say, and (3) tell them what you just said. Listen for this formula next time you attend a speech or a lecture.

In pop music the chorus provides the repetition that pulls the song together. If it is a message song, the message is usually written into the part that gets repeated. If it is a love song, the lyrics that are repeated in the chorus are usually the from-the-heart part of the song. In symphonic music, a theme is created around which the whole symphony is built. To keep the different parts related, the composer will often repeat sections of the theme throughout the full-length work.

Look for repetition in architecture. A shape or design from the outside may be repeated inside as a way of tying the look of the building together. Repetition can be used to create a sense of stability and harmony.

In dance the choreographer must strike a delicate balance between providing enough

INSIDE INSIGHT

Repetition is another good starting place if you are stuck for a way to get going on a composition. It is also a good device to use when feeling pressured to be inventive. By limiting your options for invention, you are likely to discover some of the nuances of a phrase, theme, or motif that might have escaped you if you had moved on to new material. Here are a few structures for repetition that you may find useful:

~ Repeat in a different body part.

~ Repeat facing in a different direction.

~ Repeat at a different speed.

~ Repeat at a different level.

~ Repeat with different force.

~ Repeat either accelerating or decelerating.

INSIDE INSIGHT

Laura Dean (1945-) is a choreographer known for her use of geometric patterns, driving rhythms, spinning, and repetition. But according to Dean, there is no such thing as repetition. Is this a variation on the ancient observation "You can't put your toe in the same river twice"?

repetition so that it is clear what is going on and providing enough contrast so that the audience does not become bored. As long as you do not beat a repetition to death, it can actually be a comfort to the audience to see something familiar.

How much repetition is enough? How much is too much? Maybe you know people who tell you that they love you. If they say it too often, the phrase loses its power and starts to sound like "Have a nice day." But if they hardly *ever* say "I love you" and cannot seem to say it when it is most important to you, then you might start to wonder if they really *do* love you. "And if they do," you might wonder, "why is it so hard to tell me?" As you improve in the craft of relating your ideas to other people, you will develop your own sense of how much repetition is appropriate for your statements. This

sense is applicable to dance, to other artistic pursuits, and to living.

Transition

"You can't get there from here."

Old Minnesota saying

Another saying often heard in dance and composition classes is that the real dance occurs not in the events (the dazzling leaps or the tricks), but rather *between* the events of choreography. It is easy to create a string of events or activities and move from one to the other as if you become invisible between these photo opportunities. In fact, the choreography will hang together only if the performance is sustained throughout—if the transitional movements are both important and inevitable. Just as our language is composed of nouns, verbs, adjectives, adverbs, and articles, so are dances composed of different parts that contribute to the sense of the movement. We might get the basic drift of thought from a collection of words such as

Wind Blows Tree Roots Falls Ground,

but a more complete thought includes a few transitional words:

When Wind Blows Tree Without Roots Falls Ground.

A graceful sentence includes even more transitional words as well as some punctuation that tells the reader when and how to pause:

When a wind blows, a tree without roots falls to the ground.

Try This Experiment

Try this experiment to get a sense of the role *transition* plays in choreography. From whatever position you are in right now as you read, prepare yourself *without moving* to stand up. Do not actually change positions yet, just prepare to make this change. When you are ready, go from your reading position to a standing position in one move, simply and directly—no bracing, hauling, or pausing allowed. When you have arrived at your standing position, prepare to go directly to your former reading position again, in one move. Try these exercises without transitions now.

Modify your reading position so that it is a contained shape. You might want to wrap your arms and draw up your knees. Whatever shape you create, get ready to move to that shape from a more relaxed position. Go.

Now get on your feet and invent a movement that goes into the air, such as a jump, turn, or hop into a designed standing shape. Now, go back to your relaxed reading position and repeat these activities in this order:

1. Relaxed reading pose
2. Contained shape
3. Movement in the air
4. Relaxed reading pose

Finally, see if you can feel a difference in the performance and the statement it makes by finding a way to connect all four events. If not, repeat the sequence and take more time between events—so that they are absolutely unrelated to each other—and work one last time through your sequence without stopping. You will start to feel what this transition business is all about!

By applying what you know about contrast and repetition, you could even build on these four activities and shapes and make a more elaborate statement, could you not?

In the experiment you just completed, you were asked to focus on the idea of making transitions from one shape or activity to another while moving almost continuously, so that one thing flowed into or was driven by another. Let us not overlook the fact that stillness can also be a useful tool for transition. Stillness is its own kind of action. There is a difference between active stillness and careless stillness, and as a choreographer you would need to be sure that the movement you create has a history—that it comes from some source inside or outside the dancer.

Moving from stillness can be a very useful tool for getting over choreographic blocks. As we said in chapter 1, the living body is never completely still. There is always movement within, and that inner movement can be a terrific source of inspiration if one is willing to be still long enough to be inspired.

Save this next experiment for a time and place where you have undisturbed privacy. Your teacher may choose to talk you through this sequence in class. If not, you might want to take turns with a friend so that each of you can be guided through the experiment without having to stop and read each step for yourself. It works best starting in a standing position, or at least a position from which you can move easily. If you start in a prone position, it tends to be more difficult to maintain the active stillness and easier to just take a nap.

Try This Experiment

Stand in a relaxed position, arms by your sides, knees easy, belly soft, and eyes relaxed and closed. Tune in to the circulation of blood through your body, the pull of gravity on your body, and the ever-so-slight compensations of balance you need to make on this spinning earth.

From this active stillness pay attention to your breathing. Try not to interfere with the pattern of your breathing; simply observe it as a pattern. As you inhale, your chest and belly expand, and, as you exhale, they collapse. Allow yourself to rest and be still between breaths.

Try expanding and softening the back on your next inhalation and exhalation. Repeat this expansion as long as it interests you. Try expanding and softening your left side on your next inhalation and exhalation. Repeat this expansion as long as it interests you. Explore expanding and softening different body parts of your choosing as you inhale and exhale. Repeat them as long as they interest you, and remember to honor the stillness between breaths.

Without inventing, allow some part of this process of inhaling and exhaling to become more exaggerated. This is the tricky part. The tendency is to want to make something happen or do something interesting. Resist this urge to place an activity on an already active body; instead, allow the movement to emerge from the inside. Eventually, you may find yourself moving very vigorously. Keep relating to your breath as you literally re-inspire your movement. You may find that you are actively still for long periods. Again, keep relating to your breath pattern as you explore the subtleties of minimal movement.

You will learn from experimenting with active stillness that movement is always occurring, whether or not it is outwardly visible, and that your body, if you pay attention, will guide you transitionally from what you may have thought was merely one movement to the next.

According to Martha Graham, "All action is born of necessity." Whether you choose to choreograph transitions that show a violent cause and effect, a seamless flow, or no apparent relationship at all, the way you deal with transition as a principle of composition will affect your work.

Variation

"The most deeply instinctual aesthetic form is the A B A: the beginning, middle, and end. It is the universal pattern of life itself: We are born, we live, we return to the unknown."

Louis Horst, *Modern Dance Forms*

In choreography the process of developing form is called *theme and variation*. You start with a theme, and you work from that by making one or several variations that highlight different facets of the theme. In the end, you have a nice, long dance in which many interesting things have happened. We hope. But we can do better than hope by looking at some options for creating variations that will be a gift to watch.

Variations of movement themes can consist of

1. the statement of the theme, followed by a contrast: A B;

2. theme, variation, and repetition of original theme: A B A;

3. theme, contrasting variation, repetition of theme, a second contrasting variation, and theme again: A B A C A (this is called *rondo form*); and

4. theme, variation, another variation, another, and so on: A A1 A2 A3.

You are still working with a theme as long as its elements remain in the same order (or sequence). Let us look at these variations one by one.

A B Variation

This is the simplest form of all. A B variation is the on-the-other-hand form where you set up one theme and then present a contrast. Light and dark. Open and closed. Earth and sky. Love and hate.

With A B variation you generally use B to highlight some aspect of A, and that highlight provides the statement that the dance makes. The song "America the Beautiful" is an example of this kind of variation. The "Oh beautiful . . ." part is the A and "America, America, God shed His grace on thee . . ." is the B variation, differing in melodic theme from the first half.

A B A Variation

The children's song "Three Blind Mice" is a good example of A B A variation. The melody is established and repeated twice, then transposed up four notes and repeated twice more. Then the "They all ran after the farmer's wife" part provides a contrast to the original theme. This variation gets repeated three times, and the song concludes with a repetition of the A theme (with the return of the words "three blind mice"). Much popular music uses this kind of variation. The melody is introduced, followed by a bridge or a B melody, and the song returns to the A melody to conclude.

A B A is a very popular form that satisfies an instinctive sense of symmetry; it's a cycle that returns to its own beginning. This kind of symmetry can be reassuring, but it can also be boring if inappropriately applied. If you are tempted to conclude as you have begun, check to make sure that something has happened in the meantime!

Suppose you do not have a narrative or dramatic theme you want to work with, but rather an abstract theme created from a string of movement words. Suppose your sequence is:

run turn drop leap

Your dance might open with a combination of steps arranged in that sequence. Section A might be about all the ways that the dancers can run, turn, drop, and leap. Let us say that the music is bright, light, and sunny. Then comes section B, which offers a contrast to A. Let us say that the dancers still try to run, turn, drop, and leap, but the music for this section is slow, somber, and somewhat dark. The music then returns to the A theme and so does the choreography, although not exactly; there are glimpses of the slow, somber, or shadowy aspects that were revealed in section B. A: introduce, B: develop, A: recapitulate.

Here's another scenario. Your dance might open with lots of running followed by lots of turning, then lots of dropping, and, finally,

you guessed it, lots of leaping. End of section 1. Section 2 might feature a solo incorporating all the ways you could run. Section 3 might feature another dancer who explores only turning. Thus, the recapitulation section calls into focus the importance of turning.

A B A C A D—Rondo Form

The rondo is a very old musical form dating back at least to 15th-century music. In this form the theme is stated followed by some contrast or digression, after which the theme is restated and yet another contrast or digression is offered. This process makes up the piece.

In dance, things work the same way. Let us take the sequence we worked with previously as our theme and suppose that the dancers begin with a sophisticated version of run, turn, drop, and leap, followed by a phrase that includes only running, and after which we see the run-turn-drop-leap sequence repeated. What might be a good contrast or digression around which to build the C variation?

A A1 A2 A3

The last sectional form in our list of strategies for variations is the add-in form in which the original theme is still perceptible but with each new variation the dance moves on, never to return to the original form. This is a cumulative, evolutionary form.

These forms are intended to be used as guides to help you structure your variations, not as rigid molds into which you pour your dances. These forms are also useful to bear in mind when watching other people's choreography. Looking for the ways in which material is introduced and reintroduced gives you a sense of what the choreographer feels is important in the dance.

Development

"A journey that begins with a question raised through disbelief, fueled by faith, navigated by instinct, and in search of the truth."

Nomad

Consider this story line: She was attracted to him, but he was involved with cars and did not know she was alive. He becomes attracted to her, but she has lost interest. Finally, they both like each other. They have an argument, and they both hate each other. They get back together. Love-hate, love-hate, love-hate. Then she is abducted by aliens from another galaxy; he realizes he liked racing cars better than girls anyway. The end.

Floppy, loose, lazy. Alert, upright, attentive. Quick, light, whimsical. Tired, strained, compulsive. Floppy, loose, exhausted. No story line. The end. No story, but through using this development of qualities, a life experience is suggested without being detailed, allowing the audience to read this progression in their own way.

Finally, a valid answer to the question "What happens?" may well be "Nothing." Should this be the choreographer's response, then even that nothingness will have its own significance. In the work of Merce Cunningham, for instance, one might observe that nothing happens; however, if that is your observation you are, at the very least, confronting your own expectations about what might have happened! So, is it then true that "nothing happened"? What happens in many nonliteral modern or ballet performances may be equally hard to sum up.

It is your responsibility as a choreographer to identify what the news of a dance is, though often that can be identified only *after* the dance has been choreographed, when you can step back and see what mystery has been revealed to you. Then, once you have a sense of what you've got, you can go back and make modifications so that the pace of the development supports the news of the dance.

Climax

"It has an outcome that though unforeseen was predestined from the first image of the original mood—and indeed from the very mood."
Robert Frost, *The Figure a Poem Makes*

The climax of a dance is basically the same as the climax in a story, except that in a story a chronology of events culminates and in a dance an apex of energy is reached. If the dance tells a story then, most likely, a problem comes to a head. If the dance does not tell a story, then the dancers' efforts most likely carry them to some point of no return. Often, the music assists both the choreographer and the audience in determining this point of evolution. Sometimes there is a dramatic element that lets us know. Choreographic tools discussed in the section on variation give us further clues almost intuitively, as Horst suggests. If the theme has been well established and the development is intelligible, the audience can often sense the return of the A, note the changes that have occurred, and sense the head toward home. Nonliteral dance climaxes are often accomplished by embellishing the theme or complicating the tasks of the dancers

---

INSIDE INSIGHT

Development is guided by the methods of variation you use, but at the beginning stages some strategies for exploring different kinds of development might help direct the work. Here are a few structures for development that you may find useful:

~ Find a way to lose control at some point.

~ Accelerate.

~ Intensify in time, space, or effort.

~ Create an inner monologue (that is, talk to yourself as you work).

~ Talk to an invisible person as you work, describing what you are doing and why.

~ Move continuously for a set period of time, 60 seconds to start with, increasing to three minutes.

Do not allow yourself to settle on one spot at any time. Move continuously for a set period, and do not allow yourself to move from one spot at any time.

so that the piece practically explodes. Other methods of creating more subtle explosions might be to establish constraints that force the dance to finally evolve or collapse.

Resolution

"Begin at the beginning . . . and go on till you come to the end:
then stop."

Lewis Carroll, *Alice's Adventures in Wonderland*

Doris Humphrey (1895-1958) recommended establishing a beginning *and an end* to a dance before proceeding with the development. There is value in clarifying one's direction or focus at some point in the creative process. At our stage of choreographic investigation, however, I would recommend discovering the resolution to your work by using feedback from the three modes of perception.

➤ What do you want your final image to look like? Fleeting? Dying? Resting? Invigorated? Elated? Contorted?

➤ What do you want your final image to sound like? Heavy? Weightless? Shifty? Slippery?

➤ What do you feel, and what kinesthetic effect would you like your audience to have, in resolution of your efforts? Nervous? Thrilled? Pained? At ease?

The seven principles of composition must not be confused with a flowchart of creation. In real life, each is considered and reconsidered as the work assumes a life of its own. When establishing contrast, you may discover that repetition needs to be more obvious or more subtle. Thoughtful attention to transition may take you into a new variation, and suddenly the development you had so neatly anticipated is no longer relevant! Your climax may come as you speed up or slow down. Your climax and resolution may be simultaneous. You may not have a resolution. These are elements that *probably* exist in a piece that has a clear focus and makes a moving (though not necessarily explicable) impact on the audience. These principles may be a useful resource if you suspect that your work is not accomplishing what you had hoped. Consider them references more than doctrines.

How to Make a Dance

Wouldn't it be nice if the directions for dance-making were simple enough to condense into a little booklet so that all you had to do was flip through, follow the instructions, and voilà! Well, maybe it would not be so great after all. Maybe all dances would look the same or so similar that if you have seen one dance, you have seen them all. Maybe it is just as well that composing a dance still requires a lot of experimentation, discovery, and trial and error. And maybe it is just as well that not everyone agrees on what makes a good dance and what makes a not-so-good dance. Tastes, styles, and designs of any art evolve to suit the needs of the culture they serve. Dance tastes, styles, and designs hopefully evolve along with the culture they serve.

Dance composition is an ongoing process. Even supposedly finished work often changes as new dancers learn old roles, a dance is adapted to a new space, or a slight variation is suggested that might improve the work. In fact, it has been said that one can never see the same dance twice. Every performance creates magic, and no one can guarantee what kind of magic that will be until the dance is over.

Composition—whether dance, literature, music, sculpture, or even engine rebuilding—has moments of magic for the creator, moments when the pieces of the puzzle suddenly fit. The frequency of these moments depends on all of the things we have considered in this chapter: the primary considerations of function, materials, and audience (Why? How? For whom?); the investment of the composer, and her willingness to do the exploratory work necessary to go beyond simply rearranging what has already been done, to risk making a personal leap of faith into composing; the ability to respond to the world and integrate new information so that the composition's perspective is a creative unity; and the use of the principles of composition in expanding the work beyond simply being personal into a gift that makes sense.

How to make a dance? Begin!

Think About It

1. What is the function of the opening number that the contestants at the Miss America Pageant learn and perform? If you were hired to create that dance, how would you consider function, materials, and audience when composing it?

2. Marcel Duchamps was an artist who submitted a urinal to a museum as a piece of sculpture. It was displayed as sculpture, not as a functioning toilet. An artist in New York City put a picture frame around some exposed pipes in her apartment and signed the wall in the right-hand corner of the framed area. In these two cases, how do function, materials, and audience relate to composition? Do you think these artists can be credited with composition? If a dancer takes steps he has learned in class and uses them in a dance, has he composed a dance?

3. How are function, materials, and audience part of your work in class? That is, would you handle an assignment differently if you were going to show your work to a church group? Or the entire student body? Or a local TV news reporter? Or a close friend? How are you influenced by the fact that your work is graded rather than merely applauded?

4. How would you describe the difference between a composition and an arrangement? Do you think the creative process involved with each one is different? How important is tradition to either process? Under which circumstances would one approach be preferable to the other? Which do you find easier as a creative process? How would you distinguish between composition and arrangement in music? In writing reports?

5. A composer is responsible for integrating life experience through composition. Think of one experience you had today that could be developed into a dance composition. Think of one experience you had today that could be developed into a composition in another medium (music, sculpture, literature, or video).

6. Is form preferable to chaos? How? Why?

7. How do the principles of composition apply to the writing of a lab report? How might they be applied to make a repetitive job more interesting? How might they be applied to a friendship or a relationship?

Your Turn to Dance

Pretty Dance

What do you think is pretty movement? What do you think are pretty patterns? What part of "pretty" has to do with familiarity?

In this composition, you will explore the abstract notion of prettiness and create a dance with

1. attention to the principles of composition,
2. a thesis (a point of view introduced and developed in the work), and
3. a conclusion.

You will need to confront and synthesize several important concepts that have been presented in this book, so as you create your composition, keep a running journal of the concepts you encounter. For instance, in chapter 1 the idea of culturally patterned sequences was introduced as a precondition of dance as an art form. What is the common ground shared by a culturally patterned sequence and something you identify as pretty? Can a movement be both a cliché and pretty? In that journal also keep track of how your concepts of "pretty" change as you do your research. Oh, right! There's another important concept: the six stages of the creative process. As these concepts come to you, go back and reread the text. You'll be amazed by how much you can get out of it the second time.

What If

In this composition, you will work simply with shapes and patterns and forms, avoiding any narrative or literal through-line. As you did previously, you will

1. attend to the principles of composition,
2. define a thesis (what if . . . ?), and
3. offer a conclusion or perspective.

Your thesis may be a purely physical one, such as falling and getting up; a geometric one, such as circling; a time-based one, such as a polyrhythmic structure (8-5-6-8-5-6); or a kind of effort study. If you commit to this structure and find you have discovered a narrative, try to return to the original thesis and continue exploring new solutions. You will need to confront and synthesize several important concepts that have been presented in this book so, as you create your composition, keep a running journal of the concepts you encounter.

Is This Dance Good?

$\mathcal{E}$ ager to expose students to the wonderful world of modern dance, a dance teacher arranged to have several first-year students attend a concert of a well-known New York dance company appearing in a nearby town. The lights dimmed and the first piece began. It was an abstract work with no specific plot or message. The set was nonexistent, and the dancers wore plain dark leotards. The dancers were leaping and balancing, apparently according to plan, but about 15 minutes into the piece, one of the students tapped the teacher on the shoulder and whispered cautiously, "Excuse me, but is this a good dance?"

Have you ever found yourself wondering the same thing as you watch the work of your peers or professional dancers (figure 14.1)? Have you ever wondered how to judge the merit of your creative endeavors? This chapter will give you the tools needed to help you identify the goals of a dance so that you will be in a better position to evaluate its success in a constructive and supportive framework. In other chapters we have discussed similarities between the creative processes in dance and other activities. In the same way, the evaluation process that we pursue here will help develop skills for evaluating other creative activities.

FIGURE 14.1   *The Nutcracker* has been produced millions of times by both amateur and professional companies. Audiences choose which performance they attend for various reasons.

The Creative Act

The creative act is motivated from many different sources. Some people create to satisfy their own curiosity, gain notoriety, solve problems, or prompt questions. Whatever the source, there is ultimately an idea or a product that its creator offers to the world—the result of that person's best effort at synthesizing experiences, perceptions, sensations, and personal wisdom, all formed to be shared as a gift. A 10-year-old's piano rendition of "Frère Jacques" is as much a gift to the world as the PhD's cancer research paper. A beginning dance student's 60-second study is as much a gift to the world as the evening-length work of an internationally renowned choreographer. Whether evaluating your own or others' efforts, it is important to bear in mind that the product of a creative effort is an offering that has value to its creator.

Evaluating Your Own Work

If you are evaluating your work, you will want to consider all the ways that it has value for you. What gift have you made to yourself in this creative process? When answering this question, consider the physical, social, and emotional aspects of personal growth.

➤ Through this creative process have you discovered new physical capabilities?

➤ Through this creative process have you developed any new insights about yourself as

INSIDE INSIGHT

Dr. Rollo May identifies four kinds of courage in his book, *The Courage to Create* (New York: Norton, 1975): *physical courage*, which he hopes will eventually evolve from its frontier mythology to the cultivation of sensitivity; *moral courage*, which arises out of compassion; *social courage*, the capacity to risk one's self in the hope of achieving meaningful intimacy; and *creative courage*, which he feels is the most important of all. It is the willingness to struggle to bring into existence new kinds of being that give harmony and integration. When evaluating your own and the work of others keep that aspect of courage in mind.

a social being? New insights about other people? About the way the world works?

➤ Through this creative process have you grown emotionally? Have you stretched yourself through risk-taking? Have you persevered through frustration?

➤ Through this creative process what gift have you made to the world? Is your personal development gift enough, or do you have another agenda for being an effective and vital part of the planet?

Evaluating the Work of Others

If you are evaluating the work of others, you will want to be clear about the purpose of your evaluation. In other words, for whose benefit is it? Are you describing the work for the benefit of someone who missed the performance? Are you placing the work in a social or historical context for someone who did not understand it? Are you attempting to provide helpful feedback for the choreographer? Are you using the work as a soapbox to discuss your own ideas or aesthetics?

When evaluating someone else's work, you are going through a process of critical thinking that enables you to determine the value of that work in a particular context. If your goal is to place the work in the context of your life experience, then it is appropriate to respond personally and consider the ways in which you were affected by the piece, the things you liked or did not like, what you would have done differently, what you admired, and so on. This kind of evaluation is self-serving.

Another kind of evaluation serves the work's creator. If your goal is to help the creator determine the value of the work, then your own agenda is less relevant (if at all). Your task is to help the creator by entertaining specific questions about the work and asking neutral, nonjudgmental questions of the artist. This process works best if the creator has specific questions to which you, the critic, can respond. Questions such as "Did you think it was too boring?" invite the critic to judge the piece rather than assist in its evaluation. A better question might

be "Was there too much repetition in the first section?" This invites a discussion of the value of the repetition rather than one person's definition of what is boring.

A third kind of evaluation assesses the value of the work in social or historical contexts. A reporter does this when describing the work for a public who did not attend. A description of the work accompanies an informal or formal judgment that supposedly enables the readers to assume the value this piece would have had in their lives had they been present.

There are three focuses in an evaluation:

1. Evaluation can be self-serving, enabling the critic to find the value of the work in the context of her life.

2. Evaluation can be creator-serving, where the critic's function is to assist the creator in determining which aspects of the piece have value for the creator.

3. Evaluation can be public-serving, enabling the public—those who did not witness the actual performance—to suppose what value the piece would have had in their lives had they been present.

Words of Criticism

We have tossed around several words that belong in the realm of criticism without clarifying some of their applications. Let us look at the language of criticism. Begin with the critic. Giving criticism has come to mean describing all that is wrong with something, but that is not using the word with complete accuracy. The root of "criticism" obviously comes from "critic," derived from the Greek *kritikos*, meaning "able to discern or judge." The critic is someone who expresses a reasoned opinion on any matter involving a judgment of value, truth, or righteousness; the opinion may also be an appreciation of the work's beauty, technique, or interpretation (figure 14.2).

Value. Truth. Righteousness. Beauty. Those are some fairly broad concepts on which to offer a reasoned opinion. Who *is* entitled to offer such opinions? Are you? Are your friends? Are your classmates? Are your teachers? And who gets to decide what is a reasoned opinion? We

FIGURE 14.2   Criticism can make a person feel vulnerable; be kind and choose your words carefully.

based on personal experience or feelings, as in "I think the costume is ugly." These two perspectives can easily become muddled in the arena of criticism.

Other words that often come up in critical discussions have vastly different meanings for different people and are, therefore, dangerous to interject unless you know that your value system and aesthetics are the same as those of your audience. Consider beauty. What are *your* criteria for beauty? To some, a trimmed-out Harley Davidson is a thing of beauty; to others it is just a motorcycle. To some, purple-dyed, spiked hair is a beautiful style; to others it is an aberration.

"Context" is another all-important word. The way you choose to address your criticism (as self-serving, artist-serving, or public-serving) will indicate the context of your remarks. Honest, self-serving criticism includes a lot of ownership of the opinions, as in, "I thought it looked like a swamp of alligators," or "I found it hard to look at the color red for so long." These personal statements remind the listener that the criticism being expressed relates directly and subjectively to the life and experience of the speaker. With self-serving criticism, the speaker is obliged only to share personal experience of the work, not to second-guess the intentions of the choreographer or the relation of the work to other dances.

Criticism made in the context of serving the artist obliges the critic to consider the intentions of the artist and personally respond to the effectiveness with which those intentions were revealed. As we shall discuss, if the artist does not invite these responses or cannot be clear about the intentions of the piece, then the criticism ceases to be artist-serving and reverts to being self-serving.

Criticism made in the context of serving the public is the most suspicious of all; the critic's personal preferences are quite likely to be woven into the evaluation, but they may be presented as fact rather than opinion. To be sure, there are many who are able to be objective, place their remarks in the frame of history, and accurately describe a piece so that those who missed the performance would have a sense of what they had missed. Critics who are good at composing this kind of evaluation

have also used the word "evaluate" in place of "criticize." How would you say these two words differ?

"Consider" is another word we have used in almost the same way as "criticize." Do these terms have different connotations? Are they interchangeable? Do they each imply a different commitment to the judgment being offered? A different breadth of experience or level of objectivity?

What about "objective" and "subjective"? Are you clear on the difference between them? Objective assessments are based on impersonal observation, as in "The costume was green, yellow, and orange." Objective criticism is impartial, without the interference of personal taste or judgment. Subjective assessments are

are able to create a context in which the value of a piece can be assessed.

Recognizing, Interpreting, and Creating Relevance

If your evaluation is self-serving, then it will focus on the value the dance had in the context of your life and experiences. The process of determining this value involves recognizing, interpreting, or creating some relevance between your experiences and the dance you have seen. It is not necessary that you correctly guess the intentions of the choreographer in order to do so. It is only necessary that you consider the work's images and ideas in the context of your life.

For instance, let us suppose that you have attended a performance of *The Nutcracker.* Let us further suppose that the reason you attended is not out of some deep love for the music or the ballet itself but to support a friend who was in the performance. The value you find in this dance experience may have less to do with the aesthetics of ballet and more to do with admiring your graceful friend. Finding a value for the dance in the context of your life and experiences, you might reflect on your friend's attraction to dance or level of physical fitness relative to your own. It may be that what impresses you most about the production is not the dancing itself but the elaborate sets and costumes. What value could such spectacle have in your life? If, however, your evaluation is not self-serving, that is, if your motivation is to assist the creator or report on the work for the benefit of others, then you must consider the choreographer's intention. You can assume that she has contemplated what the function of the piece should be, which materials would be best to work with, and who the target audience would be (figure 14.3).

Function

Some questions to consider relative to function include:

➤ What was the driving force that created this piece?

➤ What was the vision being pursued?

➤ What was the primary purpose? To instruct? To explore? To expose? To inspire? To entertain?

FIGURE 14.3   A well-constructed dance leaves the audience with images that resonate weeks after the performance.

INSIDE INSIGHT
To make a statement that a thing is beautiful or ugly, you need to establish some context for your observation. Otherwise, your observation, however valid, will be meaningless. As you become more adept at criticizing your own work and the work of others, you will probably discover that your vocabulary for description expands considerably. Early efforts to communicate critically usually involve words such as "nice," "funny," "pretty," and other adjectives, which do more to establish the context of a piece in the viewer's experience than to address the piece directly and objectively.

Let us look at evaluating function in your own work and in the work of others.

In the process of creating a piece one does not necessarily know what its function will be. In fact, as we discussed in the chapter on composition, it is quite likely that the original impetus will be substantially modified by the time you have finished your improvisational research.

Let us suppose you have been given an assignment to choreograph a study based on the contrast between open and closed. In this case, the driving force to create the piece is grade motivated. However, in the course of experimenting with open and closed shapes and movements you discover that what interests you is your personal discovery that closed shapes and movements make you feel safe, while open shapes and movements make you feel vulnerable. As you continue to explore being safe and being vulnerable, the driving force changes from just wanting to get a good grade to wanting to understand and to express something that has meaning for you. You now have a vision, and the piece has a purpose.

By the time you're ready to polish the work, it should be possible for you, the creator, to assess what has been made and to direct the work toward a coherent function. After all, when you ultimately present your work you will be asking your audience to find a context for your ideas in their own lives, so it does behoove you to at least have a point of view.

Ideally, when you present your work you should be able to articulate the function the piece has for you. The value of this piece—its function in your life—may pertain to physical, emotional, or social interests you wish to explore.

When you can be clear about the function you wish your piece to serve, you can be equally clear about the kind of criticism that you are most interested in receiving. If the function was to stretch yourself technically by trying to work at a speed that was uncommon for you, you might be interested in hearing from people who could evaluate your success based on a perspective that includes your earlier work. You might be interested in knowing if your audience found your movement choices interesting, attractive, compelling, or otherwise worth watching.

If the function of your piece was to arouse empathy, you might be curious to know whether anyone was moved emotionally by your work. Having specific questions will help your critics respond with information that is useful to you. For example, asking, "Did you like it?" will probably not generate feedback that is specific enough to help you to make improvements. However, asking, "Which images were particularly strong?" or "Which adjectives or adverbs would you use to describe the piece?" will give you responses that help you to gauge how well the work served the function you intended.

If the function of your piece was to educate or testify, you might not care at all about people's comments on the technical aspects of the work; you might be interested only in whether they were persuaded to adopt your point of view.

When evaluating your own work, start by examining its function. Look at both the product and the process. "Is this a good dance?" is a question you will have answered when you have found the value that the dance has in your life.

If you are evaluating the function of someone else's work, you will need to be aware of who is being served by your evaluation. If the evaluation is for your own benefit, it will be up to you to find a function that the piece can serve in your experience. Sometimes this is easy; sometimes it takes generous thought.

Materials

We said in the previous chapter that the materials for a dance come from the choreographer's experiences. When criticizing a dance—your own or someone else's—you need to consider what experiences this person might or might not have to offer.

Beginning composition students are often extraordinarily inventive because their (usually limited) exposure to dance leaves them little to compare with their own work. They often solve problems in a simple, direct, and unpretentious way because they are not trying to duplicate someone else's work. The person criticizing a beginning composition, therefore, needs to maintain the perspective of a beginning student and find value in the freshness of the composition and the skill of this person's early attempts to work with the principles of composition.

Without apologizing, both creator and critic need to keep in mind the materials that have been chosen for the work. What is the scope of the work? Is it within the capacity of the

choreographer to address this scope? What technical requirements have been placed on the dancers? Are these requirements within their capacities? What choices have been made pertaining to supporting structures, such as music, text, props, costumes, and lighting? Do these choices serve the goals of the piece, or does the piece serve these structures?

The same questions are applicable to criticizing the work of a more mature choreographer, but one would expect the standards to be more sophisticated and rigorous. When considering scope, for instance, a beginning student might be faulted for adopting too broad a theme while an advanced student might be encouraged to tackle an issue more fully and deeply. And technically, it would be assumed that a more advanced dancer and choreographer would make more specific demands on the dancers, not necessarily in terms of human tricks, but requiring completed lines, pointed feet, extended limbs, and so on. It would also be assumed that the choreography would have its own integrity, rather than relying on the supporting structures.

Audience

The intention of the piece must finally be considered in terms of the audience for which it was designed. Just as it would be unfair to reprimand a 5-year-old for not recognizing the value of a fine piece of crystal, so it would be inappropriate to expect that audiences new to dance will have the experiences they need to find a context for abstract work. When creating, you need to make decisions about what your target audience is going to be in order to offer a gift that will make sense to them. It is not different from buying a sweater for a gift. You consider what is going to fit, which colors would be appreciated, and what climate the receiver inhabits as you narrow your choices. It is similar to choosing your words carefully and deliberately when trying to express yourself in a foreign language. You want to be understood, so you put effort into speaking in intelligible terms.

When considering the audience, function and material considerations still play a part. For instance, if you are preparing a study knowing that the audience will be your composition class, you might be less inclined to throw in some sure-fire crowd pleasers than you would be if you were preparing an audition piece. Consider which risks are important to take and which circumstances you would consider safe for such risk-taking.

When evaluating someone else's work, consider which audience the work was intended to serve. The general public? Young audiences? Those familiar to dance? Those expecting a challenge? Those who hope to be reassured by something familiar?

What Does This Dance Have to Do With Me?

How are you supposed to evaluate something that you did not understand? The process of evaluating dance, or any creative endeavor, is in itself a creative act. Whether you are evaluating your work or someone else's, you are asking yourself the question, "What does this have to do with me?"

Think back to the artist, audience, and content triangle in chapter 12, page 161. Remember that each corner of the triangle can be a starting place for understanding the other two. As an audience, you can use the work to understand the artist or you can use the artist to understand the work. The wonderful thing about the dialogue, either way it goes, is that it establishes a kind of community between you and the artist. Art creates community.

In a composition class, you will be called on to respond to the work of your peers. This kind of evaluation requires generosity, creativity, and often a good bit of tact because you will want to preserve good relations while maintaining your own integrity. Your goal should be to create a critical dialogue that is nonthreatening and positive. Here are some examples of affirmative, nonthreatening responses:

1. Use adjectives creatively and honestly: "I thought the piece was very . . . (powerful, graceful, touching, humorous, clever, provocative, disturbing, and so on)."

2. Comment about the execution: "It was well rehearsed." "You made good use of the skills of the performers." "You used the space in an interesting manner."

3. Comment on the development of the artist as evidenced by the work: "You are using more contrast and variety in this work than in previous pieces." "The repetition of the phrase was very effective."

4. Ask the artist for explanations instead of voicing your opinion: Rather than saying, "Why did you use those stupid shoes?" try, "I was surprised by the choice of shoes. Can you talk about that choice?" Rather than saying, "It didn't make any sense to me when you kept going back to the wall," try, "Can you talk about the repetition of the return to the wall?"

Your responsibility as a critic is twofold: (1) not to bring your own agenda to the work you are responding to and (2) to have a desire for the artist to do his best work. You should attempt to help the artist create a piece, not to create your own. As hard as this may be, it is important for you to leave your biases and expectations out of the process.

A Reporter's Evaluation

When you do not have the benefit of conferring with the artist and you feel obliged to evaluate, as a reporter would, for the benefit of someone who did not witness the performance, what guidelines are appropriate?

First, take notice of your audience. Try to place the work in the context of other, related dance works so that the value of the piece you are describing has relevance to your audience's experience, independent of your own.

Second, make your subjective assessments (opinions) clearly identifiable and distinguishable from general wisdom. Rather than implying that everyone in the audience found a piece to be boring, stimulating, dull, or challenging, make it clear that these are *your* opinions.

Third, try to be as objectively descriptive as possible. The dancer wore red. The men wore the same costumes—which happened to be dresses—as the women. The music was contemporary, atonal, melodic, whatever. Again, this kind of description allows the listeners to determine the supposed value of the piece in the context of their lives rather than in the context of yours.

Finally, use the elements of dance and the principles of composition as a structure and framework for your comments.

Is This a Good Dance?

Ultimately, you are the best and only true judge of a work of art because you alone will be able or unable to find value in it. As promised at the beginning of this chapter, the guidelines discussed can be applied to evaluating any creative endeavor, yours or someone else's.

A dance is good if it has relevance to your life. This relevance may be immediately obvious or it may take some effort to discover. Figure 14.3 contains questions that may help you to discover the value of a work of art.

Some Considerations for Critical Feedback

1. What was the piece about?
2. Who is it coming from—out of what community?
3. What is the artist trying to do? Teach? Tell a story? Create a feeling? Change your mind? Change your vision?
4. At what point in the piece did you realize that? Should it have come earlier?
5. How did the structure of the piece reveal itself to you?
6. Was the form suitable to the content?
7. What part did language, visual elements, sound elements play in the piece, and how did it (they) communicate?
8. Was the artist in control of the medium?
9. Did the artist *push* the subject matter or rely on available stereotypes and media clichés?
10. Was the piece lazy? Obvious?
11. Where did the artist go in deep and take a chance?
12. Did the artist try to take clichés and stereotypes and turn them inside out?
13. Whose experience informs this piece—the artist's own?
14. Did the artist attempt to make art outside of his own culture?
15. Did the artist show us workable ways to draw on the experience of others?
16. What cultural symbols were used, and how were they treated—thoughtfully or casually?
17. Were they loaded symbols—highly significant to one or more cultures?
18. Did you learn something about the world that you did not know before?
19. Did the piece take a global view? Did it contribute to the picture of our multicultural society?
20. Did it show us how we can share each other's experience without losing individual identities and making a bland mush of the culture? How?
21. Was the artist guilty of cultural piracy? How?
22. If you go away from this piece with just one image, what will it be and how will you feel about holding it?
23. On a scale of 1 to 10, did you like it?

FIGURE 14.4 *Answering these questions will help you uncover the value of a dance.*

The questions were developed by Linda Burnham, founder of *High Performance* magazine, co-director of Art in the Public Interest, Saxapahaw, NC (first presented at an annual meeting of Alternate ROOTS, Black Mountain, NC).

Think About It

1. Do you think it is possible to create dances in which you have no investment, that offer no physical, emotional, or social challenges to you? What value could these dances have for you?

2. What brand of criticism is most comfortable for you to give: self-serving, artist-serving, or public-serving? What brand of criticism is most comfortable for you to receive?

3. By what criteria do you measure your success as a creative person?

4. Do you "help" someone by giving them your opinion? What makes an opinion valuable?

5. When you ask for feedback, do you usually get information that is useful to you? If so, how are you able to solicit useful feedback? If not, what might you change in the way you ask for feedback?

Your Turn to...Talk!

Obtaining Useful Feedback

As an exercise in getting useful feedback, consider a dance you've made that you feel was well developed but not completed. *Write down on paper* (not just in your head) two specific questions about each of the following:

~ Technical execution

~ Content

~ Structure

~ The principles of composition

~ History

Keep the following in mind as you write your questions:

~ Try to avoid yes-or-no questions. In this structure, the respondent is allowed to answer *only* the question you ask; he is not invited to guess why you are asking a question and venture into that guess. For instance, "Did you think the opening was effective?" is a yes-or-no question. That's all you get in this format. Yes or no. If the answer is yes, you still don't know how or why. If the answer is no, you still don't know what to fix. But if you ask, "Please describe the effect the opening had on you," then you've got something! It may be that the answer you want is yes or no. "Were we in unison?" is not a question of opinion, but it may be that in your opinion unison in a section is really important and you need to know if it still needs rehearsal. "How were we in unison?" is kind of a dumb question!

~ Try not to phrase these questions in such a way that the respondents could say they liked or didn't like whatever you're asking about. "Did you like the part where we all stood on our heads?" is a yes-or-no question and useful only if the dance is going to be valued using an applause-o-meter. The answer to the question "What did you like about it?" is a nice way to learn about your audience's experiences and tastes but it is less useful in helping you pursue your own aesthetic. The questions must be phrased in such a way that they can be answered on your terms. "When," "where," "how," and "why" questions are going to be a much better bet than "Did you . . .?" questions.

~ You control the feedback process. Sometimes it's helpful to have a moderator who can listen to the responses and keep folks on track. "That's not the question that was asked." The moderator is also responsible for steering the feedback process away from dialogue. In other words, if you ask, "Where might we use stillness?" and the respondent suggests, "The very beginning movements might be broken into staccato/still contrasts," it's not appropriate then to explain that the point of the beginning was to create a flurry of movement, so that suggestion is no good. You asked; she answered. Your response should be *only* "Thank you."

Who, What, Why?

Take a finished work, either a dance made by your peers or a professional performance, and address the following questions in formal review:

1. Who is performing?
    a. Level?
    b. Community?
    c. Expectations?
2. What is the work?
3. What's it made of; how is it put together? What do you think it means?
4. What difference does it make?
5. How does this dance relate to your life?

Photo Credits

Courtesy of Bill Arnold: Photo on p. 119

©Richard Babb: Figure 13.2

Courtesy of Heather de Manigold: Figure 3.2, photos on p. 112

©Digital Vision: Figure 9.5

©Brian Drake: Figure 1.4c

Empics: Figure 1.4b

©Dale Garvey: Figure 5.5

©Getty Images: Figure 9.4

Courtesy of the Martha Graham Center for Contemporary Dance: Photo on p. 8

©Kelly Huff : Figures 3.4b, 5.3, 12.1

©Ernst Jahn/Bruce Coleman, Inc.: Figure 10.1

©Group III Kerr/Bruce Coleman, Inc.: Figure 13.1

©Elisa Leonell/Bruce Coleman, Inc.: Photo on p. 192

©Richard B. Levine and/or Frances M. Roberts: Figures 1.3a, 3.4a, 5.4, 7.5, 14.3, photo on p. 175

©Sonya Libow: Figure 14.2

©David Liebman: Figure 1.2

©B. LittleHales/Raw Talent Photo: Figure 7.1

©David Madison/MADIS/Bruce Coleman, Inc.: Figure 4.1

©Mary Messenger: Figure 3.1

Courtesy of Tony Mills: Author photo on p. 206.

©Anthony Neste: Figure 9.2

Courtesy of the North Carolina Dance Theatre: Figures 1.1b, 14.1

©Photri/E Burciaga: Figure 7.2b

©Photri Inc: Figure 1.4a

©Photri Inc/Mauritius GMBH: Figure 3.3b

©Photri Inc/STIM: Figure 1.3b, 3.3a

©Photri/Llewellyn: Figure 7.2a

©Radford Images: Figure 9.3

©Brad Rickerby/RICKE/Bruce Coleman, Inc.: Figure 2.1

©Rischgitz/Hulton Archive: sketch (a) on p. 76

©Ken Sherman: Figure 1.1a

©Sovfoto: Photo on p. 131 (Isadora Duncan)

Helen Tamiris/Collection Daniel Nagrin: Photo (b) on p. 76

Courtesy of George Tarbay: Figures 2.3, a through e, and 2.4, a through e

©Norman Owen Tomalin/Bruce Coleman, Inc.: Figure 5.1

©Jack Vartoogian: Photos on pp. 82 and 91

Courtesy of Dr. Jochen Viehoff: Photo on p. 146

Courtesy of the Charles Weidman Dance Foundation: Figure 2.6

Index

About the Author

Constance Schrader, MA, is an independent artist and a lecturer at the University of North Carolina at Asheville, where she founded and directs the dance program. She received her master's degree in dance from Mills College in Oakland, California, in 1979. Schrader is a member of the North Carolina Dance Alliance and Alternate ROOTS, a national organization of performing artists.

Throughout her dance career Schrader has been awarded many grants and scholarships, including consecutive scholarships to attend the American Dance Festival. She has toured internationally with Meredith Monk/The House and has presented her own choreography nationally and internationally. She has worked as an associate director of a dance company and is affiliated with a regional movement theater company. Schrader is also a certified Pilates instructor.

In addition to being a teacher, choreographer, and a national and international performing artist for more than 30 years, Schrader has a rich variety of real-life experiences that have helped her make dance an art form that is accessible to a wide range of people. In fact, her greatest sense of accomplishment doesn't come from diplomas or awards, but from teaching 3,000 Japanese people to clap a rhythm at a festival in Togamura and coaxing U.S. executives to loosen their ties, kick off their shoes, and leap and laugh.

Schrader lives in Asheville, North Carolina, with her husband, Clayton, and their children, where she pursues her other passion, gardening.